THE

CONVICTION

OF THINGS

NOT SEEN

THE

CONVICTION

OF THINGS

NOT SEEN

Worship and Ministry
in the 21st Century

Todd E. Johnson

Brazos Press

A Division of Baker Book House Co
Grand Rapids, Michigan 49516

Published by Brazos Press
a division of Baker Book House Company
P.O. Box 6287, Grand Rapids, MI 49516-6287

Printed in the United States of America

Library of Congress Cataloging-in-Publication Data

The conviction of things not seen : worship and ministry in the 21st century / [edited by] Todd E. Johnson.
     p.   cm.
Includes bibliographical references.
ISBN 1-58743-032-0 (pbk.)
1. Public worship. 2. Pastoral theology. I. Johnson, Todd Eric, 1960–
BV15 .C635 2002
253—dc21   2002008659

For current information about all releases from Brazos Press, visit our web site:
http://www.brazospress.com

To Robert Webber

Amicus Dei,
Amicus Ecclesiae

Now faith is the assurance of things hoped for,
the conviction of things not seen.

Hebrews 11:1

Contents

Foreword

Webster's Third New International Dictionary defines *festschrift* as "a miscellaneous volume of writings from several hands for a celebration, especially one of learned essays contributed by students, colleagues, and admirers to honor a scholar on a special anniversary," and so this book is—a collection of writings by different people to honor Robert Webber, one of the leaders of worship studies and renewal. As with other *festschrifts,* this one contains many voices, not just one; it has many themes, but no single plot line. Nevertheless, all the essays do seem to share a common assumption: if it is going to carry out effectively Christ's mission in the world, the North American church must think carefully about what it means to minister not only in a new century but also in a new culture. Each essay in its own way invites readers to look at things from a new perspective.

Bob Webber is a man who thrives on new perspectives. I first met him in the late 1970s, not long after *Common Roots* was published. I was a relatively new assistant professor at Denver Seminary when Bob came to campus to lecture on themes from his book. As often happens to instructors with little seniority, I was assigned to be Bob's "go-for" during his visit. I picked him up at the airport, drove him between hotel and seminary, and made sure he was where he was supposed to be. I was also responsible for introducing him before his first lecture. I had been provided his bio, so I worked hard to do him justice. After recounting his many degrees and his teaching experience at Covenant and Wheaton colleges, I sat down in the front row and momentarily focused my attention on getting my note-taking materials ready. Suddenly from behind me I heard a gasp from the audience. I looked up to see Bob Webber standing on top of the desk/lectern. Neither I nor anyone else in that audience had expected such acrobatics from a theology professor, but there Bob stood, perched high on the desk looking down at our upturned and incredulous faces. Once he had everyone's attention, he made his point: "Sometimes you just have to put yourself in another place to see things from a different point of view." (Ten years later I watched Robin Williams pull off a similar stunt as the innovative teacher in the film *Dead Poets Society.*) Here, clearly, was a theologian who could command and keep one's attention.

Our paths did not cross again for two decades, though it was easy to keep track of Bob's comings and goings in the academic world. Bob wrote a number of books on Christians living in a secular and a highly politicized world, but mostly he followed the theological trajectories in *Common Roots:* evangelical religion is anything but monolithic, but has been shaped by a rich diversity of traditions, and to be authentic, worship must be rooted in the church's historic beliefs and practices, no matter where or when it takes place. I watched Bob forge a new trail in worship studies, publishing book after book on the subject. In the process, he became a sought-after guest lecturer and adjunct professor and kept up an exhausting schedule of workshops and conferences.

Bob and I finally reconnected in the late 1990s, after I became dean at Northern Baptist Seminary. When I arrived, I discovered that Bob already had well-developed Northern ties. His Baptist minister father was a Northern graduate, and for almost twenty years, Bob himself had been an adjunct professor at the seminary, teaching occasional courses in early church history, theology, and worship. Then, in the early 1990s, he became the lead professor in Northern's new doctor of ministry in worship degree program.

When the William R. and Geraldyne B. Myers Professor of Ministry chair became available, the seminary did not have far to look for its ideal candidate. Could we induce Bob to come to Northern to direct a new master of arts in worship and spirituality program after he had been so long at Wheaton? In the end the answer was "yes."

Bob has been a wonderful addition to Northern Baptist Seminary. He has become a valued colleague, a popular and provocative teacher, and a mentor *par excellance.* Bob's appointment as an endowed chair came with a reduced teaching load, affording him the time to get some more writing done. Amazing as it seems, Bob's productivity has become even more prodigious since he joined us.

As dean, I am delighted to report that Bob has more than met our expectations. In almost no time, he established himself as an important partner with the rest of us in our ongoing conversation about the kind of future we envision for theological education and for the church at large. It does not take long to find out what Bob believes in and what keeps him up at night. He believes that the renewal of Christian worship must be rooted in serious biblical, theological, and historical study, not the latest fad or the flashiest tricks of technology. He believes that it is possible to survive the "worship wars" in local congregations with "blended worship" practices. He is convinced that postmodern people think and experience reality differently than their parents or grandparents did and that ministry and worship must adjust accordingly. He has a deep interest in changing the way we educate future religious leaders so that they can minister effectively in the world as it is and not as it used to be. Most fundamentally, Bob is convinced that the answers to our present and future questions about worship may be found in the church's past, in what he calls "ancient-future faith." He sees in the rising generation a deep longing for worship that moves them toward a transcendent experience of God that is also deeply rooted in corporate experience. It is in the "premodern" interaction with symbols and creeds and in the new application of the early church's strategy for bringing pagans into the family of faith through the catechumenate that postmodern people will find their questions answered and their longings satisfied.

This *festschrift* reflects the agenda of Bob's own work: envisioning a ministry that is historically rooted and future focused. The themes that engage him are easily found in the essays that follow. For example, in one way or another, most of the essays address the demands of doing ministry in a *post-everything* world. It is now common to characterize our times as post-Constantinian, post-Enlightenment, postdenominational, post-Christian, and, of course, postmodern. As a descriptor, "post-" has its limits: we often use the prefix when we think we know where we have been, but are not at all sure where we are now or where we are going. In other words, we call something *post-* when we do not know what else to call it. Furthermore, these terms can be quite misleading if the people who use them think that the old world has in fact neatly and totally given way to the new. While it is true that signs of postmodernity abound, much of modernity remains. Expressive individualism has not been replaced by communal values, not all metanarratives have disappeared into obscurity, intuition has not completely overwhelmed the claims of science, and not everyone has jettisoned their commitment to cold logic and linear thinking. "Moderns" and "postmoderns" often inhabit the same educational and political institutions or live under the same roof, as baby-boomer parents of Generation-Xers are bound to discover.

Each of the contributors to this volume brought their own particular expertise to these issues, acknowledging the historical roots of Christianity as well as its ever-changing context. Todd Johnson's chapter shows how Willow Creek Community Church's distinctive strategy grew out of the changing youth ministry paradigms within the evangelical movement after World War II. Johnson shows what happens when evangelism, catechesis, and worship are not connected in the life of the local church. Kathleen Black's contribution is a fascinating study of how hard it is to create a single new and shared story when separate ethnic and cultural stories already exist and the necessary challenge of accommodation. Gilson Waldkoenig examines the new forms that denominationalism is taking in the postmodern world. Growing numbers of local churches no longer welcome the goods and services offered by traditional denominations. While old denominational programs and the headquarters that support them languish, new voluntary associations of independent evangelical churches such as the Willow Creek Association are on the rise. In addition, numerous mainline congregations are willing to overlook denominational labels, histories, and practices to do cooperative ministries that are revitalizing rural communities. Denominationalism may not be dying all; it is just changing into something else.

Two other essays address how differently people in the new culture view reality and understand the gospel that is preached to them. Veteran theologian Donald G. Bloesch compares three theological models from the last century (Paul Tillich, Karl Barth, and Frank Buchman) to suggest a more effective way of "penetrating the world with the gospel." He argues that what is needed in our new context is a theology of Word and Spirit that takes religious experience more seriously than in the past. The importance of experience is also a major theme in Robert Johnston's chapter. Johnston notes the lack of appreciation by most Protestants for the visual arts, especially as ministry resources. While many of the most successful churches give little to no attention to the visual arts in worship, people in the wider culture get strong and steady doses of symbolic communication from the movies and on the Internet. Johnston sees in the "catholic" understanding of symbol a much more viable way of communicating the power and truth of the gospel to people today.

Three authors deal directly with various aspects of worship in the life of the church. Lester Ruth provides a much needed taxonomy of worship types. After reviewing various current popular and scholarly labeling approaches, Ruth offers a taxonomy of worship types of his own. Likewise, John Witvliet takes on the issue that causes and perpetuates "worship wars" in local churches: the selection of music in worship. He recognizes that music has often been crucial in defining group identity and that those in charge of selecting music for worship need evaluative standards and theological integrity to do their work well. Ruth Meyers focuses her attention on the renewed interest in the ancient catechumenate. Meyers examines those churches in the United States and Canada that have adapted for their own uses the early church's practice of gradually incorporating new believers into the community of faith through a step-by-step process of conversion and instruction that culminates in baptism, confirmation, and first communion. In this way, many believe, churches will not only have an effective way of "christianizing" new adult converts who come to faith without any prior Christian knowledge or experience but also of revitalizing the faith of those congregations who seek them out and receive them.

Two other veteran authors speak directly to the shaping power of worship in the lives of those who participate in it. Rodney Clapp asks if and how people are shaped by their participation in Christian worship. These are important questions in light of the many recent studies that conclude that Christians do not behave much differently than nonbelievers. Clapp argues that worship can and should have the power to shape real beliefs and behaviors, especially as Christians move away from individualistic and privatized views of the Christian faith and toward more corporate or communal ones. William Willimon leans heavily on the ritual studies of Victor Turner and D.W. Winnicott to make his point that by participating in the corporate rituals of Christian worship, which point primarily to the majesty and glory of God, believers often experience God's love and care for them. Thus ritual and pastoral care are vitally connected.

Two of the other authors look at new ways of educating religious leaders and innovative ways of understanding ministry today. Mary Hess examines postmodernism and Christian higher education. She understands that many churches in the postmodern world no longer look to theological seminaries as the source for new ministers or as the place to find answers to their most pressing questions. How can seminaries relate to churches that no longer view them as valuable or relevant? What kind of education is required for leaders of religious communities that are in decline and no longer seem able to minister effectively in the postmodern context? Hess walks us through the process of her own seminary (Luther Seminary in the Twin Cities) in developing a "missional" curriculum to meet these challenges. Constance Cherry takes the reader through a survey of twentieth-century ministry and worship practices to see how the churches passed through stages of orientation and disorientation and are now moving toward a new period of reorientation whose content is not yet clear. She suggests that the work of constructing this new ministry and worship paradigm will include the following: awareness of the global nature of ministry, the importance of spirituality, the centrality of Christian community, and new ways of communicating the gospel in a culture that is no longer eager to hear it.

Of course, one author offers the obligatory *festschrift* biographical chapter and bibliography, yet even in this, Dennis Okholm captures a vision of Bob beyond his chronology of publications and theological shifts. Okholm presents a man whose teaching is a mission and who is equally passionate about his subject as he is his students, a truth reflected in the fact that so many of the contributors to this volume are, directly or indirectly, his students. Once again relevant to postmodern thought, maybe the best way to judge Bob Webber is less by what he has written on paper and more what he has written on the hearts of many of his students, readers, and conferees.

These essays will help serious readers look at things from a new point of view. In that way, they do honor Bob Webber, the one who climbed on top of that desk so many years ago. As dean at Northern, I get to speak for Bob's colleagues on the faculty and in the student body. He is our teacher and friend. It is a great privilege to walk down the same road with him, and to crane our necks to look at one who has dared to put himself in a new place, inviting us to see the world from a different point of view.

Timothy Weber
Dean, Northern Baptist Seminary

Introduction

Therefore every scribe who has been trained for the kingdom of heaven is like the master of a household who brings out of his treasure what is new and what is old.

Matthew 13:52

It was an unlikely gathering on the eighth floor of Hesburgh Library at the University of Notre Dame. That one winter day, like so many other days, we had gathered outside our closet-like study carrels that lined the walls. Although it is not uncommon for doctoral students at Notre Dame to congregate after class in the library, our backgrounds set us apart. There we were, graduates from some of the most prominent evangelical schools in the United States—Wheaton, North Park, Calvin, Asbury, Gordon—all of us studying liturgy at Notre Dame.

What was it that drew so many of us from ordinarily low church traditions to study liturgy at one of the preeminent Catholic liturgy programs in the world? One by one, we each told our story, and inevitably one name was common to all: Robert Webber. It was Webber, we agreed that exposed us to the larger world of catholic worship. Time and again Webber's writings, workshop presentations, or college courses were cited as pivotal or influential. Interestingly, Webber himself does not claim to be a liturgist but is a historical theologian interested in worship. He has commented more than once that if he had to do it all over again, he would study liturgy. Instead, he has made a career disseminating teachings and resources about the broader catholic tradition to evangelicals. We all agreed that Bob Webber may be the most influential nonliturgist in liturgy.

Our connection to Bob Webber as evangelicals in liturgy was further strengthened as Bob began working on his massive seven-volume series entitled *The Complete Library of Christian Worship,* or what we affectionately referred to as the "Notre Dame encyclopedia of worship," because so many of us were involved in it in some way or another. Now many of us teach those volumes for Bob's Institute of Worship Studies in the United States and Canada.

15

Each of us has our own story of how we came to know Bob. Mine begins by knowing Bob from afar: hearing him lecture at North Park while I was a seminary student there, reading (and rereading) *Worship is a Verb* and *Evangelicals on the Canterbury Trail*. I found affinity with few conversation partners concerning the state of Protestant worship, but I clung to Bob's writings like driftwood from a shipwreck. Finally the day came that I called Bob at Wheaton to introduce myself simply to thank him for his work. While trying to negotiate the landmines of evangelical worship, Bob's writings were a light in the dark—a light I followed for a number of years.

After taking in much of Bob's work throughout my ministry in the church, I decided I needed to learn more about worship and chose to do doctoral work in liturgy. Once again, I contacted Bob for advice on where to go to study liturgy. He was most gracious each time I contacted him out of the blue, encouraging my pursuit and offering good counsel along the way. I know from those eighth-floor conversations my story is not unique.

The next time our paths crossed was undoubtedly the most important. I was in my third year of doctoral studies, still very much a neophyte in the academy. I was asked at the last minute to respond to a paper Bob was delivering at a conference. I was simultaneously honored, thrilled, and apprehensive. My fears were only magnified by the fact that I would be rooming with Bob at this conference. That weekend was a watershed for me professionally, as it was my first public presentation in the academy, but it was equally important personally as I caught a glimpse of Bob's vision of writing about worship for the person in the pew, empowering them to worship with greater understanding and deeper spiritual engagement.

In the years that have passed since that conference, I have been fortunate to be able to call Bob a colleague, mentor, and friend, but I had no idea how deep his influence in my life had been until I was preparing for a presentation at a joint meeting of evangelical and Orthodox theologians and stumbled across a book entitled *The Orthodox Evangelicals: Who They Are and What They Are Saying*. This book, edited by Bob Webber and Donald Bloesch, described a meeting of evangelical scholars and pastors in May of 1977 in which a declaration was made proclaiming the evangelical tradition largely lacked the breadth and depth of the larger Christian tradition. This statement, entitled "The Chicago Call," invited the evangelical community to reconsider what had been lost in many of the Protestant traditions since the Reformation (and particularly the Great Awakenings) in terms of sacraments, creeds, ecumenism, and the riches of Christian spirituality.

Two things immediately jumped out at me. The first was the spiritual pilgrimage of three of the contributors: Webber, who became an Episcopalian (chronicled in *Evangelicals on the Canterbury Trail*); Thomas Howard, who became a Roman Catholic (chronicled in *Evangelical Is Not Enough*); and Peter Gilquist, who became Orthodox (chronicled in *Coming Home*). It made me (teaching comfortably at a Jesuit university) wonder if one could recover these elements and still remain evangelical.

The second thing that grabbed me was who signed this statement. As I looked at the list, I saw a number of professors from my *alma mater,* North Park Theological Seminary. It was as if I had found a long-lost family tree. Much of my broadly catholic orientation to the church arose out of my seminary experience with professors who sought to see the future of the church connected to its past. I realized for the first time how the vision of a Christianity that is both apostolic and evangelical, so much a part of who I am, is a result of the widespread influence of Robert Webber.

Now on the twenty-fifth anniversary of the Chicago Call, I have assembled a number of scholars who, like Bob, simultaneously look forward while looking back, what Bob has defined as an "ancient-future faith." The issues addressed in this volume touch on many of the same themes as the Chicago Call, but they ask a different question: How does one do ministry in the new century? The categories are much the same—worship and sacraments, church unity, proclamation of the gospel—but from the perspective of issues facing ministers in the third millennium.

On behalf of all the contributors, I must say that this volume has been a wonderful opportunity to celebrate Bob's work and legacy. Like Bob, we have all sought to be scribes of the kingdom, ones who bring both the old and the new out of the storehouse.

I must thank each of the contributors for their fine work. I especially offer my deepest thanks to Lester Ruth and John Witvliet, who offered such important support and counsel from this project's inception. Many thanks are also due to Rodney Clapp, who, beyond being a contributor to this volume, shepherded me through this process, all the while believing in my vision of a *festschrift* that would actually be read on its own merits as a book. To all the people at Brazos Press who have supported this project with their time and energy, I offer my sincerest thanks. They have been most generous in their patience and understanding. For every author in this volume there were easily three more scholars who wanted to be included. I thank them for understanding that the necessity of keeping this volume focused unhappily excluded their participation. Special thank yous to the Wabash Center for Teaching and Learning Theology for the grant that allowed me to edit much of this manuscript, and to my graduate assistant Neal Deles for his help with the details. And as always, thanks to my wife Susan and my children, Kyle, Kjerstin, Katherine, Kari, and Kelsey for their support of my work on this project.

Todd E. Johnson
Ash Wednesday 2002

1

Merging Tradition and Innovation in the Life of the Church

Moving from Style to Encountering God in Worship

Constance M. Cherry

Christian leaders in the world today agree that these are unsettled times for the Christian church. It could be argued that approaches to ministry in the United States have never been settled, as various groups and denominations have sought to express their distinctiveness and have continued to evolve in their own understanding of their tradition and purpose. Of course, "settled" is a subjective term that leaves plenty of room for interpretation. Admitting, however, that the ministry of the church is dynamic in nature and therefore always in motion, few would disagree that the beginning of the twenty-first century marks a particularly unsettled period for the church.

One of the signals that we are in a time of searching is the church's infatuation with what it considers to be innovation. The indications are all around us, with churches advertising new services, new styles, new times, new music, new approaches to preaching, and so on. To be innovative, according to the standard definition, is to introduce change, to implement new ideas, to create new methods in order to make inventive changes. For a religion that has historically appealed to tradition as a source of authority, innovation is becoming increasingly widespread within Christianity.

Though various aspects of ministry have merged tradition and innovation in recent years, the area that has perhaps most captivated the interest of the church is the area of Christian worship. In this chapter, we will view the worship landscape in terms of three general movements: orientation, disorientation, and reorientation. It will be shown that though some have presumed the merging of tradition and innovation to have occurred in the church's worship, the real integration of old and new still lies in our future.

This threefold movement of orientation, disorientation, and reorientation has been used by a variety of individuals for a variety of purposes. Some have used this pattern to describe the life of spiritual formation, pointing out that God works in our circumstances to change us from "one degree of glory to another" (2 Cor. 3:18). It has also been used for the purposes of identifying patterns of psychological development, developing a theology of suffering, and even analyzing the content of certain psalms from the Scriptures.[1] This same pattern of movement can serve our purposes well as we attempt to identify the state of worship during this period of transition.But before we attempt to see how this pattern applies to the church's worship, a brief explanation of the nature of these movements will be helpful.

Orientation is considered to be a time of settled familiarity. One's surroundings are comfortable and relatively untested. There is safety in what is known, assurance in the predictable, and ease in the routine. It is a time when immersion in the tradition of any significant context (whether of community, family, occupation, religion, or any organized system) provides great assurance and a sense of well-being. As Carolyn Gratton notes, "A familiar life pattern is a kind of integration (relative and more or less partial) that satisfied some of our desire for harmony or, at the very least, for predictability."[2]

Disorientation describes the upsetting of the status quo and can be the result of a variety of factors, including new leadership, cultural shifts, economic change, health issues, persecution, and so on. Disorientation, therefore, is a period of insecurity, a time when the familiar becomes unfamiliar, the settled becomes unsettled, and the comfortable becomes uncomfortable—in short, tradition is tested. There is often a sense of despair to one degree or another, because there appears to be little one can do to manage or reverse what has been put into motion. Some typical responses to disorientation include anger, resistance, aggression, and denial. Obviously, this is a painful time, as the security of the known is dismantled in favor of the unknown.

Eventually a season of *reorientation* may occur. Whether it occurs depends on several factors, not the least of which is the openness of the individual (or institution) to a new perspective. Disorientation does not automatically lead to reorientation; much depends on one's willingness to be reoriented. Many groups and individuals have lodged in a period of disorientation because of their unwillingness to trust the process, as opposed to fighting the process.

Reorientation occurs as a result of waiting for the changes in disorientation to make their full cycle, thinking and acting reflectively on the circumstances, and most of all, prayerfully considering what God is attempting to achieve through the threefold sequence. The central questions during this period are: What is God doing? and How can we cooperate with God's initiatives? There is little we can do to control the events and people around us during the period of disorientation. The challenge is to allow the status quo (the tradition) to be submitted to its full time of testing and then allow God to change us in light of his purposes for the tradition.[3]

There is no way of knowing how long each period of the sequence will last. The timetable depends on many factors, including the degree of change needed. We can, however, expect that the period of disorientation will be a lengthy one, for it is here that the greatest amount of confrontation occurs; it is in this phase that God is doing unseen work. Much time and opportunity is needed for tightly bound moorings to be loosened so that we can launch out into new waters. Attempts at expediting the process will prove futile, as the point is not for us to fix the circumstance but for the circumstance to fix us. What is true for the spiritual growth of the individual applies to the church as well.

> One of the reasons we want to "jump in and focus on fixing" is to release the tension. But remember that the process of the waiting, (to go "through"), is what moves us to the "to." The gap, the emptiness, is where we experience the transcendent. . . . The counselor tries to put life back together. The spiritual director tries to rest in the "through" because of our need to be in and experience the desert. To abort this phase is to abort the growth.[4]

Orientation

During the first half of the twentieth century in the United States, denominations and movements attempted to secure their places in the worship landscape by identifying and solidifying the lines of distinction and the core values that described their beliefs and set them apart. Though this has in itself led to the creation of more independent churches (and interdenominational organizations), oddly enough these new entities all emerged for the same reason—so that doctrine and worship practices would be clear, distinctive, affirmed, and settled.

Denominational loyalty was valued, and generations of worshipers remained within their tradition of origin when establishing their own families within the life of the church. The post—World War II years saw a ground swell of church attendance and growth in Sunday schools, youth groups, and Christian camps, as well as expanded church programming and new buildings of every type. New Christian colleges and seminaries were established. The end of the war fostered a great desire within the culture to return to the security of faith, family, and country. Though diversity among religious groups abounded, there was nevertheless a sense of orientation, stability, and clarity concerning one's distinctive identity within the larger religious community.

The rise of the liturgical movement in the early part of the twentieth century serves as an excellent example of the desire to substantiate clear doctrinal beliefs among the faithful. Though most often viewed as an awakening movement or as a renewing movement, the emphasis of the liturgical movement tended to be on "reclaiming" the church and therefore contributed to a sense of orientation in the church. An example of this is the renewal of commitment to the liturgy of the Word as an integral part of the Eucharist.[5] The liturgical movement sought to reclaim a broader and more systematic use of Scripture in worship, constituting a wider application of a Reformation principle. The wider use of Scripture reflected a reclaiming of the early church tradition and resulted in a warm receptivity among worshipers. The shapers of the movement viewed their work as a response to worship unrest, yet I argue that the nature of their response points to a return to significant traditions instead of a push forward into innovation and true reorientation. This is especially evident given that the work of the liturgical movement is frequently referred to as "reaffirmations."

According to Gordon S. Wakefield, the two primary reaffirmations of the liturgical movement are "the reaffirmation of the Eucharist as the central act of Christian worship and the source of the Church's life" and the reaffirmation of the "participation of the whole congregation. They are the celebrants, not the minister alone, who preside."[6] Both of these reaffirmations constitute a return to earlier tradition.

To this emphasis on the Eucharist and participation, John Fenwick and Bryan Spinks add the recovery of community, a rediscovery of the early church as a model, a rediscovery of the Bible, an emphasis on the vernacular, the rediscovery of other Christian traditions, and an emphasis on proclamation and social involvement as being central to the liturgical movement.[7]

While the Roman Catholic Church and mainline Protestant groups sought to articulate their fidelity to tradition through the liturgical movement, other groups of a more fundamentalist nature sought to clearly articulate their differences from other denominational bodies. Though the theological perspectives varied, what many of these groups shared was their desire to articulate their differences! For instance, the fundamentalist movement of the first half of the twentieth century resulted in the organization of many independent churches, new denominations, schools, and publishing houses that were established for the express purpose of countering what was thought to be the liberal mainline theology.[8] In the latter half of the century, a countermovement of "new Fundamentalists" wanted to distance themselves from the earlier fundamentalism. They reclaimed the nineteenth-century word "evangelical" and reversed the platform of the earlier fundamentalism. Evangelicals were prointellectual, pro-ecumenical, and pro-social action.[9] In some measure, however, both the fundamentalist movement and evangelicalism were attempts to maintain orientation and provide for greater security within their traditions.

Worship during this period was essentially more traditional in approach than not. For liturgical churches, services were defined by the church's worship book. Though content varied according to the church year, the pattern for worship generally remained unchanged from week to week. Ironically, worship services for those of the Free Church tradition also remained relatively unchanged from week to week with regard to the general order of service. Whereas the liturgical services varied primarily according to the church year, the Free Church content varied primarily according to sermon themes. Barry Liesch points out that

> Thematic worship is the favored design of perhaps the majority of evangelical churches. The desire of pastors to be free to choose their own sermon topics or series of messages cuts to the heart of the liturgical/nonliturgical issue. . . . Pastors want the planning of the service to center around and be driven by the sermon.[10]

All evaluations as to the benefit of either of these approaches to worship aside, the first part of the twentieth century was a time of orientation—a time when participants of most religious groups knew what to expect in their worship practices. Innovation was not a goal; stabilization was.

Not to be ignored as part and parcel of this era was the influence of modernism, though its moorings would soon be threatened. Typical of the modern mind-set, religious groups founded their identities on propositional arguments, believing that theological truth was arrived at by way of reason based on scholarship and logic. Modernity can be summarized as "the drive to clarity, the turn to the subject, the concern with method, the belief in sameness—modern thinkers embraced and embrace all these ideals in modernity's working out of its unique history."[11]

Disorientation

The 1960s were a decade of unprecedented social change. Along with this change came a fixation with innovation in ministry. To thoroughly examine the cultural shifts in America that began during the 1960s is far beyond the scope of this chapter. What can be mentioned, however, are several key movements that greatly influenced the ministries and worship of the church, the degree to which is still being sorted out.

C. S. Lewis offers a telling analogy for the fixation with innovation that the church acquired during the second half of the twentieth century. In The *Screwtape Letters,* the character of Satan writes to one of his ambassadors:

> The real trouble about the set your patient is living in is that it is *merely* Christian. They all have individual interests, of course, but the bond remains mere Christianity. What we want, if men become Christians at all, is to keep them in the state of mind I call "Christianity And." You know—Christianity and the Crisis, Christianity and the New Psychology, Christianity and the New Order, Christianity and Faith Healing, Christianity and Psychical Research, Chris-

tianity and Vegetarianism, Christianity and Spelling Reform. If they must be
Christians let them at least be Christians with a difference. Substitute for the
faith itself some fashion with a Christian coloring. *Work on their horror of the
Same Old Thing.*[12]

Lewis could have written "Christianity and Ministry Approaches" or "Christianity and Innovative Worship Practices," and we would have instantly recognized what he meant. Church leaders during the last half of the twentieth
century were well acquainted with the horror of "the Same Old Thing," for
they regularly experienced the tyranny of innovation. Sameness became a curse.

Perhaps nowhere was the need for innovation in greater demand than in the
worship service, especially as it relates to worship style. The issues related to
worship style raised their heads quickly, and style-driven worship has dominated the worship scene for the last quarter of the twentieth century and shows
little sign of diminishing. Several developments on the worship scene in the
1960s and 1970s brought stylistic changes to the forefront. Three notable developments were the charismatic renewal movement, the Jesus Movement, and
Vatican II. Though the focus of these movements was not on style per se, the
end results nevertheless drew attention to style in worship.

The charismatic movement began in the late 1950s as a renewal movement
within established denominations. There is speculation that it "received its
name at the fourth international convention of the Full Gospel Businessmen's
Fellowship International held in Minneapolis on June 25–29, 1956."[13] Ecumenical in nature, this "neo-Pentecostal"[14] movement quickly made its way
into many traditional churches, both Roman Catholic and Protestant, including the Episcopal, Methodist, Lutheran, and Presbyterian churches.

Characteristics of charismatic worship include the priority of the immanence of the Holy Spirit, freedom of expression in verbal participation as well
as in physical gestures (raising of hands, prostration, dancing, kneeling, and so
on), manifestation of the miraculous and revelatory gifts of the Spirit, participatory worship, prominence of Scripture-based and newly composed congregational songs, spontaneity, and resistance to set worship forms and orders.

Church leaders tended either to embrace or to discourage charismatic influences in worship; there was not much middle ground. Yet, whether churches
viewed the influences of the charismatic renewal movement as positive or not,
it did contribute to the period of disorientation in worship across the country
and around the world. What was considered traditional in any denomination
was now threatened by the possibility of new expressions of worship. The status quo was challenged, and the comfortable was made uncomfortable. Sooner
or later most churches wrestled with the influence of the charismatic renewal
movement.

The emergence of the the Jesus Movement provided its own contribution
to the period of disorientation in worship. Developing on the West Coast in
the late 1960s, the Jesus Movement was the Christian version of the counter-

cultural movement of the 1960s. Led by converted young adults who were adherents to the counterculture of the day, the Jesus Movement made its mark by emphasizing nontraditional worship style, order, location, and leadership.

The Jesus Movement was largely music driven, and Christian bands were instituted to lead corporate worship. Christian rock bands quickly developed, and large Christian rock concerts as well as the availability of the recordings made the music of the Jesus Movement readily available for traditional churches. The line between concert and worship began to be blurred and remains so to this day. This is seen clearly in a recent article in a leading worship magazine:

> Having been to lots of concerts throughout my twenties—Bruce Springsteen, Tom Petty, Elton John, The Who and more—I thought I knew what to expect from a rock concert; bravado, wild fans, marijuana and band worship. But for all of those events, I was completely unprepared for the sense of the sacred that I experienced while taking in a U2 show recently. . . . Don't get me wrong. We had a party. . . . But in the middle of this all out party, I met with God quite unexpectedly. Later on, I asked myself why it was that I felt this way. Was it because Bono prayed over the fans "in the name of God" midway through the performance? Or because Bono sang so passionately that he hardly had a voice left by the end? Or did I get lost in band veneration and mistake it for God-directed worship? No. I met with God because I'd been led to His feet by the greatest rock band on earth. The emotional catharsis, the reverence, the fun— all of it led me into genuine worship. By the end, I felt like I didn't need to go to church for a year.[15]

Locations for worship were found that would enable the gospel to come to the people, hence worship took place in storefront properties, auditoriums, parks, or on the street. Less emphasis was given to the preparation and ordination of clergy; those who felt called and were gifted to speak often provided the pastoral leadership for the movement. Tradition was viewed with suspicion, and as in the charismatic renewal movement, priority was given to the immediacy of experiencing God.

An offshoot of the Jesus Movement, the praise and worship (P&W) style developed in the early 1980s. Like the Jesus Movement, P&W is largely music driven. The praise and worship style, however, is an adaptation of the charismatic movement, especially in its incorporation of extended times of singing contemporary songs and Scripture choruses as well as the appreciation for freedom in the Spirit. Praise and worship services emphasize the intimacy of worship and build on the belief that "music and informality must connect with people of a post-Christian culture."[16]

Arguably the most far-reaching worship renewal movement of the second half of the twentieth century occurred not in the Protestant churches, but in the Catholic Church. The touchstone for this renewal was the *Constitution of the Sacred Liturgy of the Second Vatican Council* (Vatican II). "The goal of the constitution was the revival of Christian spirituality and pastoral life in bringing the faithful to the source of Christian life in the Christ mystery of the liturgy."[17] Key reforms instituted by Vatican II include full participation of the faithful in liturgical celebrations, worship instituted in the use of vernacular worldwide, more reading of the Holy Scriptures, greater emphasis on liturgical catechesis, respect for the "genius and talents of the various races and peoples" in their own rendering of the Mass,[18] and full involvement of the people at both the service of the Word and Eucharist.

Because of the depth and breadth of the reforms, along with the lack of precedent for such wholesale change, the full implementation of the reforms of Vatican II are ongoing. Implementation is underway but is not yet complete across the global expanse of Catholicism. Still, research has indicated that the reforms of Vatican II have taken hold and have reshaped Catholic parishes across North America.[19]

These three movements did not take place in a vacuum. Both the charismatic renewal movement and the Jesus Movement were transdenominational in scope and affected almost all Christian traditions, though some more than others. Likewise, many credit Vatican II with forging a trail of liturgical reform for Protestant churches to follow. This is best seen in the revisions of Protestant worship books after Vatican II, along with the widespread acceptance of the three-year Common Lectionary.

Though very different in nature, each of these movements addressed some common themes: the need to emphasize community in worship, the need for full participation of worshipers, and an allowance for, or acceptance of, various stylistic influences in worship. Each movement succeeded in challenging long-standing traditions that defined the church's mission and ministry. These movements opened the door for ecumenical convergence and interchange—both liturgically and theologically.

The result has been disorientation and an uncertainty of what were once clearly identifiable denominational boundaries. Many of the baby boomers, though they were absent from traditional churches during their young adult years, have returned to the church as young parents. This generation was the first to be influenced by the Jesus Movement and has consequently provided fodder for contemporary worship services, which now appear everywhere across the country.

> The music revolution of the 1960s set the stage for music-driven worship. As Webber states, the new approach became "Convert the musicians, bring them into the church and develop a new music-driven worship. And the Jesus movement did just that when numerous guitar-strumming and band-playing longhairs swarmed to Jesus. . . . All over the world new churches were founded by the young. At the end of the century advocates of "church growth" thinking were saying, "Go contemporary or you just will not survive."[20]

Now therefore, worship expressions that would have once been categorized as strictly charismatic now appear regularly in mainline congregations—such as the raising of hands, clapping, dancing, anointing with oil, and so on. And the reforms of Vatican II, such as the renewal of liturgical texts and formulas and the acceptance of each culture in defining ministry practice and worship, have parallels in many Protestant churches.

Most denominations are no longer "settled" into worship patterns or practices. Churches of all types have experienced, and continue to experience, disorientation as traditions are modified and styles of worship are reevaluated. To the dismay of many, worship has become a central defining element of a congregation's ministry. Confusion and anxiety over worship style may be the primary reason for disorientation in Protestant churches at the turn of the century. Citing style of worship music as the number one example of dramatic change (which brings anxiety), George Barna states, "Worship has undergone such dramatic changes in the past several decades. In fact, if we were to track the progression of corporate worship experiences over the past half-century we would identify a vast number of pivotal shifts in church wide worship practices."[21]

Another significant cause for disorientation in ministry in the second half of the twentieth century is the birth and rise of postmodernism. Historians and theologians offer various theories as to when and how the term "postmodern" arose. The term seems to have been first used in relation to certain developments in the arts in the 1930s. In the 1970s, the word was applied to architectural design, but in relation to a broader cultural phenomenon, it has only recently found its way into academic circles and the general populace. In time, "postmodernism" became the generally accepted term for the diverse social and cultural phenomena of the mid-to-late twentieth century. The significance of the movement from modern to postmodern culture cannot be overstated.[22]

At the core of postmodernism is the refusal to acknowledge the existence of absolute truth. Postmodernism is antimodern in that it rejects rational discovery through scientific method alone. The Newtonian approach to truth was primarily based on physical, discernable laws. The answers to the human dilemma (at any level) consisted of unlocking the scientific secrets that would, in turn, create a better world. The primary epistemological assumptions of the Enlightenment were that knowledge is certain, objective, intrinsically good, and obtainable. The modern thinker believed in dispassionate knowledge and believed it was possible for people to be unconditioned observers.

Postmodernists hold no such assumptions. They "reject the Enlightenment quest for universal, supracultural, timeless truth"[23] and see the world as historical, relational, and personal. They do not believe, as did their modern ancestors, that knowledge is inherently good. They need only cite contemporary examples of the abuse of technology to prove their point (the development of nuclear weapons and the threat of their use, for instance).

A second feature of postmodernism is appreciation for community. Whereas modernism emphasized and heralded the individual, postmodern culture is keenly conscious of community. Due to the dissolving center in society, smaller social units are developing that have little in common except locale. There is therefore a growing interest in participation in communities that share common goals and purposes as opposed to a common locale. Robert Webber asserts, "In the postmodern world the most effective churches will be led by those who turn their backs on the corporate market-driven view of the church and return to the theological understanding and practice of the church as the community of God's presence in the world."[24]

A third aspect of postmodernism is the loss of a metanarrative. A metanarrative consists of the collection of stories that in turn constitute a group's history, and thus, its identity. Prior to the end of the twentieth century, there were identifiable metanarratives defining shared worldviews among large communities. But postmodernists strongly believe the metanarrative no longer exists; they have no worldview, but instead, have many worlds and many views. "To the postmodern mind, metanarratives are mere human constructs, fictive devices through which we impose an order on history and make it subject to us."[25]

Where does this discussion of orientation and disorientation take us? What sense can we make of worship in transition, of the push of tradition and the pull of innovation? What does a discussion of modernism versus postmodernism lend to our understanding? I propose the following assertions:

- Worship practices are not yet in the reorientation stage but remain well entrenched in the disorientation stage.
- The renewal movements of the second half of the twentieth century have resulted in a fixation with worship style (though this was not originally their primary intent).
- The transition from one cultural era to another is lengthening the period of disorientation.
- Only when worship leaders (1) move away from style-driven worship and (2) acknowledge the coming of a new cultural age (which has only begun) will we truly move toward reorientation.

Reorientation

Some have argued that because churches across the country have adopted new worship practices, a time of reorientation has already arrived. As proof, they point to the number of churches that have adopted so-called contemporary formats, have attempted to do "blended worship," or have included other previously unknown elements of worship in their service in an effort to pursue innovation. Church growth experts have convinced many that capturing a certain worship style will result in increased church attendance and viability in the competitive church market, thus many churches have tried their hand at making stylistic changes. This had led some to conclude regrettably that "worship in the '90s . . . is a market-driven activity, shaped and defined exclusively by the perceived desires of the progressive church-going consumer. . . . Worship in the '90s equals whatever works, and what works on Sunday or Wednesday night is what fills the pews."[26]

Unfortunately, a number of the change-oriented congregations moved forward without the benefits of critical thinking, theological reflection, or liturgical analysis. In many cases, their attempts did not deliver the desired result. Consequently, numerous churches across the country have ended up with conflict within the ranks and generic worship services that resemble those of any number of other congregations.

Such change-oriented congregations did not understand a central principal of transition: Trying something new does not constitute reorientation. Innovation does not produce a new way of seeing God at work. Worship style has been the approach of choice used to convince others that the church is innovative. Yet the very thing that we hope will deliver reorientation is what holds the church hostage in a stage of disorientation, that is, the commitment to innovation.

One question seemingly drives the issue of worship style: What do people *prefer?* If we listen to the reasons given for any worship change, we will likely hear answers along the lines of "because the young people like it," "because we have to keep up with the culture," and "because so-and-so wants this type of music." The answers themselves give us away. We are chasing a magical, illusive, all-inclusive style.

Pursuing a worship style fails at the practical level because style is a moving target. Styles never stay the same. As soon as it is "cutting edge" in one part of the country, it is out of date in another. The style of worship, like the style of clothing or automobiles or anything else, is subject to change at someone else's whim. By the time one has mastered the style, the style has changed. Pragmatically driven ministry is also inappropriate for theological and practical reasons. Theologically, chasing a worship style as one's foremost endeavor is ill advised because it presumes the wrong question. The style question is always "What do people like?"

I suggest there is a better question to ask: What kind of worship helps people encounter God? This question will lead us away from preferences and toward the true goal of worship. Worship is first and foremost an encounter with the living God through Jesus Christ. Style keeps "program worship" alive (the kind of worship that invites people to observe rather than participate). Helping people encounter God suggests a means of participation rather than a style of service.

What does "participation" mean in our current North American culture? Before the participation level of a service can be addressed, we must first review where we are in relation to the current dramatic cultural shifts. At the turn of the century, our culture is neither modern nor postmodern; it is in flux, oscillating between modernity and postmodernity, and will remain so for quite some time. The shift from modernity to postmodernity is a change in *eras,* a transition that occurs much more slowly than a change in *generations.*[27] Therefore it is becoming increasingly evident that as we set the table for worship and invite people to the table, we can no longer assume that catering to their tastes will satisfy their hunger. Of greater importance will be our ability to honor the reality that the ways in which people receive information, perceive truth, and encounter God are shifting.

People are drawn to style-driven worship, not because they choose to be but because the next generations of worshipers have been inculturated to be consumers. People have become accustomed to being sold to, and churches are now viewed as products.[28] This has directly affected the way we receive and give religious information. Pierre Babin, author of *The New Era in Religious Communication,* posits that due to the communications revolution at the end of the twentieth century, people are definitely attuned to receiving messages in a new way. He proposes that people in our culture are experiencing a deep desire for meaning, for the transcendent, for love, and for the mystical—in short, for a true and deep experience with God. But he also suggests that due to the swift and dramatic change in the way in which information is presented today, people are experiencing God by way of delivery systems that are visual and image oriented as never before.[29]

Cultural scholars are in agreement: There is an increasing dependency on imagination, the visual, the symbolic, story, and picture as the primary means of communication.[30] Among them, Babin goes so far as to say that the medium itself has become the message: "The medium is not just a limited technical prop, but the totality of the infrastructures and conditions necessary for a medium to function."[31]

Prior to the development of the Gutenberg press in the mid-fifteenth century, culture was primarily an oral and visual culture. Information was transmitted orally by the religious community. This also allowed for the transmission of emotion in connection with the information, thereby adding the dimension of valuing. Feeling was combined with intellect. Information was transmitted not only orally but through the visual as well. Dramatic presentations, symbolic gestures, images that proclaimed the faith, and other forms of visual art transmitted truth.[32]

The written tradition began a new era, lasting from the late fifteenth century to the end of the twentieth. The method by which faith was learned changed dramatically. The written tradition became the way of learning faith for the next five centuries. The result was that "slowly but surely, rational analysis, the practice of making logical distinctions and connections, and the cult of obedience to formulas and to canon law became more important than feeling oneself at one with the church or taking an active part in the liturgy."[33]

The last five hundred years has emphasized cerebral faith, linear thinking, reason, logical argument, and faith arrived at by a mental acceptance of doctrines. The communication revolution of the late twentieth century, with its dependency once again on the use of image, the visual, symbol, and drama, is quickly moving our culture from the era of print to a new era of the oral and visual.

If this is true, and there is significant evidence that it is, we are back to the preferred question: What best helps people to encounter God? Because we are between a shift in eras, the answer will be "through a variety of means of encounter," and will continue to be for quite some time. Here is where we can accept and work with the idea of innovation. To innovate is to make new, but now we are speaking of innovation in a fuller way; we are endeavoring to create new and varied opportunities for modernists, postmodernists, and everyone in between to encounter God.

Modernists will continue to perceive God largely through powers of reason, appeal to the cognitive, logical argument, and printed text. Those among the first wave of postmodernists (and generations to follow) will perceive God through experiencing the transcendence and mystery of God, through story, silence, symbol, color, and image. Modernists will continue to be comfortable with an individual religious experience, even in corporate worship; postmodernists will yearn for a true sense of community in corporate worship.

The longer the church stays fixated on style-driven worship and the longer it ignores the implications of postmodernism, the longer the period of disorientation will be. As stated earlier, reorientation is a new way of seeing God's purposes through God's eyes. Reorientation is not so much what we *do,* but what *God does in us* to change our hearts and vision. The point isn't to come up with "answers" that will get us out of disorientation but to watch and pray so that we are able to recognize God moving the church toward a new way of being.

In the Meantime

As we find ourselves in a time of great transition, how can we approach our worship dilemmas? Perhaps we could develop "bilingual worship." Being bilingual means having the vocabulary, the syntax, and the inflection to communicate in two separate languages. Interestingly, people who are bilingual can flow back and forth between languages, even within one conversation. Both of the languages are native tongues for them; they do not have to stop and analyze the grammar before speaking, they simply speak and listen.

Worship language at the turn of the century would benefit from bilingual capabilities. On the one hand, we all have inherited the language of the tradition of the church. There exists a holy vocabulary that has been well crafted over twenty centuries of living faith. It contains words of biblical beauty and theological integrity and forms a vocabulary that is appropriate to all Christian groups. The written texts of worship (prayers, liturgies, songs, and creeds) utilize a language that is familiar to the whole church and treasured by the whole church. This language is passed on through generations of believers and becomes the worshiper's native tongue.

The second language to be spoken is that of sign and symbol, transcendence and mystery, picture and image, drama and gesture. It is the language of visual and oral expression and is reintroduced to us by way of our cultural orientation. The first language invites participation at the cognitive level; the second language invites participation at the affective level. Both provide genuine opportunities to encounter God in a world that is in need of experiencing the Eternal. Providing these opportunities is a far cry from providing stylistic choices. Style-driven worship attempts to please others; bilingual worship helps others to find their worship language so that they can actively minister to the one who created them and awaits their adoration.

Perhaps people in the new century don't need to find their worship style as much as they need to find their worship voice. One suggests satisfying preferences; the other suggests enabling worshipers to do the active, participatory, work of worship. I propose that the merging of tradition and innovation in the life of the church will best occur when we decide to ask better questions, admit that cultural shifts will likely keep us in transition for quite a while, and prayerfully listen to God, awaiting reorientation from God and remembering that the process of "going through" is what moves us "to"—in this case, to a new era of Christian ministry.

2

A Rose by Any Other Name

Attempts at Classifying North American Protestant Worship

Lester Ruth

How would you classify the worship of your church or parish? It is "contemporary" or "traditional"? Are those terms too limited? In that case, would the terms "linear" or "organic," as found in some recent youth ministry training materials, be more helpful? [1] Still at a loss for the right classification? Maybe these terms from a recent online worship forum would be more accurate: "multisensory worship," "indigenous worship," "innovative worship," "transformation worship," "blended worship," "praise services," "spirited traditional," "creative," or "classic worship"? [2] Or are ethnic or racial designators more descriptive of your service's character: "African-American," "Hispanic," "Euro-American," or some other similar designation? [3]

Has the term that is exactly right for your church's worship not been mentioned yet? If so, then how about "multimedia worship," "authentic worship," "liturgical worship," "praise and worship," or "seeker services"? [4] Perhaps terms rooted in various intended "audiences" would be better: "believer-oriented worship," "believer-oriented worship made visitor-friendly," or "visitor-oriented worship." [5] Some scholars now advocate classifications by generations. And so, is your worship service "boomer," "buster," "Gen-X," or "millenials'" worship?

As you can see, there exists a dizzying array of terms and classifications for worship. This diversity of classification schemes reflects the current state of Protestant worship in North America. A cacophony of terms describe the wide range of worship services. Even single resources can contribute to the Babel of classification schemes. In one recent anthology on worship, for example, the titles for the various essays showed designations derived by stylistic, theological, ethnic, and age-specific considerations. [6]

Is it possible to find some semblance of order within these widely different taxonomies for worship? In our attempt to do so, the first step will be to examine four current taxonomies and recognize their strengths and limitations. Then, building on some of these taxonomies and filtering the usable data through some categories derived from Robert Webber, I will suggest some ways of classifying North American Protestant approaches to worship that I hope are true to their breadth. While the new taxonomic schemes I will present do not exhaust all possible taxonomies, I hope they will offer some helpful designations. The taxonomy I will suggest makes classifications based on the nature of liturgical commemoration (What is remembered over time from worship service to service?), the dominant sacramental principle in a congregation's worship (What is the primary way worshipers assess God's presence in worship?), and liturgical polity (What is the method by which worship is planned in individual congregations?). These taxonomical categories are suggested because they are broad enough to be applied to all North American Protestant worship and yet are important enough to show true differences among Protestant worship today.

A Popular Scheme: The Traditional/Contemporary/Blended Worship Taxonomy

One of the most popular classification schemes today is a taxonomy that uses the terms traditional, contemporary, and blended worship. Among American Protestants, these terms are pervasive in conversations, in popular literature, and, unfortunately, in "worship wars." A sizable number of Protestant churches have moved to offering multiple worship services every week, distinguishing between the services by these labels.

Despite the pervasiveness of the three terms, and despite some kind of assumption about their general meaning, the specific meanings of these terms are unclear. Very often they are code words. *Traditional* designates "what we have been doing," usually meaning a form of mainstream Protestant worship that reflects practices of the mid-twentieth century and has roots in the Victorian Era. *Contemporary* typically designates "what we could or should be doing." Often, this term implies worship that has some combination of the following "contemporary" characteristics: worship attuned to popular culture, particularly in entertainment forms; use of music that is highly repetitive, syncopated, and reflective of pop music; reliance on electronic technology; a quick pace and rhythm in the service; minimal ceremony; an informal style of leadership; and use of worship leaders to demonstrate the physical and emotional dimensions of worship.[7] In popular usage *blended worship* tends to refer to worship that uses both traditional hymnody and contemporary choruses.[8] While some—most notably theologian Robert Webber[9]—have a more sophisticated, nuanced use of this term, it frequently amounts to little more than a quota system for music and dramatic skits.

All these terms—traditional, contemporary, and blended worship—have severe limitations and should be rejected in any serious taxonomy of worship. Simply put, as commonly used, these terms are too general for too limited a phenomenon.

That many of the works seeking to explore the best approach to contemporary worship sometimes include in "contemporary" what might be popularly designated as "traditional" shows the limited usefulness of this scheme. For example, one recent writer includes what he calls "liturgical worship" as a type of contemporary worship.[10] But what he describes as liturgical worship, others would label traditional. If the terms are that fluid, what real meaning do they have?

This popular taxonomy suffers other serious limitations. Given worship's inherent conservatism (over time even newly created congregations tend to stabilize and maintain patterns), eventually the term contemporary must fall out of usage, or churches will end up with the oxymoron of "traditional contemporary" worship in a few generations.

In addition, those who use traditional/contemporary language usually have too limited a historical horizon. From one angle, "contemporary worship" really is not contemporary. When I reviewed the multiple orders of worship for so-called contemporary worship on an online forum, for instance, the orders all reflected a very traditional order of worship that features proclamation as the climactic act. Such an order of worship has been the mainstay of much American Protestant worship for a couple of centuries. Other than a change in the stylistic veneer, what is truly contemporary about that? Similarly, from a greater historical perspective, "traditional worship" really is not traditional. When using the term traditional, most people do not have in mind deep worship traditions, whether those of the early church or of the originators of various Protestant movements like Luther or Wesley.

Consequently, the traditional/contemporary taxonomy is inadequate for describing approaches to worship, whether denominational or congregational. For example, how should we classify a vibrant congregation of Quakers worshiping in complete silence until they receive the Holy Spirit's unction to leave? Is this "traditional" because it follows a classic Quaker approach that has a long history reaching back to the seventeenth century? Or it is "contemporary" because the worshipers might be wearing casual clothing? Since there is no music at all, musical style cannot be the key to classifying this service. And what about an African-American congregation using gospel music in a classically structured Eucharist service? Is it "contemporary" because the music has been recently composed and has a beat? Or is it "traditional" because many of the texts can be traced back to the patristic era, as can the basic order of worship? Similarly, what about the two Episcopal churches close to my home that

use the *Book of Common Prayer* Eucharist service but have praise teams leading the music while the congregations follow along on PowerPoint projections?
Is this "traditional" or "contemporary"? Is it "blended" even though there is
only one style of music and leadership?

Seeing the limitations of this scheme's terminology, some scholars show signs
of moving away from the traditional/contemporary taxonomy. For instance,
in seeking a term that speaks of worship as emerging from a worshiping people rather than as something merely imitated from elsewhere, Leonard Sweet
prefers the term "indigenous" over "contemporary."[11] Others reject the all too
often antagonistic positioning of the terms (traditional versus contemporary),
noting that each speaks of qualities desirable for all worship services.

> Attempts to reform worship that rely exclusively on either traditional or con-
> temporary models are not adequate solutions to our longing for more faithful
> worship. This is actually a false dichotomy since authentic Christian worship is
> by necessity both contemporary and traditional. It is traditional because it must
> continue the story of Jesus Christ in the world in history, and it is contempo-
> rary because it must be engaged with the present, with actual people who live
> in particular cultures.[12]

Even the term "blended worship" is too limited for serious use since it too
often describes merely a kind of quota system for worship. As one scholar
recently lampooned: "[In] many congregations . . . we'll do a traditional hymn,
then we'll do a praise song. We'll have the classic structure, but we'll spice it
up with skits. A little of this and a little of that, and everyone will be happy."[13]
Such an approach to blended worship tends to deal only with the surface issues
of worship performance without dealing with the more substantial issues of
the structure, content, and purpose of worship.[14]

Given that these terms used in this popular scheme—traditional, contemporary, blended—are too ill defined and are likely to pass out of usage, a comprehensive taxonomy for North American worship must be found elsewhere.

A Polemical, Apologetic Scheme: The Taxonomy of William Easum and Thomas Bandy

Well-known church consultants William Easum and Thomas Bandy provide an example of a liturgical taxonomy shaped by a polemic that seeks to promote a certain evangelistic agenda. Easum and Bandy work together as Easum,
Bandy, and Associates, an organization that provides a range of educational
and consultation services for churches. According to its web-posted "approach
to ministry," this organization "helps leaders organize priorities, identify goals,
innovate new strategies, and motivate congregations to address the spiritually
yearning, institutionally alienated seekers of today." They claim to have pre-

pared more than 75,000 church leaders in the United States and Canada since 1988.[15]

It is somewhat inaccurate to speak of a single taxonomy by Easum and Bandy. Their writings reflect related but ever-shifting sets of terms to classify worship. In a short 1997 essay, Easum lays out an early two-term taxonomy: "traditional" and "contemporary."[16] According to Easum, traditional worship uses the printed page, a sixteenth-century style of music and "linear, somber, slow forms of printed liturgy." Creeds and periods of silence are important, too. Contemporary worship, in contrast, does not have much quiet time; it produces a visual experience and uses "indigenous" music that is "plugged-in and turned up."

In their joint book, *Growing Spiritual Redwoods*, also published in 1997, Easum and Bandy offer several taxonomies for classifying worship. The most fundamental is a variation of the traditional/contemporary scheme. Seeking to define basic categories to assist in worship planning, the authors describe three possibilities: "traditional," "praise," and "sensory" worship.[17] In traditional worship, "participants give thanks in formal, historically grounded, rational ways." This "track" is for those who prefer "robes, hymnals, creeds, quiet time, and Elizabethan-type music." Praise worship "seeks to release the emotions and express the joy many people who were formerly estranged from relationship with Jesus now feel." Praise worship is a "celebration" focused on a certain kind of music. It is a "spectator or entertainment style of worship, with little quiet time and no emphasis on guilt." Sensory worship is characterized by a heavy use of sensory experience other than hearing. It occurs "less in words, and more in the sights and sounds, images and music, that surround the worship experience." It consists of permeating sights and sounds, video and visuals, rather than print or verbal speech and uses "extra-loud, plugged-in, turned-up music."[18] Easum and Bandy connect this taxonomy to generational appeal: traditional worship appeals to those who "by physical age or mental orientation" find "some form of Christendom worship meaningful," praise worship to baby boomers, and sensory worship to the vast majority of people born after 1965.[19]

This traditional/praise/sensory taxonomy is not the only one Easum and Bandy offer in *Growing Spiritual Redwoods*. Elsewhere they speak of "transactive" worship (conveys the gospel across gaps), "interactive" worship (involves participants in a reciprocal or mutually shared thanksgiving), and "actualized" worship (makes faith as realistic and comprehensive as possible).[20] Later in the book, they provide a taxonomy based on different ways worship services can address human need. This taxonomy offers four options: "healing," "coaching," "cherishing," and "rejoicing" worship.[21] They also provide another taxonomy of a sort when they describe the characteristics of "indigenous" worship. Such worship makes experience more important than content, is interconnected with everyday life, uses indigenous music, uses video and sound systems as crucial elements, replaces choir practices with technology rehearsals, and has "constant, uninterrupted flow."[22]

In subsequent writings, Easum and Bandy have continued to evolve their taxonomies. In a 2000 article on "multi-tracking" worship in a congregation (that is, providing multiple worship opportunities targeted at different groups' spiritual needs), Bandy expands a taxonomy laid out earlier, noting differences in "healing," "coaching," "cherishing," "celebration," and "traditional" worship.[23] Similarly, Easum takes the earlier traditional/contemporary or traditional/praise/sensory categories and adds some qualitative adjectives. Easum now sees four kinds of worship services: "spiritless traditional," "spirited traditional," "praise," and "postmodern."[24] According to Easum, the category of spiritless traditional is the most prevalent and is found in 80 percent of churches. It is "slow, linear, and predictable," enabling people to sleep through the services. The music is slow and played on organs. The service is filled with dead spots. To outsiders, these services feel lifeless, dull, and boring. The spirited traditional form of worship is found in less than 10 percent of churches, according to Easum. It is characterized by passion in the pulpit and vitality in the pews. It moves with precision and has an abundance of good music. Despite its current vitality, however, it reflects a "culture whose day has long passed." Praise worship is used by 90 percent of growing churches in Easum's opinion. The most notable element of the service is the music itself. Other common characteristics include solid preaching, drama, an informal atmosphere, and no "dead spots." Postmodern worship uses a variety of musical styles in an ever-changing tide of services. It uses every form of technology, offers a clear and uncompromising message, and develops authenticity, intimacy, and community.

Although the precise terms vary from publication to publication, there are several constants in Easum's and Bandy's taxonomies. Their tone does not vary. The taxonomies are polemical and apologetic throughout. The two men bring an iconoclastic tendency to their descriptions. Determined to advocate measures that will achieve evangelistic success, the two consultants attach descriptions to their categories that will make what they are advocating the most attractive and what they consider problematic the least attractive. They show no concern for detached, objective descriptions.

Indeed, there tends to be a certain kind of dualism running throughout the liturgical writings of Easum and Bandy. In their opinion, some forms of worship are bad; others are good. Generally, those forms of worship they associate with mainstream Protestantism of the latter half of the twentieth century are found to be bad because they show so little potential for accomplishing Easum's and Bandy's evangelistic goals. In Easum's terminology, these are the spiritless traditional services, and the two men describe these services in very harsh terms. In contrast, they portray other kinds of worship in glowing terms.

Standing behind this dualism is Easum's and Bandy's fundamental concern: positive personal experience in worship. Their classification schemes are really taxonomies of how they perceive and believe people to be responding to the current variety in worship. Their taxonomical method is rooted in a concern for a positive personal experience in worship. Consider the emphasis on personal experience as a fundamental category in Easum's summary of worship: "No matter what type of worship a church uses, one thing is important: People must experience the transforming presence of God. Anything less isn't worship, no matter the style."[25] The two consultants typically see newer forms of mainstream Protestant worship as creating positive experiences.

This concern for experience has two facets within their thought. One is assessing people's immediate reaction to different kinds of worship. The other is an emphasis on culturally accessible communication as the primary purpose of worship. Thus Bandy can suggest two reasons why people are not attending his reader's worship service. Either "your current worship service does not address their spiritual needs" or "your current worship service does not communicate in their cultural forms."[26] These concerns thoroughly color the taxonomies of Easum and Bandy. They view a category of worship highly if they believe it gives people a positive experience of Christ.[27] Likewise, since a primary purpose of worship is communication, worship practices that use newer communication forms receive more glowing endorsements.

There are several limitations in Easum's and Bandy's taxonomies. The first comes from the polemical nature of their writings. They are so eager to advocate a certain approach that their descriptions too often fall into caricatures. This is true even for the types of worship that they advocate. Their writings universalize their own experiences and perceptions of the struggles in mainstream Protestantism.[28] Their biases seep into their writings, cutting off consideration of worship's true breadth. Consider, for example, two depictions of traditional worship. Traditional worship involves "robes, hymnals, creeds, quiet time, and Elizabethan-type music" and "the linear, somber, slow forms of printed liturgy."[29] How would this description apply to an African-American congregation using a gospel music setting for their weekly eucharistic service or to an Episcopal eucharistic service using so-called contemporary music? Consider another caricature: the idea that sensory worship that appeals to younger adults will use "extra-loud, plugged-in, turned-up music."[30] How does this caricature square with the increasingly popular phenomenon of young adults attracted to services using the quiet, contemplative music of Taizé, the ecumenical community of France?[31] Unfortunately, if one does not read carefully, Easum's and Bandy's prescriptions for worship too often verge on being absolute—but inaccurate—descriptions of worship.

Another limitation found in the writings of Easum and Bandy is their lack of emphasis on the theological content of worship. Given their liturgical method (the use of qualitative categories based on worshipers' positive responses and the presumption that numerical growth validates worship practices), it would be possible to misuse their categories to legitimize forms of worship that should be illegitimate for Christians. For example, the shallowness of their categories that connect "inspirational" and "spirited" to "transformative" could be used to affirm classic Shaker worship of the nineteenth century, despite its hetero-dox anti-Trinitarian theology. The Shakers were evangelizing effectively with new forms of worship that moved people (literally) and transformed lives. Could not Easum's and Bandy's categories be used to affirm this worship, even though it was clearly unorthodox? Admittedly, the two men do not overtly advocate unorthodox worship, but given the lack of theological concern in their taxonomies, one wonders why Shaker worship would not fall into their "good" categories. That is precisely the problem with an intentionally dualis-tic, polemical taxonomy like theirs: too little thoughtfulness stands behind the categories.

In addition, the classification schemes of Easum and Bandy are limited in that any taxonomies in which the classifications are rooted in worshipers' per-sonal reactions tell us more about the worshipers (or classifiers) than the wor-ship itself. Using categories based in experience or reaction is too highly sub-jective, since different people could have a completely different reaction to the same worship service. Different theologies, cultural backgrounds, capacities for ritual activity, and spiritual inclinations among worshipers could result in vastly varying interpretations of the same worship service. In that case what does "spirited" or "inspirational" worship mean? One suspects that in Easum's and Bandy's writings such terms always mean a kind of worship they like.

An Evangelical, Pastoral Scheme: The Taxonomy of Paul Basden

Paul Basden provides another recent taxonomy of North American wor-ship.[32] Basden, a Baptist pastor, created his taxonomy for a different purpose and audience. Compiled to help evangelical churches understand different approaches to worship that they may follow, Basden's taxonomy is instructive in that it shows how a current American evangelical might see the diversity of North American worship. As a comprehensive taxonomy for North American worship, however, it is incomplete.

Basden constructs his taxonomy as a one-dimensional, horizontal spectrum using popular, nontechnical labels. The distinct categories assess different kinds of worship "styles," which Basden appears to use as a broad term for forms of worship. The elements he assesses to determine different styles of worship include the following: attitude, mood, order of worship, "target audience," congregational singing, special music, musical instrumentation, amount of Scripture, offering, manner of preaching, manner of "invitation," and approach to ordinances and sacraments.[33] He develops a five-point spectrum in order to go beyond the simple traditional/nontraditional or traditional/contemporary/ blended categories often used today.[34]

With the goal of discerning distinct styles of worship, Basden identifies five main styles and places them along a spectrum, the left-hand side being the most traditional, and the right, the least.[35] In chart form, Basden's spectrum looks like this:

Liturgical   Traditional   Revivalist   Praise and Worship   Seeker

Basden's main concern is to describe the nature of each of these styles. Identification of each category with a particular denomination, ethnic group, or historical figure is offered, but is a secondary concern. When such details are specifically identified, Basden's spectrum looks like this:

Liturgical	Traditional	Revivalist	Praise and Worship	Seeker
Lutheran	Reformed	Zwingli	Black worship	Willow Creek
Anglican	Separatist	Quaker	Pentecostal	Saddleback
	Puritan	Wesleyan		
		Frontier		

Basden details what he means by each category. Generally, "liturgical" worship has the strongest historical roots; its goal is "to bow before the holiness of God in structured reverence."[36] Liturgical worship is the form of worship used by most mainline Protestant and Roman Catholic churches. "Traditional" worship is a hybrid of its two neighbors, "liturgical" and "revivalist."[37] From its liturgical roots comes a sense of dignity and reverence; from its revivalist connections comes a concern with moving the hearts of the worshipers. "Revivalist" worship derives from American frontier roots. It is characterized by "informality, exuberance, zeal and aggressive preaching," all of which are aimed to convert sinners.[38] Basden identifies "praise and worship" mainly with Pentecostal worship. It is worship aimed at bringing believers into an intimate sense of God's presence through music.[39] The "seeker" approach is a rehash of the revivalist goal, albeit in a toned-down format. Seeker worship attempts to present the gospel to unbelievers.[40]

Basden's taxonomy has several strengths. It focuses on congregational phenomena, and thus, offers itself as a possible taxonomy for assessing what is currently happening in North American Protestant worship. It recognizes diversity within denominations. It is concerned with God's presence in worship, which, as I will argue, is an important way to distinguish among approaches to worship. And importantly, Basden attempts to be open-minded as he tries to provide a fair, attractive description of each worship style.

Basden's taxonomy does have some flaws, however. Because he does not limit himself to current expressions of worship, Basden at times makes historical overstatements. For example, it is quite surprising to find the sixteenth-century Reformer Ulrich Zwingli, the seventeenth-century Quaker founder George Fox, and the eighteenth-century Anglican priest and founder of the Methodist movement John Wesley grouped together as examples of the revivalist category.[41] Those preferring a history-based taxonomy would do better with James White's more historically accurate taxonomy, which I will describe later.

A severe flaw occurs in the use of "liturgical" as a taxonomical category. Such usage must be questioned on theological grounds. Basden, following popular evangelical usage, seems to intend this term to mean a certain way of doing worship that involves a high level of ceremony, use of historically grounded texts, and a certain reverential tone. Although this usage might be common among evangelicals, it is poor theology to limit "liturgical" to one "style" of Christian worship, because it implies that the rest of Christian worship is not "liturgical." In a theological sense, "liturgical" does not refer to a certain style of worship—formal with much ceremony—but to a church's worship participating in the ongoing ministry of Jesus Christ before God the Father (Heb. 8:1–2). "Liturgical" refers to worship as a work of the people, a public service. It can refer to both Christ's work on humanity's behalf and the church's participation as the body of Christ in the ongoing ministry of Christ for all people. In this theological sense, all Christian worship must be "liturgical" to be truly Christian. Thus the theological question is not whether any certain kind of Christian worship is liturgical or not, but *how* it is liturgical. "Liturgical" should not be used as a classifying term to distinguish a worship style.

Basden's spectrum breaks down at some points. Looking at whether the different styles of worship address primarily Christians or non-Christians, a style's placement on the spectrum does not indicate its approach to this issue. Thus "revivalist" (in the center of the spectrum) and "seeker" (on the far right end) target non-Christians, while "praise and worship," located between these two, is concerned with leading Christians into worship (as are "liturgical" and "traditional").

Basden's taxonomy is also limited in that it is not comprehensive enough. Basden is Baptist, and that perspective, naturally enough, seems to be his real point of reference. Many of his examples of each type of worship are Baptist examples. Because his intended audience seems to be evangelical churches trying to find their way through the worship "maze," he tends to underemphasize approaches to worship that are not viable options for mainstream evangelicals.

Basden's taxonomy tends toward caricature at several points. For instance, because it makes classifications based on worshipers' reactions, Basden can paint a picture that presumes all Christian approaches to worship have as a primary purpose a desire to elicit responses from the worshipers—possibly a projection of Basden's own experience. But that is not necessarily the case for all Protestant approaches to worship.

Likewise, even some strengths of his taxonomy, such as assessing the manner of God's presence in worship, can lead to caricature. Basden spends quite a bit of time linking what he sees as different dimensions of God's presence to different types of worship. Thus "liturgical" worship cultivates a sense of God's transcendence but not immanence.[42] "Traditional" worship, in comparison, yields both a sense of God's transcendence and immanence, while "praise and worship" focuses on a sense of God's immanence.[43]

Examining the way in which God's presence is experienced in the different forms of worship has potential for a solid taxonomy—and will be revisited below—but Basden's use of this aspect of worship is too subjective and can lead to inaccurate caricatures. It would not be too hard to find "liturgical" churches with active, deep fellowships in which a tremendous sense of God's immanence is experienced during the exchange of the peace of Christ or reception of the Eucharist. Similarly, one can imagine a Pentecostal church bowed before a sense of God's transcendence after a particularly moving word of prophecy embedded within the time of music. Basden's taxonomy would benefit from looking not at a subjective, qualitative sense of God's presence but at the ordinary means by which the worshiping congregation senses God's presence. In other words, not whether the God's presence is experienced as transcendent or immanent but whether the people expect to find his presence in their music, their preaching, or in their sacraments.

Finally, Basden's taxonomy suffers from his overstatements. For example, he describes the purpose of praise and worship services as guiding worshipers "to offer a sacrifice of praise . . . in a spirit of joyful adoration." Surely, this is such a broad and basic statement that one wonders who in Basden's taxonomy would not want to claim it.

A Thorough Historical Scheme: The Taxonomy of James White

Noted liturgical historian James White has created perhaps the most thorough Protestant liturgical taxonomy. This thoughtful scheme reflects the breadth of White's knowledge and is the place to ground any serious study of Protestant liturgical classification. White's evenhanded scholarship is evident as one views the continual development of his taxonomy over fifteen years to its present, mature form. White began intentionally publishing a comprehensive taxonomy for Protestant worship in 1975. Several revisions followed until he published a final form of the taxonomy in 1989.[44] White's goal is a comprehensive taxonomy to classify the different traditions of Protestant worship from their origins to their present expressions.

The heart of White's taxonomy is his identification of nine Protestant worship traditions: Lutheran, Anglican, Reformed, Methodist, Puritan, Anabaptist, Quaker, Frontier, and Pentecostal. White identifies these nine traditions based on key enduring characteristics of each. He emphasizes this ethos of each tradition's approach rather than the older approach in his discipline that emphasized each tradition's liturgical texts. White chooses to emphasize each tradition's ethos rather than its liturgical texts because, as White himself points out, some Protestants do not have liturgical texts, having rejected their use in worship as part of the tradition's ethos.

From his first published taxonomy to its mature form in *Protestant Worship: Traditions in Transition* (1989), White is fairly consistent in the list of elements he uses to determine the distinctive ethos of the various Protestant liturgical traditions. These "central elements" that distinguish one Protestant tradition from another include the use or absence of service books, the importance or unimportance of sacraments, tendencies to uniformity based on codification or lack thereof, congregational autonomy or connectionalism, the varying roles of music and the other arts, ceremony or its absence, variety and predictability, and various sociological factors.[45] White builds his taxonomy on these factors, first identifying a cluster of characteristics that constitute a distinctive ethos, then labeling that ethos as a Protestant worship tradition, and finally describing how those characteristics define that Protestant tradition. Thus the Lutheran tradition shows a basic conservatism, a love of music, a concern for preaching, and a toleration of indifferent matters (for example, robes) as long as they do not suggest works righteousness. The Methodist tradition is a hybrid tradition that mixes certain Anglican roots with a Free Church attitude. Added to this mix are a good dose of pragmatism and, at least originally, an interest in examples from the early church. The Quaker tradition, in comparison, emphasizes direct access to the Holy Spirit and waiting for the Spirit to move before any action is taken in worship. It is a form of corporate mysticism, as a classic Quaker approach abolishes all presupposed outward forms of worship. White's earlier works describe each tradition in an abbreviated form. His 1989 book, *Protestant Worship*, gives a chapter-length examination to each.

Differences in essential character or ethos is how White distinguishes between the various Protestant traditions. Having established a distinctive identity for each, White places the nine traditions under three broad classifications: left wing, central, and right wing. While acknowledging that these terms are pulled from the political arena, White does not mean them in a literal political sense.[46] Instead, White intends to show in these broad political terms a tradition's relative position to late medieval Western liturgical roots, one of his main criteria for distinguishing among Protestant worship traditions. White labels two of the Protestant traditions (Lutheran and Anglican) as right wing, meaning that, with respect to late-medieval liturgical forms, their worship practices have reflected a more restrained revision. In contrast, the central groups (Reformed and Methodist) reflect a more remote attachment to the ways of worship of the late Middle Ages. The left-wing groups (Anabaptist, Quaker, Puritan, Frontier, and Pentecostal) show the least connection to medieval roots.[47]

In addition to these two bases for distinction—a tradition's enduring characteristics of ethos and its relative position to the medieval past—White also notes each tradition's date of origin to develop his full taxonomy. The result is a two-dimensional spectrum that visually represents the relative position of each Protestant tradition to the others and to its medieval roots. The horizontal access in this spectrum represents the relative connection to medieval roots with the right-wing traditions, as might be guessed, on the right hand side of the spectrum and vice versa. The vertical axis represents each tradition's point of origin in history. The older Protestant traditions appear at the top of the vertical axis, and the younger toward the bottom. This mature taxonomical chart first appeared in 1989 and is reproduced below.

White's Chart of the Protestant Traditions of Worship[48]

Origins	Left Wing		Central	Right Wing	
16th century		Anabaptist	Reformed	Anglican	Lutheran
17th century	Quaker	Puritan			
18th century			Methodist		
19th century	Frontier				
20th century	Pentecostal				

A subsequent version included lines to show shifts and developments. In another adaptation, White has also produced a version of the taxonomy that links the different traditions to European regions when appropriate.[49]

White's taxonomy has both strengths and limitations. It is strongest when used for describing the origins of historically distinct approaches. White's tremendous grasp of liturgical history is evident. Not surprisingly, his taxonomy is therefore a good tool for showing the nature of distinct approaches to Protestant worship in their original forms. In addition, the characteristics he identifies for assessing each tradition's ethos are very perceptive and remain useful.

The taxonomy is less useful for showing the actual types of Protestant worship in use *now*.[50] White himself hints at this limitation in his classification scheme when he notes that it is easier to define the center of a tradition than its periphery.[51] In addition, White recognizes that cultural and ethnic differences can deeply affect the expression of a tradition in any context. Moreover, White recognizes a degree of blurring among the traditions, as certain cultural shifts (for example, the Enlightenment) can cause similar fallout among the traditions.[52] White also recognizes that ecumenical sharing can cause the blurring of lines between traditions.[53]

Failure to recognize these limitations could lead to a false picture of the current state of Protestant worship in North America. If a reader failed to see the factors that lead to blurring over time, it would be possible to overemphasize a distinction between, for example, Methodist and Reformed worship. In actuality, due to a variety of factors, many of the traditions named by White can now represent a rather wide spectrum of worship practices. Put more simply, can anyone really say what it means to worship according to the Methodist or the Reformed tradition right now in North America? Churches belonging to a tradition identified by White—even to the same denomination within that tradition—can vary widely in worship practices today, even if they are located on the same street in the same city. White's own prophecy, written in the first publication of his taxonomy, seems to have come true: "It is quite possible that the greatest differences will soon be discernible within groups that previously would have been reckoned distinct traditions."[54] That would suggest that a different set of labels other than the ones suggested by White, which tend to be historically based, would be helpful for describing the current diversity of Protestant worship in North America.

Suggestions for a New Taxonomy

Where does our examination of these taxonomies leave us? If we desire a taxonomy that is simple enough to distinguish basic differences among Protestant churches, yet broad enough to cover the full range of current North American practices, whose taxonomy offers the most guidance? The popular traditional/contemporary/blended taxonomy is hopelessly simplistic. Easum's and Bandy's taxonomies are too polemical; they provide more information about the agenda of these two men than they do about the true range of Christian worship practices. Basden's taxonomy has some helpful points but is too narrow and, at times, inaccurate. James White's taxonomy is the most thorough, well developed, and historically sound. It is strongest, however, as a *historical* taxonomy for Protestant worship. Its categories are not as helpful in distinguishing the variety of current approaches to Christian worship

All is not lost with these taxonomies. I believe it is possible to take the root information behind White's taxonomy—his notion of the ethos of each tradition—and combine it with some insights from Robert Webber in order to achieve the goal of a simple, accurate, yet broad set of classifying terms for Christian worship in North America today.[55]

In speaking about the planning of worship, Robert Webber often makes a distinction between content, structure, and style in worship.[56] This framework is itself a helpful step because it takes us beyond simply looking at stylistic issues, which is where some popular taxonomies stop. In fact, I suggest that it is the other two elements (content and structure) that are the most helpful for developing categories to classify worship. This takes Webber's terms beyond what he himself does with them. For Webber, who tends to advocate a certain approach to worship in his publications, believes the content and structure of worship should remain fairly steady. The content and structure he suggests is derived from the Bible and based on deep historical norms.[57] I believe the fact that he must *advocate* certain classic content and structure in worship highlights that it is precisely on these crucial matters that diversity abounds in Christian worship.

And so, taking White's notion that different liturgical approaches can be defined by differences in ethos and Webber's distinctions between content and structure, I suggest two initial ways of classifying worship today. The first deals with the question of content. Specifically, what is the content of a church's worship in terms of whose story is told: the personal story of the believer or the cosmic story of God? No one service or Sunday is likely to fully disclose how to classify a congregation. This must be assessed over a longer period of time, evaluating the worship from week to week. I suggest two categories for classifying content: personal-story churches and cosmic-story churches. There are churches whose worship over time is most focused on the personal stories of the worshipers and how God interacts with their stories. In contrast, there are churches whose worship over time unfolds a more cosmic remembrance of the grand sweep of God's saving activity. The goal here will be to show how worshipers have a share in salvation history. These two categories represent a continuum rather than an absolute distinction, since few churches appear to exist strictly in one mode or the other.

Personal-story churches and cosmic-story churches can be distinguished by how their worship answers this question: What needs to be remembered corporately in worship? The different answers may not be readily identifiable in a single element in a single congregation. Rather, over time, one must assess how a church selects the Scripture it will read, the normal purpose of the sermon, the regular content of prayers and music, the nature of any dramatic presentations, and the special holidays that are observed. Evaluate, for example, the content of a church's worship music. Over time, are the main metaphors and content relational, emphasizing our relationship to a wonderful God? Are there few references to a historical man Jesus or to biblical stories of God acting within human history? In comparison, is the content mainly historical, using this remembrance to make statements about a saving God? One could also look at how the congregation explains the meaning of baptism and the Lord's Supper. Are these events about each individual's personal experience of a gracious God who has given us life abundant, or are they signs by which, to use the language of the newest United Methodist baptismal service, we are "incorporated into God's mighty acts of salvation"?[58]

A few examples may clarify the difference between personal-story and cosmic-story churches. An example of the first is a church that plans its worship based on themes of particular interest to the worshipers. This approach usually creates personal-story based worship, particularly if the church is intentional about identifying its participants' "felt needs." Ginghamsburg United Methodist Church in Ohio represents this approach. Planning wor-

ship begins with naming a felt need in the church's target audience. Based
on this need, worship planners then develop a theme and a metaphor that
serves as the root visual image for the service. Everything else is selected on
that basis.[59] In contrast, the worship of a Methodist church strictly following the Revised Common Lectionary operates on a much different basis. If
the musical texts, prayers, readings, and sermon content were all connected
to the lectionary texts, the result would be a telling of a very different story
than that of the Ginghamburg church.

The second approach I suggest for classifying worship deals with the different structures of worship services. When Webber discusses structure, he
usually is advocating a fourfold order rooted in the services of the early
church.[60] I do not intend such a narrow focus here in using different structures as a key to classifying different kinds of worship. I use structure in a
broader sense to designate the organizing principle in a congregation's worship. Put more specifically, where is the most time and energy spent within a
service, and what gets the most prominent space and most expensive fur-
nishings and equipment? When these questions are answered, I believe that
most North American worship services are organized around one of three categories: music, Word/preaching, or table (meaning the Lord's Supper). In
other words, one of these usually serves as the dominant aspect of worship
around which other things orbit.

I also suggest that these three categories are not just the main organizing
principles in what gets the most time, energy, and dominant position in the
order of worship. I believe they also serve as the primary sacramental principles at work in different approaches to North American worship today. In other
words, one of these three categories is usually the normal means by which a
congregation assesses God's presence in worship or believes that God is made
present in worship. This assessment or belief does not have to be at the level
of formal theology. It can be at the level of popular piety. The point is the same.
A congregation will devote time, energy, attention, and money to the worship
activity in which the people find God's presence.

I am not the first to suggest this threefold approach to different sacramental principles. Reformed liturgical scholar John Witvliet has suggested a similar thing.

> Worshipers in nearly every Christian tradition experience some of what hap-
> pens in worship as divine encounter. Differences in Christian worship arise not
> so much whether or not God is understood to be present, but rather in what
> sense. Those who mock supposedly simplistic theories of sacramental realism at
> the Lord's Supper wind up preserving sacramental language for preaching or for
> music. Speaking only somewhat simplistically: the Roman Catholics reserve
> their sacramental language for the Eucharist, Presbyterians reserve theirs for
> preaching, and the charismatics save theirs for music. In a recent pastors' con-
> ference, one evangelical pastor solicited applications for a music director/wor-

ship leader position by calling for someone who could "make God present through music." No medieval sacramental theologian could have said it more strongly.[61]

I suggest that Witvliet's description of different approaches to sacramentality is accurate enough that it can form the basis for a new kind of liturgical taxonomy, although Witvliet himself does not take it that far. Everyone speaks of encountering God's presence in worship. The difference, which can offer categories for a liturgical taxonomy, is how and where they expect to have that encounter in worship.[62]

Some may be surprised by the notion of attaching the experience of God's presence to music itself, although they understand doing so with the Word of God or the Lord's Supper. Such a connection to music, however, is quite prevalent in some current approaches to worship. It is the basic premise, for example, in any praise and worship service based on a typology of the Old Testament temple. In that case, music is the vehicle that moves worshipers into the Holy of Holies of God's presence.[63] One book based on this approach states the matter bluntly in its title: *God's Presence through Music.*[64] Even the very recent sociological study from the Hartford Institute for Religion Research suggests a connection between a stronger sense of the "immediacy of the Holy Spirit" and those churches using newer musical styles and electronic instrumentation.[65] These are often the churches that have a central role for extended music in their services.

The categories in this taxonomy can be overlaid on White's chart in order to update his approach. One could place the music-organized, Word/preaching-organized, and table-organized categories on top of his chart. The result would show tendencies in North American worship today. Traditions on the right-hand side of the chart tend to have worship that is organized around the table. Centrist traditions' worship tend to be organized around the Word and preaching. The left-hand traditions are those in which one tends to find music-organized services and an emphasis on music as sacrament.

Such a scheme is too simple, however, in two respects. For a more accurate picture, this kind of taxonomy must take diversity into account, whether we are speaking of denominations or White's traditions. Yet in spite of this, this classification scheme can be helpful. For one thing, I suggest that churches at either end of an expanded version of White's chart are more likely to be in line with the tendency of that end of the sacramental-principle spectrum. Thus Pentecostal churches currently are more likely to have music-organized services, but not exclusively so. Lutheran and Anglican churches, in contrast, are more likely to have table-organized services, but not exclusively so. This sacramental-principle spectrum can suggest what might be the second most likely kind of service for a church. In other words, a Pentecostal church is more likely to have a Word/preaching-organized service than a table-organized one. Similarly, one is more likely to find a Word/preaching-organized service in a

Lutheran or Anglican setting than a music-organized one. An example would be an Episcopal church I once attended whose services had no music at all. For White's central traditions, particularly Methodist and Reformed, this sacramental-principle spectrum suggests the true diversity—and fights—that now take place within these traditions. Within these central traditions some forces pull churches toward a music-sacramentality, while other forces pull toward a sacramentality in which God's presence is most acutely experienced in the Lord's Supper. Thus it is currently possible to find services within these centrist traditions that fall anywhere within the spectrum of sacramentalities.

In addition, to show the true diversity of today's approaches to worship, this scheme must take into account the possible combinations of sacramental principles.[66] In other words, there are churches whose services balance music-organized and Word-organized sacramentalities and churches whose services balance Word-organized and table-organized sacramentalities. Less likely are churches that combine music-organized and table-organized sacramentalities. Less likely, too, are churches that combine all three. These combinations suggest a different meaning for the term "blended worship." Rather than referring to a blending of music or even worship styles, perhaps it is better used to describe congregations that sense God's presence in worship through a variety of means.

Finally, I would like to suggest another set of classifying labels for North American worship today that are rooted in White's assessment of ethos but that are not connected to Webber's. I believe that one of the aspects White uses to distinguish the ethos of a tradition still serves as a clear and crucial element in classifying worship today. The aspect is whether a church, in its liturgical planning, operates as an independent congregation or starts with the assumption that it will use resources common to its tradition or denomination.[67] The first approach I call "congregational," and the second "connectional." (Non-Methodists must excuse my selecting for the second approach a term that has roots in my Methodist heritage.) Of course, there is a third option: churches that are officially connectional but actually operate as autonomous congregations. (I could point to my own Methodist church.)

These labels are useful for understanding how it is that single congregations are likely to make worship decisions. I believe, for example, that the literature on liturgical inculturation can be separated along this congregational/connectional divide. There is one set of writings on how we should adapt worship to fit different cultures that presumes a connectional method. In this perspective, the goal is to take a common resource, whether created by the denomination or derived from history, and then adapt it to different cultural groups. Most of the literature from Anglican and Lutheran sources fits this approach. In contrast, literature on culturally adapted worship from church growth experts, including Easum and Bandy, emphasize the absolute autonomy of local congregations in creating new worship forms.

This classification scheme can line up generally with White's chart, too. Churches on the left-hand side of his chart will tend to have a congregational liturgical method, whereas churches on the right will have a connectional one. As before, the central traditions will be split. Individual denominations there might officially be connectional but act congregationally.

Conclusion

And so, back to our original question: How would you classify your church's worship? Using the new classifying terms I have suggested, does your church's worship usually tell a personal story or a cosmic story? How do people organize the worship service and assess God's presence? Is your service music organized, Word organized, or table organized? How do people expect to encounter God in worship? In the music, in the preaching, or in the Lord's Supper? And finally, is your church's worship planned using a method that is congregational or connectional in its approach?

Given the variety of liturgical taxonomies now in use, it is a daunting task to suggest another scheme. I hope the categories given in this new taxonomy can provide some real insight about the substance and diversity of North American worship today.

3

Disconnected Rituals

The Origins of the Seeker Service Movement

Todd E. Johnson

Few topics can polarize a conversation within Christian circles the way the subject of Willow Creek Community Church can. In its twenty-five-year history Willow Creek has created the most imitated approach to church ministry and evangelism in the world. In the opinion of many, Willow Creek and its market-driven, seeker-sensitive approach is the tonic the church sorely needs to cure the ills of an increasingly secular and pluralistic world. Others believe Willow Creek is a poison that kills the apostolic ministry of Word and sacrament, replacing it with entertainment and "chicken soup for the soul" spirituality.

Regardless of how favorably one views Willow Creek, most believe it is a unique phenomenon in the history of the Christian church. Its orientation toward the unchurched, though not without precedent, is beyond what other churches have done. Liturgically, Willow Creek has inverted the calendar. Sunday mornings and Saturday evenings, traditionally time for worship by believers, has become a time for "seeker services," rituals whose primary focus is not the adoration of God but communicating about this God to open-minded unbelievers. Worship services at Willow Creek are held on Wednesday and Thursday evenings, an obvious break from even the most rudimentary understanding of Christian time.

There are, however, some who have argued that Willow Creek and its approach to ministry is anything but new. Churches with nontraditional buildings, thousands of people attending services each week, services that border on spectacle, and multifaceted ministries eclipsing the ritual center of the church are as old as the revivals in North America. From Philadelphia's Baptist Temple, through Chicago's Gospel Tabernacle, to Los Angeles's Angelus Temple, by the 1920s, megachurches were evident from coast to coast in North America.[1] Likewise, many would suggest that Willow Creek's two-tiered seeker sensitive ritual program is not new but is instead an updated form of "frontier worship," and in this regard is nothing new at all. For example, Lutheran liturgical scholar Gordon Lathrop argues that the structure or *ordo* of "megachurch worship" simply follows the pattern of worship growing out of the camp meetings of American revivalism.[2]

The origins of the rituals of revivalism can be traced to Great Britain. Scottish Presbyterians migrating to America brought with them a practice known as "sacramental seasons."[3] Sacramental seasons were regional gatherings of clans who met for a period of days when they would hear numerous sermons leading them to introspection and confession. The gathering would conclude with a service of Holy Communion.

When this practice was brought to North America, a new twist developed, as the people who gathered at these rituals were not necessarily baptized believers. This required calling the repentant and unbaptized women and men forward for baptism before they would receive the Lord's Supper. The result is what we now call the "altar call," which climaxed a ritual best described as preliminaries, preaching, and response. When these newly baptized converts established churches in their home regions, they used this threefold pattern of worship, excluding the Lord's Supper for lack of ordained clergy. This pattern is known as "frontier worship" and has influenced every Protestant denomination in the United States in this century.[4] It exemplifies a long-standing liturgical principle: the language of faith given through evangelism and catechesis determines the language that one uses for God in one's ongoing life of faith.[5]

This insight is not new, however, as the early Christian churches intentionally connected the prebaptismal instruction and postbaptismal mystagogical catechesis (or teaching the newly baptized the meanings of the sacraments) to the liturgical and social life of the church of one's baptism.[6] This model has been revived in the recovery of the catechumenate in the Roman Catholic tradition through the Rite of Christian Initiation of Adults and the Catechesis of the Good Shepherd for children. Imitations of both of these models for Protestant churches are abundant on the bookshelves, if not in parishes.[7]

It is this relationship between evangelism, instruction, and worship that gives rise to the thesis of this chapter. The new phenomenon in Christian worship known as the "seeker service" arose from practices of evangelism and catechesis that were not explicitly connected to the church's worship. This resulted in the creation of worship patterns that matched the language given in the evangelism and faith development of a large segment of the American population through youth ministries from the 1950s on. This chapter will demonstrate how uniquely postmodern the seeker service is compared to traditional forms of evangelical worship. In the end, it will be argued that liturgically, the legacy of Willow Creek and its seeker service is a new and innovative form of Christian ritual.

Understanding the Postwar Protestant Church

The period after the Second World War was a time for revising the American dream. Although America remained a predominantly Protestant country, demographics were changing. The typical American family was more and more apt to be found in the city or in the suburbs. American parents were increasingly likely to have a high school or even a college education, and their children were likely to have access to cars and television. This was a time when the church no longer ministered to generations of families in rural communities but reached out to relocated family units in suburban America. With the challenges imposed on the society by technological change and the fear of Communism, the church assumed the task of socialization as well as supporting the values of democracy and capitalism.[8]

As Robert Wuthnow has demonstrated, history and tradition were devalued across Protestant denominations after the war. On the one hand, there was a critical lack of clergy, which left many churches served by pastors with little or no theological training (that is, people who were ignorant of the tradition). On the other hand, those who knew the tradition wished to put the past behind them, because the immediate past brought memories of war and poverty. Emphasis was placed on the tomorrow yet to be created, not the past to be reclaimed. Traditions, according to Harold Emerson Fosdick and others, were necessarily in constant need of revision. The only tradition that Protestants maintained was a Biblical tradition, which was open to a variety of interpretations.[9]

As the church became more of a socializing agent for a society in transition, the goal of the church became one of providing programs to create a new sense of community and to reinforce "traditional" values. Churches, becoming more of a central social and cultural resource for their families, began to hire multiple ministers. This created larger church staffs, which included expanding secretarial support to assist in the growing administrative needs. Simultaneously, a growing interchurch or parachurch movement also provided religious programs. Youth ministry was one of these expanding programs.[10]

The 1950s were a high point in the growth of Protestant churches. From *Time* magazine to President Eisenhower, the resurgence of Protestantism was acknowledged and claimed as a benefit for the nation and the world.[11] Yet in the 1960s and 1970s there was a drastic decline in membership and attendance of Protestant churches, with the majority of the loss identified as the absence of those who were thirty and younger. This loss can largely be attributed to the lack of commitment to the institutional church.[12]

Wuthnow also points out the decline of denominational allegiance in the postwar era. In the 1950s about 10 percent of the population had left its denomination of origin, whereas by the 1970s this number had reached 33 percent. Although some of this can be credited to a lessening of class distinctions between denominations, a larger factor was the growing tendency to marry outside of one's ethnicity or denomination after the war. This led to the phenomenon of "church shopping." For couples, especially those with children, a church's programs were crucial in selecting a church. Judging from the growth of Protestant churches in the1950s, programmatic Protestant churches were rather successful in their initial attempts.[13]

The change that occurred in the 1960s within American Christianity was incisively described by sociologist Peter Berger. Writing in the mid-1960s, Berger both described the religious milieu of the times as well as insightfully predicted much of what was to come. Berger describes the Protestant church as, for the greater part, having rejected the "mystery," or supernatural elements, of the faith. The church also responded to the growing pluralism of the world— what he calls a "crisis of credibility"—with a focus on the interior life of the individual. In this context one's internal realities and beliefs were trusted, and those external realities, such as doctrines and their institutions, were suspect. Further, Berger describes the first stages of what he calls a religion of the marketplace and sees the Protestant church accommodating an increasingly consumeristic culture by peddling its religious wares to a culture of consumers in order to survive.[14]

The Genesis of Youth Culture and the Evolution of Youth Ministry

The concept of an extended period of transition between childhood and adulthood is a modern idea. In 1875, the Supreme Court ruled that tax money could be used for high school education. Before this, only one in fifty people attended high school. Now a growing population of adolescents began to remain at home and in school instead of entering the work force. In fact the term "adolescent" did not come into prominence until Stanley Hall's two-volume work of that name appeared in 1905.[15] The term "teenager" did not even enter into the American vocabulary until 1938.[16] By the 1950s, adolescence was not only a social reality; it was a social movement. An entire youth culture was forming for the first time.

For many, adolescence soon stretched beyond high school to college age. After the Second World War, the GI Bill made higher education available to a larger segment of the population than ever before imaginable. In doing so, it set an educational standard for the growing middle class for years to come.[17]

The roots of youth ministry can be traced to the early-nineteenth-century response to the growing industrialization and secularization of England and the United States. Precursors of youth ministry are the Sunday school movement and the YMCA. The initial focus of youth ministry was reinforcing the transmission of values from one generation to the next in the face of growing cultural resistance to religion. As "adolescence" came to mean more time away from family, youth ministry later became a central agent for the transmission of values.[18]

The methods used for youth ministry immediately after the Second World War focused primarily on large weekly youth rallies, often on Saturday night. In the era following ten years of depression and six years of war, youth ministry provided the opportunity for public gatherings and painted the picture of a brighter tomorrow through personal faith. Although these rallies existed into the 1960s, their effectiveness was long since past, as the times had changed drastically.[19] These rallies also coincided with the growing urbanization of the United States. It was in the cities where thousands of teenagers would gather at revivals to hear youth speakers such as Billy Graham.[20] The model of these meetings followed the typical pattern of frontier worship: preliminaries, preaching, and response.

The effectiveness of these rallies varied depending on the audience and its predominant view of scriptural authority. The evangelists at these rallies assumed the Bible to be authoritative. To say that something was in the Bible was to appeal to the highest authority possible. But for a growing number of people, this authority was seriously in question.

A watershed in youth ministry occurred in the national debate over evolution, whose touchstone was the trial known as the "Scopes Monkey Trial." Here, the authority of the Bible was publicly challenged and defeated in the eyes of many Americans. High school education, which by the 1920s had become the norm for teens, increasingly emphasized "secular" values. No longer were Protestant Christian values seen as entirely compatible with a liberal arts education. This began the erosion of authoritarian presentations of the Bible.[21]

In light of lessened certainty of biblical authority, new models of youth ministry sprouted in the 1940s and flowered in the 1950s. It is in this context that one should view the development of Youth for Christ and particularly Young Life and their relational approach to ministry. Young Life had its origins in the 1940 vision of Texan Jim Rayburn, who initiated the transition from the rally model of youth ministry to the group meeting model. At these group meetings, the leader would not presume that the Bible had any authority for the students but would try to gain the trust of the high school students by developing a relationship with them and establishing the "right to be heard." Rayburn's conversational approach to public speaking was distinctive of Young Life's ministry. He was different from other preachers of his day, neither shouting nor pounding the pulpit. Instead, he just talked.[22]

The Young Life model of a weekly meeting changed little between their leaders' manuals of 1941 and 1970. From 1950 on, these weekly club meetings replaced Saturday evening rallies as the focus of youth ministry in America. A weekly meeting opened with fast-paced songs, followed by skits and games, leading to slow songs. With a shift in mood accomplished, a message was presented. Though biblically based, it was more thematic and practical than biblical exposition. The meeting concluded with music and prayer. The goal was to make the students as relaxed as possible to "break down the barriers" and earn "the right to be heard."[23]

There was more to the Young Life model than simply weekly meetings. There were annual trips to camps that provided the finest recreational opportunities available in some of the most attractive vacation settings. There were also occasional youth rallies and other large group meetings, all of which had the goal of conversion. These activities were supplemented by the Campaigners program. The Young Life leader's manual defines Campaigners in the following way: "The club work is primarily outreach, introducing young people to the Person of Jesus Christ, while the Campaigners ministry is designed to continue in the Christian life in a vital growth process."[24] Though the goal of Young Life was to engraft the Campaigner program into the local church, "the effectiveness of getting new believers into the local churches was unsatisfactory both to Young Life staff members and to (clergy)."[25]

The Young Life model and its correlative "Incarnational/Relational Theology" was disseminated through professional youth ministry journals, books, and organizations and quickly became the norm for parish and parachurch youth ministries in the 1970s.[26] It standardized a relational and conversational method of delivering a talk, in contrast to the authoritative biblical preaching of the youth rallies.

Further insight is gained into the methods of youth ministry when it is compared to the burgeoning youth culture of the1950s. Through the postwar baby boom, a growing number of people had access to both time and money, making teenagers a target market for the first time. Music, movies, magazines, books, and products of all sorts were created exclusively for adolescents. As one would imagine, teenagers became the target of a significant amount of advertising energy. Youth ministries had to compete with Madison Avenue in promoting their "product" that would provide meaning for the rock and roll generation.

In his provocative history of the relationship of advertising and American culture, James Twitchell cites the religious roots of advertising in the late nineteenth century as the impetus that gave rise to the religious quality of advertising in our century. It was literally the sons and daughters of Protestant clergy who took the message that "you are sinful, God offers salvation, accept God's offer and you will be saved" and transformed it into "you have a ring around the collar, Wisk can get the ring out; use Wisk and be saved from your dilemma." Like the holy relics of Christendom, access to these powerful items can in some way stave off the powers that threaten you.[27] By the 1950s, advertising had come full circle, and the church was competing against its creation—the religion of advertising.

The church's response to this newly formed culture of consumerism was thorough and significant. A survey of the American interpretations of Christian history and theology from the 1880s through today provides examples of reimaging the Jesus of the Bible as a white, middle-class male. Jesus has been seen as a marketer, politician, corporate CEO, and advertising executive intent on capturing the market share for his heavenly Father. Jesus quickly became a businessman, and his parables became ads—in much the same way that many of our current ads have become parables that point us in the way to eternal fulfillment.[28]

In a developing consumer culture, youth ministry was competing with many other "products" in an expanding market. The growing tendency was to try to reach youth with the same techniques used by Madison Avenue on the Pepsi generation: a confluence of message with media in which the two became indistinguishable. In a consumer culture, Christianity became a product to be tested, sampled, and compared to all of the other options available in the culture. The market-driven rituals of evangelism and catechesis provided an entire generation with a new language for God that was not being used in worship. Herein lies the difficulty in moving teenagers from youth ministry into the church. Youth ministry sold Jesus to adolescents because it was relevant, entertaining, and they would "get something out of it." Now where would they worship?

From Youth Ministry to the Development of the "Seeker Service"

According to Mark Senter, youth ministry historian, 1979 marked a shift in youth ministry outreach from parachurch ministries like Young Life to the parish. Much of this shift followed the model developed by youth ministers Dave Holmbo and Bill Hybels in Park Ridge, Illinois, in 1972. Hybels at the time was twenty years old. Holmbo, who was a pastor at the Park Ridge church, asked Hybels to lead a Bible study for the youth group. Hybels led about twenty high school students in a weekly meeting that lasted an hour and a half. Although some singing and a few skits were involved, the meeting was primarily a Bible study—one hour of the meeting was devoted to Bible study. When Hybels asked the teens if they would bring their non-Christian friends to the study, they responded with incredulity. "You know we like you and we'll listen to you, but my friends don't even know you! I don't think they can last that long."[29]

Hybels took the concerns of his youth group to heart and established a new youth service for unchurched friends of youth group members. These weekly meetings, called "Son City," offered youth gatherings that included competitive games, group activities, polished musical and dramatic performances, and an "evangelistic or pre-evangelistic message." By 1974, the meeting had grown to one thousand students a week and was divided into two meetings.

In May of 1974, Son City held an outreach event in which three hundred teens came forward to dedicate their lives to Christ. Hybels realized at this point that he could never work in a traditional church. Within a year Hybels resigned from Son City and left with a core of the Park Ridge youth group to start a church to evangelize the youths' parents. This ministry was the beginning of Willow Creek Community Church and became "perhaps the best known and widely imitated church youth group in the nation in the 1980s."[30]

When he was twenty-three, Hybels began Willow Creek as a youth ministry to 150 high school students, at that time meeting in a theater. As Hybels began to envision what sort of church could be built around this youth ministry, he canvassed the surrounding area, targeting white males ages 25–50 who were not attending church. Hybels surveyed the area, trying to identify what kept people away from church and what would bring them back. Hybels then proceeded to give the people what they wanted, what Hybels calls "biblical worship," which uses a variety of entertainment to avoid boredom.[31] Within a year it was a congregation of 1000; in three years, 3000. Today over 17,000 people attend on any given weekend, and the church plans both to expand its physical plant and extend its ministry to satellite churches.[32]

Charles Finney and his 1835 work, *Lectures on Revivals of Religion,* embodied the growing sense of pragmatism among Protestants in issues pertaining to evangelism and worship. In this work, Finney gave a step-by-step outline on how to orchestrate a revival. Liturgical historian James F. White succinctly describes the pragmatic attitude of Finney: "If something produces results, i.e., converts, then keep it. If it fails, discard it. This allows for plenty of experimentation, but unsuccessful ties are quickly eliminated. So pragmatism became the essential criterion in worship."[33] White also points to the origins of the seeker service movement (what he also calls the megachurch movement or high-tech worship) as being the work of the church growth movement and its dean, Donald McGavran. It was McGavran who wrote, "Those interested in liturgy find that church growth may say very little about their concerns."[34]

The method used by Hybels to facilitate the growth of his church demonstrates both Finney's sense of pragmatism and McGavran's liturgical indifference. This is not to say that his method doesn't have serious liturgical consequences. Hybels established a seven-step method of enfolding people into the life of Willow Creek.[35] The seven-step method began with a relationship between a Willow Creek member and an unchurched friend. The member was to invite the unchurched friend to a seeker service on Sunday morning or Saturday evening, when seekers were most likely to attend. The person was then invited into a small group Bible study, where they would enter into a less autonomous setting. It was assumed that the individual would acquire personal faith in Christ either before or after entering the small group. Once a believer, the new person would be baptized, join the church, and begin attending worship on Wednesday or Thursday nights.[36]

When comparing this formula for evangelization and church growth—especially in light of Hybels' experience with Son City—it is apparent that he followed the Young Life model of two ministry tracks when he established Willow Creek. On the one hand, he had seeker services, which were not worship services per se, but outreach gatherings akin to the Young Life group meeting. According to Willow Creek materials, "Seekers are those people who are in the process of making a decision for Christ or examining Christianity."[37] The basic assumption that Hybels has worked with since the inception of Son City is that you must communicate differently to seekers than you do to believers.[38] The goal is to move these people from a decision for Christ into church membership, affiliation in a small group Bible study, and attendance at Willow Creek's worship services on Wednesday or Thursday night. This goal parallels the Campaigners component of the Young Life model.

The seeker services of Willow Creek follow fairly closely to the Young Life model of ritual as well. They begin with upbeat, contemporary music, and include drama and the finest technical equipment available for multimedia presentations. Slower music is used as a transition to the talk, which, as in the Young Life model, has biblical themes but is ultimately practical in orientation. What the seeker services offer are relevant sermons that blend Scriptural themes with practical advice on self-improvement for a harried middle class. The preaching walks a fine line between preaching the gospel and simply dispensing pop psychology.[39]

In a thorough study of Willow Creek, Gregory Pritchard has analyzed the messages preached by Hybels and others staff members. Although they claim to preach the trade-off between the blessings of the faith and the cost of discipleship, the evidence shows a decided imbalance on the side of spiritual gain.[40] This nonthreatening message continues to attract seekers to Willow Creek.

The source of Willow Creek's life has not been abandoned, as Willow Creek's focus remains on youth. High School youth meetings and Sunday school are high-tech and multimedia. Nationwide, megachurches are reaching out to the young by mimicking some of the most seductive elements of pop culture. The focus on youth arises from the reality that adults often look for churches that meet the needs of their children. Once they are inside the door, the church has the opportunity to present the Christian message. At Willow Creek, more than 60 percent of its teenage worshipers joined independently of their families.[41] Willow Creek has further adapted to the needs of Generations X and Y by establishing "Axis," in which youth sit around tables and discuss the message presented, leaving open multiple interpretations. This provides still more evidence of Willow Creek's willingness to adapt to the new understandings of authority in postmodernity.[42]

Willow Creek is not only successful; it is a cottage industry with numerous churches subscribing to its materials and attempting to duplicate its success. Some of these churches, denominational and independent, are less careful in their distinction between the "seeker service" and worship. Megachurches without this distinction often offer a variety of services, from traditional worship to seeker services, not unlike the offerings at the nearby movie theater in the shopping mall.[43] Like the local shopping mall, megachurches are offering a cornucopia of consumer items to attract seekers into their midsts. Megachurches offer numerous opportunities for involvement, most of which are amenities. Alongside small-group Bible studies and counseling, they offer aerobics classes, health clubs, day care and preschools, bowling alleys, and bookstores that sell a variety of related books and recordings.[44]

Disconnected Rituals: Evangelism, Catechesis, and Liturgy

In the recent analysis of American Protestantism, one case study illustrating the perceived lack of relevance of mainline churches describes a person who explicitly contrasts her church with the personable and accessible ministry she experienced in Young Life, particularly ritually.[45] Although not everyone would identify the contrast between their youth ministry experience and its incompatibility with Christian liturgy, statistics suggest that this is a common experience. It is estimated that over 75 percent of Protestants under fifty had their primary religious experience through youth ministry and the marketing language we have identified.[46]

E. Byron Anderson summarizes a growing body of material from theology, religious education, and anthropology, maintaining that ritual is the primary way one learns faith, for in ritual one is most fully engaged in the religious message. Anderson asserts that "liturgical practice is intrinsically formational and transformational. It is a means by which we come to know ourselves as people of faith and to know the God whom we worship."[47] Supporting John Westerhoff's argument, Anderson asserts that ritual is the most important influence in shaping faith, character, and consciousness.[48] Succinctly put, it is through ritual that we learn how to be a Christian.

Ethnographic research by Keith Roberts reinforces Anderson's conclusions: Myths are set forth in ritual, and those myths define a worldview and a faith for the participant. Ritual norms in a changing world contribute to the plausibility of the mythic system it purports. Roberts' research indicates that the very sequence of the ritual defines the myth. Similarly, the language used in ritual conveys the implied sense of immanence or transcendence of God defined in the myth. Ritual is a primary vehicle for transmitting the tenets of the faith and teaching the worshiper how to interact with God.[49]

In a recent essay, Thomas Troeger has further extended the applications of these theories. Troeger suggests that humans exist in culture in the same way fish live in water; it is simply the assumed environment for existence. One can fully understand the unique qualities of one's culture only when contrasted with another. Culture is primarily passed on indirectly through imitation, not by directly teaching doctrine. Culture shapes the way we move, the values we have, and how we imagine the world—particularly the world of faith.[50] By implication, the language of faith inculturates the new believer through the rituals of evangelism and catechesis into a particular faith. For those whose culture of faith is the culture of relational youth ministry, this spiritual culture becomes normative, simply the water in which one is swimming.

The implications of these conclusions for the seeker service are clear: Since the '50s, a large segment of the population have been evangelized and cate-chized with rituals that presented a mythic system incompatible with the rit-uals and accompanying mythic system of traditional Christian worship. The development of the seeker service was inevitable; for those who had come to accept the interpretation of Christianity presented through youth ministries, a vehicle for its ritual expression was necessary. Although there are obvious pre-cursors to seeker service worship (for example, Robert Schuller's Crystal Cathe-dral in Garden Grove, California), it was Bill Hybels who made the connec-tion between evangelism, catechesis, and worship for the baby boomers. One is left wondering how the transition from one culture of faith to another is negotiated if the language of the youth ministry differs from that of the larger church's worship? It appears that this is often done by simply accommodating to other cultures of faith, in this case by adding "Youth Worship" or "Con-temporary Worship" services as options to traditional services.

Even those who have never been exposed to youth ministry find seeker ser-vices accessible because they use the "religious" language of our society: adver-tising. In a culture saturated by consumerism, no translation to the mythic lan-guage of the "seeker service" is necessary. It has already translated the gospel into the categories of self-improvement and entertainment and has explicitly created a ritual setting that reflects the business and consumer world of middle-class suburbia.[51]

A startling example of this is found in a recent study of the symbol of the cross at Willow Creek. Because there is an explicit attempt to avoid traditional Christian symbols, the use of the cross at Willow Creek is limited. A quota-tion from a guide at Willow Creek is revealing.

> In fact, you will see no Christian symbolism here at all. The metaphor or image we are trying to project here is corporate or business, not traditional church. Now, we do have a cross. We bring it out for special occasions, like baptism. When I was baptized here, all of us were asked to write our sins on pieces of paper and stick them on the cross as we came forward. I'll never forget looking

up from the baptistery at the cross, covered in paper. I had not really understood atonement until that moment. So we think of the cross as a *prop*.[52]

Though considering a focal religious symbol[53] a prop seems to diminish its
value, the research of Stewart Hoover suggests that in our contemporary American culture, this is high praise. Hoover argues from a fascinating synthesis of
theological, cultural, and philosophical theories to suggest that in a culture of
commerce, using the cross occasionally and inviting personal spiritual connections allows it to become the currency of a religious/cultural exchange.[54]
The limited use of symbols at Willow Creek allows symbols to function as
expressions of personal faith, not as authoritarian signs defining one's faith, as
is often the case.[55] This is another indication of Willow Creek's accommodation of postmodernism.

Reconnected Rituals: Evangelism, Catechesis, and Liturgy

Although there are many churches following Willow Creek's lead in creating rituals that build on the language of youth ministry evangelism, there are
other models being advocated also. There are youth ministers who orient their
ministry toward preparation for the worship of the church. Some from the
Lutheran tradition see the Lutheran liturgy as normative. The presentation of
the gospel and the order in which theological issues are presented to youth
within the church are determined by the liturgy. Further, the explanation of
elements of the liturgy is suggested as an important topic of youth ministry
meetings. Youth evangelism is geared to offer young men and women the gospel
of Jesus Christ, just as in the relational model. But in this model, acceptance
of the gospel leads not to private faith but to life in a community, with a language for God that is predetermined by the liturgy. Evangelism and catechesis
are explicitly geared to teach the language of worship.[56]
It is also important to note that both the revival and relational models of
youth ministry are uniquely American. Although there has been a transatlantic
sharing of methods of evangelism since the day of Whitefield and Wesley, the
Young Life model of youth ministry did not catch on as quickly in Europe.
Although there has been a good deal of time and energy spent on updating
music style and teaching methods in order to remain relevant, much of European youth ministry up to the 1980s was explicitly geared toward the liturgical traditions of the churches. A fine example of this is a study of English youth
ministry by Pete Ward, the Archbishop of Canterbury's Advisor for Youth Ministry, who describes the recent disconnection between youth ministry and preparation for church life, which indicates that the effects of relational youth ministry are just beginning to be noticed in Europe.[57]

There has been no shortage of criticism of Willow Creek and any number of worship styles that fall under the category of "contemporary worship." Criticisms of contemporary youth ministry models are less frequent. A recent essay by Mark Yaconelli, son of the director of Youth Specialties, Mike Yaconelli, raises the crucial question about the contemporary state of youth ministry: Have we forgotten how to pass on our faith, or can't we find a faith to pass on? Yaconelli's quick overview of the history of youth ministry identifies it as a reflection of upper-middle-class white suburban culture. He then identifies the three types of "successful" youth ministries: entertainment/programmatic, in which success is gauged by how many events each youth group member attends; charismatic leader, in which the youth minister takes on the role of savior; and information-centered, in which the youth ministry is a catechetical school that often indoctrinates without nurturing its members. Yaconelli's own journey as a charismatic programmer was leading him to burnout and frustration, as he was not seeing the spiritual growth that he had expected in his youth group. He then discovered traditional forms of spiritual formation, particularly contemplative prayer. He took the desperate and radical step of introducing spiritual disciplines to his youth group and, through the youth group, to the whole church. His model was not "give the people what they want" but instead drew upon the rich traditions of Christianity to offer them what they needed.[58] Likewise, it should be added that any number of young people in their twenties are finding spiritual homes in churches with liturgical traditions, because these churches have abandoned attempts to be relevant.[59]

Regardless of one's evaluation of Willow Creek and other seeker-sensitive worship styles, it should be made clear that the Willow Creek model is not a one-size-fits-all solution to the problem of evangelization in the postmodern world. There are other models that are working just as effectively, even if on a smaller scale. What they all have in common is the congruence of language used in evangelism, catechesis, and prayer—whether individual (spirituality) or corporate (liturgy). What this chapter has made clear is how Bill Hybels almost singlehandedly recast worship and evangelism to meet the unique needs of the evangelical tradition within the context of the postmodern crisis of authority and the tradition's history of youth evangelism.

One must ask if the end justifies the means in this case. Is Willow Creek's method of evangelization and worship as good as any other? Gregory Pritchard's research suggests that it is not. Pritchard's thorough study draws many sharp and critical conclusions; of particular relevance to our discussion are his conclusions that the Christianity promoted at Willow Creek is little more than a program of self-improvement,[60] that the church conforms more to the desires of the audience being evangelized than to the God whom they worship,[61] and that in an attempt to be relevant, the gospel is often superseded by psychology as the primary text.[62] Pritchard's study suggests that the program of evangelism and worship at Willow Creek has been so driven by an advertising model that it has to some degree compromised the cost of discipleship.

This chapter has surveyed the historical origins of the seeker service. In doing so, it has shown that this most contemporary liturgical form has validated one of the more ancient understandings of the church: *lex orandi, lex credendi;* the language you use for God will determine the belief you have of God. In this case, the language used in evangelization and catechesis will in the end determine the language that will be used in worship. The question remaining is one of priority: Does one use the most effective means of evangelism possible and then create worship that is congruent with this process, or does one have a liturgical standard in place and evangelize and catechize with language that leads to that end? This is the question all Christian communities are facing in this new millennium: How do we reconnect our rituals?

4

Beyond Style

Rethinking the Role of Music in Worship

John D. Witvliet

Arguably no other religion in recorded history features such a dazzling variety of liturgical music as does Christianity. For twenty centuries, Christians at worship have sung everything from contemplative Byzantine chants to exuberant Methodist frontier songs, from the trancelike music of Taizé refrains to the precise rhetoric of Watts and Wesley, from songs with the Dionysian ecstasy of African-American gospel anthems to those with the Apollonian reserve of a Presbyterian metrical psalm, from the serene beauty of a Palestrina motet to the rugged earthiness of an Appalachian folk tune, and from the enforced silence of Quaker corporate mysticism to the sustained exuberance of an African-American ring-shout sermon.

These forms of music are not just adornments to Christian experience. They are the pulse of faith, integral to the different ways in which Christians have experienced worship and God's presence for over two thousand years. For many Christians, it would be difficult to imagine worship without music. In some churches the music starts when the community gathers and doesn't stop until the service ends. Even in congregations where music is subservient to preaching or other acts of worship, often it is the music that has the staying power to stick with people all week long. It is the music of worship that echoes in our minds during sleepless nights and that we whistle on the way to work.

Correspondingly, music is a source of Christian identity. One of the ways to tell what kind of Christian you are—what "species" of the Christian "genus" you belong to—is to think about the kind of liturgical music that has shaped your soul. Music identifies us as belonging to a particular denomination, tradition, ethnic group, or generation. One of the most reliable methods for grasping the inner pulse of a given community—whether from centuries ago or miles away—is to understand that community's music.

This is nowhere more evident than in today's North American church climate. Today, people gravitate to a given congregation more for the music that is sung than for the doctrine that is taught. A given congregation is as likely to advertise its identity by reference to its music as it is by reference to its denominational affiliation. Indeed, omnipresent stylistic terms like "traditional," "contemporary," and "blended" are generally understood to refer primarily (if not exclusively) to music, despite the fact that liturgical "style" is just as variable in other dimensions of worship, including preaching, liturgical leadership, and prayer.[1]

The centrality of music both in Christian experience and in congregational identity is part of the reason why Christians spend so much time fighting about it. Ninety-nine times out of a hundred, the worship wars of the past decades (although frankly, when hasn't there been a worship war?) are about nothing more than music—what music will be sung, what style will it be, who will lead it, what instruments will be used, and how loud will it be.

All of this recent bickering is also explained by how significantly Christian liturgical music has changed in the last few decades.[2] Some churches are singing from the wealth of hymnody generated by the late–twentieth-century hymn renaissance (more hymns in traditional forms have perhaps been written in the last thirty years than in any period except during Charles Wesley's lifetime).[3] Others are packing up their hymnals and singing an exclusive diet of recently written praise songs. Some churches are reclaiming ancient patterns for worship, including the Christian year, lectionaries, and traditional structures of the eucharistic prayer. Indeed, this liturgical movement has led Methodists and Presbyterians to sing their eucharistic prayers, evangelicals to light Advent candles, Roman Catholics and Episcopalians to nurture congregational participation in psalmody, and some Mennonites, Brethren, and Nazarenes to form lectionary study groups. At the same time, other congregations are becoming more market driven. Church growth theorists—of both mainline and evangelical stripes—invite us to purchase subscriptions to *Net Results* and to buy books with such titles as *Entertainment Evangelism.* There is a great concern for a congregation's market niche and the way that music can function as a tool to appeal to a wide spectrum of people. These competing impulses have put enormous pressure on musicians in congregations to meet competing demands and expectations. They have also fueled intense debates and even divides within countless congregations.

Problematic Discussions

Frequently, the deep emotions that well up inside us over these matters confuse our ability to think straight. Critics of "contemporary music" lament the simplistic repetition of words in most praise songs, neglecting the fact that cyclic form and textual repetition has a storied and time-honored history in Judeo-Christian worship. (One congregational music committee recently spent most of its meeting bashing textual repetition, only to end its meeting by selecting Handel's "Hallelujah Chorus" for an upcoming Easter service). Meanwhile, proponents of "contemporary" music argue that most praise songs are straight from Scripture, while neglecting to note that the overwhelming majority of praise songs set only a small portion of certain kinds of scriptural texts to music.

Some of our arguments in these matters are just plain vague. We tolerate abstract and nebulous arguments that call for a "better hymnody" that embodies "higher musical quality" without specifying what that means. Who determines what that looks like? On what standards is it based? Such statements often conceal our unwitting reliance on aesthetic sensibilities geared toward other forms of musical expression, such as concert music of either classical or popular forms—sensibilities that may not be particularly helpful for assessing liturgical music.

Among the most tendentious arguments are those that involve the use of history. Proponents of contemporary music based on the pop forms claim that since Luther and Wesley used musical tunes from the barrooms, so should we.[4] Others respond by holding up the meticulous craftsmanship of Bach or Buxtehude, seemingly unaware of their concern for congregational song. Almost everyone discusses such historical precedents on the basis of which argument they want to advance in the contemporary situation, with a striking disregard for historical facts.

History is not the only form of propaganda. Contemporary cultural judgments function in the same way. So, there are some who have never seen a Gallup poll they didn't like. They argue that if a plurality of Americans like music of a certain style, then that's what we ought to use in church. By this way of thinking, a given congregation's music ought to sound a lot like the music that most worshipers have preset on their car stereos, whether or not music in worship has a different function in our life. On the other hand, there are others who either refuse to be aware of the musical dimensions of ambient culture or refuse to find anything of value there. By this way of thinking, every musical innovation is dismissed as a part of our "individualistic, materialistic, hedonistic" culture without a moment's consideration. The bewildered observer, sensing that most cultures are an ambiguous mixture of good and bad, is rightfully frustrated with either side.

Beyond the Fight

Fighting about music—especially with such jumbled arguments—is not a body-of-Christ way to solve our problems. These kinds of arguments simplify complex issues, cut off discerning communication, and fail to embody the virtues that are part of the grateful Christian life.

Consider a different vision. Near the opening of the book of Philippians, Paul records his prayer for the Philippian Christians: "And this is my prayer, that your love may overflow more and more with knowledge and full insight to help you *to determine* what is best, so that in the day of Christ you may be pure and blameless, having produced the harvest of righteousness that comes through Jesus Christ for the glory and praise of God" (Phil. 1:9–11, emphasis mine). At the heart of this prayer is Paul's desire that his readers will exercise the virtue of discernment. He wants them to be able to make good choices, to "determine what is best."

What does it mean to discern? Discernment is what Solomon asked for when he asked for "an understanding mind . . . to discern good from evil." Augustine defined it as "love making a right distinction between what helps us move toward God and what might hinder us."[5] Discernment requires making choices, saying "yes" to some things and "no" to others.

Paul gives us a short recipe for discernment. Knowledge and insight are two key ingredients. They provide a measuring stick by which to judge a given innovation or practice. To make good choices, we need to ask probing questions and search for penetrating insight into truth. We need the mind of Christ.

Another ingredient is love—not a sentimental love that baptizes every fad but a deep, pastoral love that nurtures long-term spiritual health. Such pastoral love requires a community. Psalm 19:12 asks "Who can detect their errors?" reminding us that no one by themselves alone has the perspective to see the whole picture. That's why Paul prays for "you all" (second person *plural*) to determine what is best.

Finally, discernment, like every virtue, is less an accomplishment to achieve than a gift to receive. The chief ally and agent in any communal discernment process is none less than the Spirit of God. Discernment is a Pentecost virtue, a gift of the Spirit, and so, something for which we should pray.

Toward Criteria for Music in Christian Worship

Robert Webber knows about the criteria for music in Christian worship. Robert Webber has recognized music's power. He has also entered into the middle of the worship wars, serving as a witness to the importance of theological reflection in the middle of contemporary discussions. As he has traveled all over North America teaching and lecturing, he has addressed countless questions about the practice of music. Along the way, he has articulated in common, accessible language the kinds of criteria that don't merely perpetuate the problem but actually can lead toward resolution. In this chapter, I will expand on Webber's work and place his work in conversation with other recent writers. The goal of this chapter is to propose categories for thinking about the valid and healthy use of music in the context of Christian worship, categories that are accessible enough to function well in the next worship committee meeting in most North American congregations. I will introduce these categories by means of six overarching questions that every congregation and every church musician might profitably address. These questions are designed to help congregations "determine what is best."

Question 1, a theological question: *Do we have the imagination and resolve to speak and make music in a way that both celebrates and limits the role of music as a conduit for experiencing God?*

At a conference some time ago, a pastor stood to advertise a search for a church musician. When asked what kind of person was needed, the pastor replied in a stammering, stuttering way—the kind of speech that tells you the person is probably saying what he or she really thinks rather than giving an edited, politically correct version of the same. The answer came back: "Someone who can make God present in my congregation." Now this, to put it mildly, is a rather loaded expectation![6]

Yet, language like this is increasingly present in want ads for parish musicians. Churches are looking for people whose creativity and charismatic personality can turn an ordinary moment into a holy moment. This tendency is not limited to charismatics. Churches with names not only like Community Church of the Happy Valley but also Tall Steeple Presbyterian Church want to hire musicians who aspire to make holy moments. One attempts to do this on a pipe organ with a loud trumpet stop and one attempts it with microphone and drum set, but both are striving to make God *present,* in some true, if elusive, sense. In congregations today, our strongest sacramental language is often not used to speak about what happens at the pulpit, font, and table, but rather what comes from our conga drums, synthesizers, and swell box. Even the architecture of many worship spaces (which rarely lies about what is most important) conveys the "sacramentalization" of music. The front-and-center space formerly reserved for pulpit, font, and table or altar is now reserved for worship bands or towering pipe organs.

Certainly, this concern for attending to holy moments is important. Arguably, most Christian musicians (in every style) are drawn to music because of a transformative musical experience. Yet no one, no matter how charismatic, can make a moment holy by his or her own creativity, ingenuity, or effort. Scripture records a long line of those who tried: the prophets of Baal at Carmel (1 Kings 18), old Uzzah, the servant who wanted to help along the cause of God by rescuing the ark of the covenant from the shaking ox cart that was carrying it (2 Sam. 6, 1 Chron. 13), and Simon, the magician, who longed for the divine power of healing to reside in his hands (Acts 8).

To avoid a similar temptation, some years ago choral conductor Westin Noble selected an anthem on the Pauline text "God does not dwell in temples made of human hands" for (of all things) a chapel consecration service. The choir proclaimed the Word of the Lord through music that day, echoing Paul's sermon in Acts 17:24: "The God who made the world and everything in it, he who is Lord of heaven and earth, does not live in shrines made by human hands, nor is he served by human hands, as though he needed anything, since he himself gives to all mortals life and breath and all things." This word guarded against the assumption that a certain kind of building could enshrine or produce God's presence. It served as a powerful reminder that God's presence is to be received as a gift, that it cannot be engineered, produced, or embodied automatically (though one does wonder how the building committee felt about that statement!).

Westin Noble's choice reflects a well-established Christian instinct about the arts in worship. Augustine was nervous about sung alleluias that distract our attention from the God who gave us voices and was worryied when "the music itself was more moving than the truth it conveys."[7] John Wesley advised, "Above all, sing spiritually. Have an eye to God in every word you sing. Aim at pleasing him more than yourself, or any other creature. In order to do this *attend strictly to the sense of what you sing, and see that your heart is not carried away with the sound, but offered to God continually;* so shall your singing be such as the Lord will approve here, and reward you when he cometh in the clouds of heaven."[8] More recently, Thomas Long has warned, "If one desires an intimate encounter with the holy at every service, then go to the Temple of Baal. Yahweh, the true and living God, sometimes withdraws from present experience. In sum, God does not always move us, and everything that moves us is not God."[9]

There is no doubt that music has great significance in the divine-human encounter of worship. In spoken prayer, word mediates divine-human interpersonal encounter. In sung prayer, music does this multivalently. Augustine is right: "To sing is to pray twice." Pipe organ music, an African drum, unified unaccompanied voices, all of these and many more forms of music do function to inspire praise, evoke wonder, reveal new insight, and generate qualitatively different religious experiences.

But can we safely take the next step and believe that music generates an experience of *God*? By no means. That places far too much power in music itself. Music is not God, nor is music an automatic tool for generating God's presence. Rather, in Robert Webber's words, music "*witnesses* to the transcendence of God . . . it elicits the sense of awe and mystery that accompanies a meeting with God."[10] Music is an instrument by which the Holy Spirit draws us to God, a tool by which we enact our relationship with God. It is not a magical medium for conjuring up God's presence.

Imagine a church musician agreeing to take a new position in a congregation, provided that she or he would be able to lead one service without music at all. Most congregations would be perplexed at the thought of an entire service without music. Yet this would be a prophetic demonstration that while music was incredibly important, it is also not absolutely *necessary*. Rhetorically, musicians gain credibility when they are willing to both promote and limit their statements about the power and beauty and universal significance of pipe organ music. Spiritually, we gain great freedom in Christ when we celebrate the fact that a divine-human encounter is not finally dependent on our musical achievement, but is a Spirit-given gift.

Question 2, a liturgical question: *Do we have the imagination and persistence to develop and play music that enables and enacts the primary actions of Christian worship?*

Some time ago, I asked a group of elementary students—always one of the best barometers of the "living theology" of a congregation—to talk with me about the meaning of worship. We took out a bulletin, and I asked them to tell me what was going on at every point of the service. When I pointed to the "prayers of the people," they told me "well, there we are talking to God." When I pointed to the Scripture reading, they told me "well, there God is talking to us." So far, so good. But when I pointed to the opening hymn, they told me "well, there we are singing." They told me this even though the first hymn was a prayer.

In other words, when it came to the music, they had no theological explanation of what was happening. They could only refer to what we were doing on the surface. This response is very instructive. So often we experience music in worship not as a means of praying or proclaiming the Christian gospel but as an end in itself. This is not only a problem for children in worship but also for adults—and for the musicians that lead them in worship.

This is precisely the worry of philosopher Nicholas Wolterstorff. "It is," Wolterstorff writes,

> habitual for musicians trained within our institutions of high art to approach the music of the liturgy by insisting that it be good music, and to justify that insistence by saying that God wants us to present our very best to Him—all the while judging good music not by reference to the purposes of the liturgy but by reference to the purpose of aesthetic contemplation."[11]

This concern applies equally to forms of church music derived from popular culture chosen for its emotional or entertainment value. In contrast, Wolterstorff calls for liturgical artworks that "serve effectively the actions of the liturgy . . . without distraction, awkwardness, and difficulty."[12]

The primary elements of worship are those that express and enact our relationship with God: God speaks to us through Scripture, God nourishes us at the table; we thank God, we confess our sins to God, and we declare our faith to each other before God's face. Music always serves to accomplish one of these actions. Some music helps us confess sins. Some helps us express thanks. Some of it is the means by which we proclaim God's words. Music is always a means to a greater spiritual end, a means for enacting our relationship with God.

Thus, Robert Webber speaks of music as "the wheel upon which the Word and Eucharist ride" and the arts as "the means by which Christ is encountered."[13] Music must support—in unique and invaluable ways—the primary actions of worship rather than serving as an end itself. As Webber concludes, "Worship is never to be arts-driven, but arts-enhanced. What should be prominent is the celebration of God's great deed of salvation in Jesus Christ. When the arts serve that message, they serve and assist our worship."[14]

This functional view of music has direct implications for congregational practice. For congregations with an established pattern or liturgy, it means that musicians must select music that enables the congregation to truly do what the liturgy requires. A piece of music that accompanies a penitential prayer must actually allow the congregation to confess their its sins. Having an orthodox text set to a memorable melody is not enough; music must also enable the action it accompanies. For congregations without an established pattern, the challenge is greater. In this case, a worship leader must lead the congregation in such a way that the deep purposes of a given song or hymn are clear. A lament text introduced as simply "another good song for us to learn" will likely not be experienced by most worshipers as a lament—even if the text is clear. Music—in any style—becomes problematic when we don't experience it as helping us to accomplish the primary tasks of worship, when we respond to a piece of music by saying "wow, that was impressive," rather than "that music really helped me pray more honestly."

Question 3, an ecclesial question: *Do we have the imagination and persistence to make music that truly serves the gathered congregation, rather than the musician, composer, or marketing company that promotes it?*

Nearly every tradition agrees that Christian worship is the work of God's people, a corporate activity in which the sum is greater than the parts, in which our being together as liturgical agents is primary. Music has a significant role in making this corporate dimension of worship palpable. Whether at a Bobby McFerrin, U2, or B. B. King concert, a Columbine memorial service, or a Notre Dame football game, music forges first-person-plural experiences.

As communal song, congregational song differs from many of the genres and institutions of high art in Western culture. In concert music, we value the proficiency of the solo artist. In worship, the pinnacle of musical virtue is to find an entire congregation singing well—honestly, musically, imaginatively, prayerfully, beautifully. In his book *Holy Things*, Gordon Lathrop makes this point as follows:

> In current European-American culture, certain kinds of art will be misplaced in the meeting: art that is primarily focused on the self-expression of the alienated artist or performer; art that is a self-contained performance; art that cannot open itself to sing around a people hearing the word and holding a meal; art that is

merely religious in the sense of dealing with a religious theme or enabling individual and personal meditation but not communal engagement; art that is realistic rather than iconic; art, in other words, that directly and uncritically expresses the values of our current culture.[15]

In liturgical art, no pride of place is offered to the autonomous, solitary, artistic genius. Instead, the liturgical artist is called to take the role of servant, giving worshipers a voice they never knew they had to sing praise and offer prayer to God.

Thus service as pastoral musician-liturgists requires not only theological and artistic conviction but also hospitality. The fourth-century "Constitutions of the Holy Apostles" advised bishops: "When you call together an assembly of the Church, it is as if you were the commander of a great ship. Set up the enterprise to be accomplished with all possible skill, charging the deacons as mariners to prepare places for the congregation as for passengers, with all due care and decency."[16] The craft and coordination and "performance" in the work of the church musician finds its ultimate goal and purpose in welcoming the people of God to experience the power and joy of profound and communal liturgical participation. As Alice Parker reminds us, "There are churches in all denominations in this country where congregations do sing well, and it is always because there is at least one person who is actively expecting it."[17]

This raises several significant questions: Whom do we welcome to our musical feasts? Do we actually welcome a community? Do our texts have a breadth of viewpoint? Are our tunes more communal than soloistic? Do we welcome children? Do we welcome persons who speak other musical languages?

But if we do these things, the response typically goes, there will be no time for really good music. Good music, however, is partly a matter of what we say it is, what standard we use to judge it, what virtues we aspire to. All composition (and music making) is in part the ability to create works of integrity and imagination within a set of constraints. The organ stop list is one set of constraints. So is the liturgical pattern used by your community. So is the musical skill of your congregation. It may be true that one ultimate test for the pinnacle of achievement in worship music led by a contemporary worship band is to see how supple and powerful a sound can be created with $200,000 worth of sound equipment, or how seamlessly a group of twelve instrumentalists can improvise off music charts, or how hot a combination of new guitar and percussion riffs a band can generate. It may be true that one ultimate test for the pinnacle of achievement in worship music led by an organist is to see what an organist and builder can do with a $2 million dollar budget for building a new instrument; another is how well an organist can play a featured recital at an American Guild of Organists convention. A more important test, however—which also needs to be recognized, celebrated, affirmed, and credentialed—is to see how effectively, honestly, and knowingly a worship band or organist can get a congregation to sing well together. Music in worship is not primarily about individual choice, participation, or preferences, but about the entire congregation.

And many voices would extend this reasoning one step further to argue that music in worship is not only about individual congregations but also about the whole body of Christ, the whole catholic church. In his description of liturgical music, Dietrich Bonhöffer explores this catholic impulse:

> It is the voice of the *Church* that is heard in singing together. It is not you that sings, it is the Church that is singing, and you, as a member of the Church, may share in its song. Thus all singing together . . . serves to widen our spiritual horizon, make us see our little company as a member of the great Christian Church on earth, and help us willingly and gladly to join our singing, be it feeble or good, to the song of the Church.[18]

In a culture that celebrates individual choices and preferences, this vision calls us to a new way of experiencing music. This vision invites us not to ask, "Did I like that music?" but rather, "Did that music give me a powerful sense of joining with Christians in other times and places?"

Question 4, a question about aesthetic attitudes: *Do we have the persistence and imagination to develop and then practice a rich understanding of "aesthetic virtue"?*

Most conversations about music in the church center on the music itself—whether it is relevant, authentic, well crafted, well chosen, or interesting. These concerns are important but incomplete. Equally important are the attitudes toward the arts that we cultivate and tolerate in the Christian community. In a winsome chapter in his book *Religious Aesthetics,* Frank Burch Brown identifies four distinct attitudinal problems about the arts—let's call them "aesthetic sins"—that persist like viruses in the church.

First, there is the *Aesthete,* "the person whose chief goal is not glorifying and enjoying God but glorying in the aesthetic delights of creation." This may be the person in the church who loves to hear their Bach straight and couldn't care less if that music enables liturgical action. Or it may be the contemporary worship fan who is more a connoisseur of sound systems than of expressing gratitude to God.

Second, there is the *Philistine,* the one who "does not highly value or personally appreciate anything artistic and aesthetic that cannot be translated into practical, moral, or specifically religious terms." This is the sin, Burch Brown notes, that is exposed in Alice Walker's *The Color Purple,* where Shug says to Celie: "I think it pisses God off if you walk by the color purple in a field somewhere and don't notice it." The Philistine is the person who refuses to devote any energy to reveling in the God-given ability to create or who refuses to appreciate the creative work of others. This is the person (perhaps even a musician) who treats music like a commodity, simply a tool to attract people or increase revenue.

Third, there is the *Intolerant,* the one who "is keenly aware of aesthetic standards of appraisal, but elevates his or her own standards to the level of absolutes." This, notes Burch Brown, is "the aesthetic equivalent of the sin of pride . . . it severs human ties and does violence to the freedom, integrity, and self-hood of others." This is the sin of those in the church who don't perceive how their own critique of another musical style applies equally to their own stylistic preferences. This is the sin of those who caricature music they don't like.

Fourth, there is the *Indiscriminate,* the one who embraces "radical aesthetic relativism . . . [who] indiscriminately [embraces] all aesthetic phenomena." Indiscriminate people are those who "cannot distinguish between what in their own experience has relatively lasting value and what is just superficially appealing."[19] This is the person in our congregations who has never heard a praise song or choral anthem he or she didn't like, or the musician who simply wants to please everybody and will never admit that some music is actually inferior.

Burch Brown's way of thinking is striking, in part because it speaks of aesthetic experiences in *moral* categories (evoking the coupling of moral and aesthetic categories, which has a long history in the Christian tradition). The use of such categories is helpful, because it gives names to complexities we often fail to acknowledge. A lot of energy in the church is spent working against only one form of aesthetic sin, rather than all four. Thus some musicians are tempted to fight only Philistinism, thinking of their life's work as a sustained attack on poor aesthetic sensibilities. Likewise, some pastors spend a lot of energy working against intolerance, especially when two competing groups in a congregation seem to embody this vice in equal measure. In most communities, it remains stubbornly tempting to fight philistinism with aestheticism and to fight intolerance with indiscrimancy.

Burch Brown's vision challenges us to work for the *simultaneous* reduction of intolerance, aestheticism, indiscrimancy, and philistinism—not just in our congregations, but also in ourselves. All of us have a different prayer of confession to offer: some of us work against the sin of indiscriminancy, others the sin of intolerance. These vices cohabit in our individual souls and in our congregations. We need to name and work against all four simultaneously.

The positive side is that such vices suggest corresponding virtues. Moments of liturgical aesthetic *virtue* happen, too. Perhaps a musician will willingly embrace a piece of music in a style she doesn't prefer but at the same time help the enthusiast for that music to become more discriminating. Perhaps someone will express delight in his discovery of a canticle, psalm, or hymn that conveys his own prayers better than he could have himself. Another time, someone in your congregation may have a chest cold and, because she is not able to sing, will for the first time listen to the sounds of corporate singing around her and be moved by the power of this common expression. Yet again, someone will sing a text, be struck with the power of the thought expressed, and later add it as a quote as part of his e-mail signature. Another time, your congregation may pull off the unthinkable: they will sing a meditative prayer text softly, without singing weakly. In many musical styles, these are virtuous moments to celebrate.

Question 5, a cultural question: *Do we have a sufficiently complex understanding of the relationship between worship, music, and culture to account for how worship is at once transcultural, contextual, countercultural, and crosscultural?*

One of the many contributions of Vatican II to twentieth-century Christian worship was its insistence that liturgical expression reflect the particular cultural context of local congregations. This insistence calls to mind John Calvin's admonition that matters in worship for which we lack explicit biblical teaching that are not necessary for salvation ought "for the upbuilding of the church . . . to be variously accommodated to the customs of each nation and age."[20] Since Vatican II, a small cadre of liturgists have attempted to be conscious of how this accommodation—variously termed contextualization, indigenization, inculturation—can best take place. Spurred on in part by the postmodern concern for cultural particularity, this project has been approached enthusiastically by many ecclesiastical traditions. The Roman Catholic Church has produced a much-discussed "indigenous rite" for Zaire. Protestants have eagerly encouraged the development of indigenous musical repertoires in Africa, South America, and Southeast Asia. And many traditions are exploring the stunning variety of cultural expressions that contribute immeasurably to the liturgies of the world church.[21]

Significantly, the recent move toward inculturation has both *promoted* and *limited* indigenous forms of expression. It has encouraged the development of indigenous forms only insofar as they complement the historic structure of Christian worship. Generally speaking, this movement has argued that Christian worship should arise naturally out of its cultural environment but that it should also critique aspects of the culture that run against central tenets of the Christian faith. The movement has argued that worship should avoid *both* "cultural capitulation" and "cultural irrelevancy."[22]

One of the mature statements to come out of this movement, the "Nairobi Statement on Worship and Culture," has been produced by the Lutheran World Federation. This statement argues that healthy congregations should have worship that is self-consciously transcultural, contextual, countercultural, and cross-cultural—all at the same time.[23]

First, all Christian worship should be *transcultural,* embracing the universal dimensions of the Christian gospel and of Christian liturgy. Thus all worship should feature the centrality of the Word, honest prayers offered in the name of Jesus, the proclamation of the full gospel of Christ, the rich celebration of baptism and the Lord's Supper. Correspondingly, we should lament forms of worship that do not embody the nonnegotiable and universal components of Christian liturgy.

Second, all Christian worship should be *contextual,* reflecting the unique genius of the culture in which it is placed, speaking directly to that culture, and arising naturally from people of that culture. When the transcultural elements of worship are practiced, they will be done in vernacular languages, with forms of rhetoric, dress, gestures, postures, and symbols that enable local congregations to celebrate them in deep and rich ways. Correspondingly, we should lament worship that feels disembodied, that seems disconnected from the real living, breathing people who live and work in a given community.

Third, all Christian worship should be *countercultural,* resisting those aspects of culture that detract from deep, gospel-centered celebrations. When technology, material wealth, constant noise, or individualism threaten to erode a community's authentic faith, then worship forms should protest rather than embody these cultural traits. Correspondingly, we should lament worship that simply baptizes everything in culture that comes along.

Fourth, all Christian worship should be *cross-cultural,* incorporating elements, prayers, and music that a given community receives as gifts from Christians in other times and places. In music, this happens when even ethnically *homogenous* congregations attempt to become musically *multilingual* and sing songs and hymns from a variety of cultures. Correspondingly, we should lament worship that is insular, that gives the impression that a given congregation has no need for other parts of the body of Christ.

Like Burch Brown's work on aesthetic sins and virtues, the "Nairobi Statement on Worship and Culture" affirms four virtues that must be cultivated simultaneously. Here is a theory of inculturation that is not governed by an implicit either/or rhetoric. Rather efficiently, this document properly complicates our thinking about the proper relationship between music and culture.

Here again, each Christian leader and each community needs a different prayer of confession. Some of us need to confess our imperialism, some our cultural retrenchment, some our indiscriminate use of elements of our culture.

In most congregational discussions, the discussion of worship and culture is remarkably simplistic. Most congregations and their leaders are more excited about one of these four adjectives than the others. In one congregation, one group argues that the pipe organ should be locked up because it is irrelevant, while another group asserts that the pipe organ is necessary because it is countercultural. In another congregation, a congregation adds $200,000 per year to its budget for video production to have music videos call the congregation to worship each week, based on the idea that worship should reflect local culture.

Imagine congregational musical life in which musicians constantly pursue balance in these matters. So a worship band that was working on a hard-driving new ballad—the height of perceived contextuality—might also work on learning a Taizé refrain as a countercultural protest against overly noisy and technologized forms of music.

Question 6, an economic question: *Do we have the imagination and persistence to overcome deep divisions in the Christian church along the lines of socioeconomic class?*

Finally, we come to a troubling area that resists easy answers and challenges nearly every community to reconsider common practices. In the last generation, the church has worked at bridging barriers of color, race, ethnicity, and gender. But we have not done well with socioeconomic class. This may turn out to be the most vexing division of all.

The question before us is simply this: In a culture that is so obsessed with making and spending money, how can we promote excellent worship music but not promote the idea that it takes hundreds of thousands of dollars to worship God well? How can we celebrate the gift of music that is possible at a cathedral or megachurch (the cathedrals of Free Church Protestantism), with all their resources, without implying that that worship is somehow better than the worship offered at the small congregation eight blocks from the cathedral or two suburbs over from the megachurch, but across the tracks?

In 1853, *Presbyterian Magazine* extolled the virtues of Cincinnati's new Seventh Presbyterian Church as having a belfry "not surpassed for richness and beauty," an interior "illuminated by a superb chandelier of original design and chaste workmanship," and a gallery of "the most costly and imaginate [sic] specimens of its kind." All of this gentrified language may be true, but the impression it creates is deeply troubling. One wonders how Christians in the next century may read the Internet-archived newspaper headlines about today's megachurches or cathedrals or tall-steeple campuses.

Of course, these vexing economic questions can be wrongly used in an utterly Philistine way. Resources and the costly use of them in the service of God are not bad. What is bad is the persistent implication that it takes money to truly worship God.

Thoughtful consideration of the economic implications of our worship may lead congregations to very different strategies. What if our cathedrals and megachurches hosted a festival service in which the orchestras, sound systems, and organs were set aside for a time as a witness to the virtue of Christian simplicity? What if large distributions of funds for musical resources in worship were paired with equally large distributions of funds to communities with fewer resources? What if we designed a church culture in which the staffs of huge suburban churches and church-related colleges attended worship conferences at small, rural churches, eager to learn about the virtues of smallness and simplicity—rather than just the other way around?

Multiple Themes and Congregational Practice

At first glance, the six questions above, and the criteria they suggest, might sound entirely impractical. What musician in a local congregation has the time to promote musical, aesthetic, liturgical, theological, economic, and pastoral integrity—all at the same time?

It is true that we must not be too optimistic about criteria like these. The little boat of thoughtful discourse they are designed to promote is easily swamped by the tidal wave of aggressive marketing and personal tastes that dominate the worship music scene. In many congregations, the most important forces shaping music are a tenacious attempt to hold on to traditional practices, or, conversely, a strong desire to stay on the cutting edge of new musical forms. There seems to be little interest in thinking more deeply about music's function.

At the same time, these questions may still prove to be useful. For one, they help us have better conversations about music. They help us perceive and avoid overly simplistic arguments. We are less apt to become enthralled with a popular piece of new music if we don't perceive how that music will enable our congregation to pray more honestly next week. We are less apt to follow a simplistic cultural argument once we realize how complex the church's relationship to culture is. Our efforts toward musical integrity will bear richer fruit once we have a clearer sense of the aesthetic and liturgical virtues toward which we are aiming.

Asking these questions can also result in tangible differences in music in your congregation. Asking theological questions about music's role in mediating God's presence can lead a worship leader to change how he or she introduces a song. Asking questions about music's liturgical function can lead musicians to choose very different music for worship than if they simply were trying to please everyone. Asking questions about culture can lead musicians to choose a balanced diet of both contextual and countercultural music for next Sunday.

Sound, tangible changes are not inevitable, however. Such discernible changes require yet one more thing, signaled by the single word that has appeared in each of the six questions: the word *imagination*. Most often, the ultimate constraint on our musical life together in congregations is not the lack of money, the lack of books or articles about the subject, or the lack of consultants who will come to help us. The ultimate constraint is our lack of imagination.

We need imagination to see what is really going on under the surface of our warlike conversations about music. We need imagination to see how the weekly practice of worship music embodies different aesthetic and cultural virtues and vices. We need imagination to perceive how our practice of music can, at the same time, be made more accessible and authentic, more relevant and profound. This kind of imagination that is forged by both knowledge and love will allow us together to "determine what is best."

5

Journeys of Faith

Current Practices of Christian Initiation

Ruth A. Meyers

Jack was baptized at the Easter vigil. The congregation gathered in darkness early that Easter morning. A fire was lit and then a candle, and in the flickering light a cantor sang the *Exultet,* the ancient hymn of praise rejoicing in God's victory, proclaiming *"This* is the night"—the night when the children of Israel were led out of bondage in Egypt, the night when Christ broke the bonds of death and hell. The congregation listened to familiar stories: the creation of the world, Israel's deliverance at the Red Sea, God's promise of a new heart and a new spirit, the valley of dry bones, the gathering of God's people. Then Jack was presented by his parents and godparents, who promised to raise him as a Christian and, on his behalf, renounced Satan and promised to follow Christ. The congregation proclaimed the Apostles' Creed and reaffirmed their baptismal promises; the presider prayed over the water. At last, Jack was stripped naked and plunged into a tub of water, washed clean in the water of new life. Fragrant oil was rubbed on his head, and he was marked with the sign of the cross. A minister lit a candle, and as he presented it to Jack and his family, urged them to light that same candle every year on the anniversary of Jack's baptism and tell Jack the story of that Easter morning. Finally, the congregation gathered around the table, set with bread and wine, and after the great prayer of thanksgiving, Jack joined them in receiving the holy food and drink.

This baptism took place recently in the Episcopal Church. But it could have been celebrated by a congregation in any one of several North American denominations: the Anglican Church of Canada, the Evangelical Lutheran Church of America, the Evangelical Lutheran Church of Canada, the Presbyterian Church USA, the United Church of Canada, the United Church of Christ, or the United Methodist Church.[1] In the last quarter century, there has been a remarkable ecumenical convergence in the official worship books of these main-line Protestant churches. Anecdotal evidence suggests that practice continues to vary widely, within as well as between denominations. Nonetheless, the most recently published worship texts suggest that a significant transition is under-way in the understanding and practice of Christian initiation, the process by which a person becomes a Christian, part of the body of Christ.

For most of Christian history, the celebration of baptism has been the prin-cipal rite that makes one a Christian, although that celebration has been at times as simple as the use of water in the name of the Father, Son, and Holy Spirit or in the name of Jesus and at other times as rich and elaborate as the Easter vigil at which Jack was baptized. But becoming a Christian involves far more than a single rite. When believers are baptized, conversion and forma-tion usually precede baptism. And whether one is baptized upon profession of faith or as an infant, a life of ongoing formation and discipleship follows (or ought to follow) baptism. Various rites may mark both the period before bap-tism and occasions of reaffirmation after baptism.

By the early twentieth century, many Protestant churches had developed similar patterns of Christian initiation, although the ritual expression of those patterns varied widely. A rite marking birth—infant baptism or, in many believer baptist traditions, infant dedication—was followed by Christian for-mation during childhood, which led to a rite of personal affirmation of faith—confirmation (or a rite of membership)—and first reception of communion, or believer's baptism. For many Protestants influenced by revivalism and later by Pentecostalism, these rites were secondary to the individual experience of conversion, or "baptism of the Spirit."[2]

By the end of the twentieth century, these rites had changed dramatically. The liturgical movement, the liturgical scholarship that both fueled and was stimulated by the liturgical movement, and ecumenism all contributed to the ecumenical convergence found in the initiatory rites in contemporary North American liturgical books. Moreover, the emerging post-Christendom context of contemporary North America has increasingly required new ways of think-ing about and ritually enacting initiation into Christian faith and life. Of par-ticular influence in this ecumenical convergence were the 1979 *Book of Com-mon Prayer* of the Episcopal Church and the Rite of Christian Initiation of Adults (RCIA) of the Roman Catholic Church.

Baptism in the 1979 *Book of Common Prayer*

The Episcopal Church did not set out to lead the way in developing a bap-tismal rite for a post-Christendom world. Nor had liturgical scholars reached an ecumenical consensus as to the best way to revise the rites of Christian initiation. But as Daniel Stevick points out, the timetable for revision of the 1979 *Book of Common Prayer* placed the Episcopal Church on a schedule slightly ahead of other churches in their revision processes, and the resultant rite proved influential.[3]

A primary feature of the 1979 Episcopal Church baptismal rite is its public nature. "Holy Baptism is appropriately administered within the Eucharist as the chief service on a Sunday or other feast."[4] The baptisms envisioned by this rubric are a far cry from the baptisms I recall from my childhood—the baptism of a cousin during the early 1960s and my youngest brother's baptism nearly ten years later. What stands out for me from each of these baptisms is the memory of a large, nearly empty church, where immediate family gathered on a Sunday afternoon. In the Episcopal Church and other churches that baptize infants, this had been common practice for generations. With the liturgical movement of the mid-twentieth century, which emphasized the active participation of all the faithful in worship, the practice of essentially private baptism was increasingly challenged. By the time the 1979 rite was introduced, there was little resistance to celebrating baptism at the principal Sunday service in the presence of the congregation, and public celebrations such as Jack's baptism described above are now the norm throughout the Episcopal Church.

Yet there is more here than just baptizing new members in the presence of the body of Christ into which these members are being incorporated. The congregation promises to support those being baptized in their life of Christ, joins adult candidates and their sponsors in responding to the "Baptismal Covenant" (which includes the Apostles' Creed in interrogatory form and additional questions of Christian commitment), and welcomes the newly baptized with a formal statement of welcome and the exchange of the peace. All of these actions underscore that baptism directly forms the church and that candidates are being incorporated into a living body. Moreover, participation in the baptism of new Christians is an opportunity for everyone present to renew their baptismal commitment; by witnessing the baptism of another, Christians are reminded of their own baptism, and by responding to the questions of the Baptismal Covenant, worshipers affirm their own commitment to Christian faith and life.

The context of the Eucharist is also significant. Previous Anglican prayer books had specified that none could be admitted to communion until they were confirmed.[5] In effect, this stipulation required formation and personal affirmation of faith in order to receive communion, since these were required for confirmation. The 1979 prayer book eliminated the requirement of confirmation before communion, opening the way for all the baptized, including infants, to receive communion.

Several factors brought about the contemporary Episcopal practice of communion of all the baptized. Liturgical scholars had recognized that separating baptism from confirmation and first reception of communion had not been the practice of the Western church for the first thousand years of Christianity and has never been a practice of Eastern churches. Rather, participation in the Eucharist had been the culmination of initiation into the body of Christ, a celebration that also included administration of water, anointing before and/or after the water, laying on of hands, and signing with the sign of the cross.

A second factor had its origins in the developmental approach of the religious education movement that flourished after World War II. Christian educators began to recognize the ability of children to respond to the symbolic nature of the Eucharist, a developmental ability that precedes by several years the capacity for abstract reasoning. At a communion service one day, my four-year-old grandson, listening to the words over the cup in the eucharistic prayer ("Drink this, all of you: This is my Blood of the new Covenant."), turned to me and said, "You mean that stuff is Jesus' blood? Cool!" If children can comprehend the significance of communion on a nonverbal and nonrational level, religious educators argued, perhaps they ought to receive communion and be able to grow in their understanding as they reflect on their experience.

Another important factor leading to the Episcopal practice of communion of all the baptized was the liturgical movement. As leaders of the liturgical movement stressed the importance of the Eucharist, celebration of the Eucharist as the principal Sunday service became more and more common in the Episcopal Church, and Episcopalians began to view the Eucharist as the principal ritual that nourishes and sustains the Christian community. In that context, the exclusion of children from the church's principal source of sustenance was increasingly questioned.

The 1979 prayer book does not explicitly direct that infants be given communion at the time of their baptism. But it neither forbids the practice nor designates any other occasion or prerequisite for the first reception of communion. In 1988, the General Convention of the Episcopal Church approved guidelines for the preparation of the parents and godparents for the baptism of infants. These guidelines specify that at baptism the infant "may receive Holy Communion (in the form of a few drops of wine if the child is not yet weaned)."[6] Practice varies throughout the Episcopal Church, but it is not uncommon for infants, such as Jack (who was four months old when he was baptized), to receive communion at the same service at which they are baptized. Participation of infants and very young children in communion emphasizes their full membership in the body of Christ, a body in which all are one in Christ Jesus (Gal. 3:28).

In addition to calling for baptism to be celebrated within the Eucharist as the principal service on Sundays or other major feasts, the 1979 prayer book further suggests that baptisms be reserved for four feasts—the Easter vigil, Pentecost, All Saints' Day (or the Sunday after All Saints' Day), and the baptism of Jesus, which is celebrated the first Sunday after the Epiphany.[7] All of these feasts except All Saints' Day were principal occasions for baptism in various geographical regions at least as early as the fourth century, and the liturgical scholarship of the twentieth century drew attention to the significance of these occasions. But the designation of these days as baptismal feasts is due to more than their historic importance. Each of them points to an important aspect of the meaning of baptism: Jesus' death and resurrection and the baptized person's dying and rising to life in Christ; the outpouring of the Holy Spirit on the disciples and the church and on the person being baptized; entrance into the communion of saints in every time and place; our participation in Jesus' baptism, which inaugurated his ministry. These meanings are central to Christian identity. When Jack was baptized at the Easter vigil, the congregation heard some of the central stories of Christian faith. As he grows and his parents tell him the story of his baptism, he will be reminded of who he is: a child of God, created in God's image, freed from slavery to sin, united with Christ in his death and resurrection, living in hope of eternal life with God.

Connection with biblical narrative is also evident in the prayers and ceremonial actions of the 1979 service of baptism. The prayer of thanksgiving over the water recalls the significance of water in salvation history—the Spirit moving over the waters of creation (Gen. 1:1), the passage of Israel through the Red Sea (Ex. 14–15), and the baptism of Jesus. For the administration of the water, the 1979 *Book of Common Prayer* directs that the minister "immerses, or pours water upon, the candidate,"[8] giving precedence to baptism by immersion in a manner more forceful than previous texts, which directed the minister to "dip [the candidate] in the water discreetly, or . . . pour water upon [the candidate]."[9] Although immersion baptism is not common in the Episcopal Church, many clergy use far more copious amounts of water than the barely moistened fingertips that had been the most widespread practice for many decades, providing a stronger connection to the water imagery of the biblical narrative.

After the water is administered, hands are laid upon the person being baptized as the individual is marked with the sign of the cross and (optionally) anointed with chrism (traditionally, olive oil mixed with oil of balsam or some other fragrant oil). The prayer for consecration of the chrism relates this anointing to Jesus' anointing by the Holy Spirit (Acts 10:38) and suggests that it signifies participation in the royal priesthood of Christ (1 Peter 2:9–10). A candle, suggesting the light of Christ and the Christian call to let our light shine before others (Matt. 5:16), may also be presented to the newly baptized.

With these texts and actions, as well as with the expectation of a public celebration in the context of the Eucharist, the baptismal rite in the 1979 *Book of Common Prayer* underscores the significance of baptism as participation in Christ's death and resurrection, conversion, forgiveness, cleansing, incorporation into the body of Christ, receipt of the gift of the Spirit, new birth, enlightenment, liberation, entrance into the reign of God, and empowerment for mission and ministry. Certainly these understandings of baptism are not new; they are well established in Scripture and Christian tradition. But the 1979 rite is enabling the Episcopal Church to recover and reclaim the significance of these meanings for Christian life today, and so to come to new understandings of the baptismal identity of the church.

Similar claims could be made about the baptismal rites of a number of North American Protestant churches. Many of them call for public baptism at the principal Sunday service and encourage that baptism be celebrated in a service of Word and Sacrament, concluding with Holy Communion. In some places, the newly baptized then receive communion at the time of their baptism. Many of these rites include a prayer over the water that is similar to the prayer in the 1979 *Book of Common Prayer* with its narrative of salvation history. The administration of water may be accompanied by other interpretive actions—laying on of hands, anointing, marking with the sign of the cross, giving of a lighted candle, clothing in white garments. The Protestant churches, at least in their official texts, seem to be moving away from the Reformation-era suspicion of ritual action and now permit or even encourage stronger ritual expression of the power of baptism.

But there is more to becoming a Christian than the celebration of baptism. Protestant churches are increasingly attentive to the preparation of the parents and godparents of infant candidates. Moreover, many of those churches that have traditionally practiced infant baptism are seeing an increase in the numbers of adult candidates for baptism. While some adults were raised in churches that practice believer baptism and were never baptized, growing numbers of adults in North America come without any previous affiliation to a church or any prior Christian formation. In response, several churches are developing processes and rites that enable the formation and incorporation of unbaptized adults into the Christian faith. These materials are based largely on the Roman Catholic Rite of Christian Initiation of Adults, which was introduced in the early 1970s.

Rite of Christian Initiation of Adults

The Rite of Christian Initiation of Adults (RCIA) is the term for an extended process of formation and incorporation into the Christian community, a process marked by a number of rituals that culminate in baptism, confirmation, and first communion at the Easter vigil. Restoration of the catechumenate, a period of prebaptismal preparation, had been mandated by the Second Vatican Council in 1963 in the first document released from that council, *The Constitution on the Sacred Liturgy*. But the need for a process of adult formation and initiation had been evident since at least the sixteenth century, when Roman Catholic missionaries began to bring the gospel to the Far East, Africa, and the Western Hemisphere.

The missionaries brought with them liturgical books containing the late medieval Western baptismal rite. This rite began at the church door with renunciation and profession of faith, exsufflation (blowing on the candidate's face), exorcisms, marking with the sign of the cross, prayers, laying on of hands, and giving of salt. In the fourth and fifth centuries, when adult baptisms were common, these rituals had been administered during the catechumenate, usually over a period of time rather than as a single rite. As infant baptisms became the norm during the Middle Ages, the series of rites was gradually collapsed into a single preliminary rite at the church door immediately preceding the ritual at the font. The ceremonies at the church door concluded with entry into the church and a procession to the font, where the baptismal rite continued with the recitation of the Apostle's' Creed and Lord's Prayer, the *ephphatha*,[10] renunciation of Satan, anointing, profession of faith, administration of water in the triune name, anointing with chrism, and giving a white garment.

This complex rite was not well suited to a missionary context. The diary of Toribio Motolinía, a Franciscan who ministered in Mexico City during the sixteenth century, describes some of the challenges: "The missionaries faced two or three thousand baptisms a day, requiring the *ephphatha* and exsufflation, a burning candle in a windy courtyard, individual white garments and entrance into a church building in a place where there was no church building."[11] In addition to the difficulties presented by the ritual requirements, little guidance was available for missionaries as they instructed converts.

Despite the formidable obstacles, missionaries in different contexts provided at least rudimentary instruction and adapted the baptismal rite in various ways. During the eighteenth and nineteenth centuries, missionaries in China introduced a catechumenate with stages and administered some of the preliminary rites as part of the catechumenate. In Africa during the late nineteenth and early twentieth centuries, religious orders introduced a catechumenate of two stages, each lasting up to two years. A ritual marked the transition from the first stage, in which pagan faith and practices were renounced and the candidates came to believe in the God of Jesus Christ, to the second stage, which involved additional intellectual and moral formation. The second stage concluded with another examination of the candidate's behavior and understanding of Christianity, with baptism following soon thereafter.[12]

The catechumenate in Africa was so effective that in 1962 the Roman Catholic Congregation of Rites published the "Order of Baptism of Adults Arranged as a Catechumenate in Steps." This text did little other than divide the preliminary portions of the baptismal rite into seven stages. Prayers and ritual actions were not modified. Nonetheless, the order marked official acceptance of a catechumenate in stages and opened the way for further renewal a few years later, after the Second Vatican Council.[13]

Another factor contributing to the Council's restoration of the catechumenate was the introduction of an Easter vigil celebration. During the Middle

Ages, the traditional vigil was celebrated earlier and earlier on Holy Saturday, so that by the sixteenth century it was celebrated on the morning of Holy Saturday. In 1951, Pope Pius XII authorized the celebration of the Easter vigil on the evening of Holy Saturday. This restored night-time vigil did not include baptism, but it did introduce a renewal of baptismal vows. Additional reforms of Holy Week liturgies introduced in 1955 gave permission for the order of adult baptism to be divided, with the first part celebrated on the morning of Holy Saturday and the second at the vigil. These reforms gave new emphasis to the paschal character of baptism, that is, baptism as participation in Christ's death and resurrection, which was a significant shift from a focus on baptism as deliverance from original sin.[14]

Twentieth-century liturgical scholarship was a third factor in the restoration of the catechumenate. The discovery of numerous ancient documents enabled historians of liturgy to develop new understandings of liturgical practices in the early centuries of the church. Using catechetical homilies from the fourth century and ancient church orders that prescribed ritual practice, scholars reconstructed an elaborate initiatory process that included a lengthy catechumenate leading to baptism, which often took place at the Easter vigil.[15]

The form of the ancient catechumenate, its complex series of rituals, and even its terminology provided the basis for the Rite of Christian Initiation of Adults, a process that has four distinct stages and rituals that mark the transition from each stage to the next. As they developed these rites, the revisers also considered missionary experience with the catechumenate and pastoral needs in various modern contexts. Thus, they retained some components that had developed much later in history, for example, the option of marking the initiate with the sign of the cross multiple times during the rite of admission to the catechumenate, and eliminated other ceremonies that were of ancient origin, for example, the giving of salt.[16]

Period of Evangelization and Precatechumenate. This stage, which has no set structure or fixed length of time, begins when an individual first expresses interest in Jesus Christ. The gospel is proclaimed so that "those who are not yet Christians, their hearts opened by the Holy Spirit, may believe and be freely converted to the Lord."[17] No rituals are included in this period, but pastors and catechists may incorporate suitable prayers, including prayers of exorcism and blessings.

Rite of Acceptance into the Order of Catechumens. The rite of acceptance takes place publicly, in a liturgical assembly. The candidates, their sponsors, and other Christians gather outside the regular place of worship. There, the candidates make their "first acceptance of the gospel,"[18] which may be replaced by exorcism, exsufflation, and renunciation of false worship. The candidates are then marked with the sign of the cross on their foreheads (and, optionally, on all the senses), may be given a new name, and are invited to enter the church "to share with us at the table of God's word."[19] After the proclamation of the

Word and the homily, a book of Gospels and a cross may be presented to the candidate. Intercession for the catechumens follows, and the catechumens are then dismissed from the assembly.

Period of the Catechumenate. This time of nurturing the catechumens in their faith journey ordinarily lasts at least a year and may last several years.[20] During this time, the catechumens participate in the liturgy of the Word, receive instruction, and participate with other Christians in the church's life of service and mission. The instruction involves far more than the intellect: it "should be of a kind that while presenting Catholic teaching in its entirety also enlightens faith, directs the heart toward God, fosters participation in the liturgy, inspires apostolic activity, and nurtures a life completely in accord with the spirit of Christ."[21] In addition to celebrations of the Word, this period may include exorcisms, blessings, and anointing with the oil of catechumens. Catechumens regularly attend Sunday celebrations of the Eucharist and are ritually dismissed from the liturgy after the homily, before the intercessions take place. The Lutheran scholar Maxwell Johnson explains:

> While [this] may strike moderns as a bit of liturgical-historical romanticism, especially given the fact that any person today—believer and nonbeliever alike— is usually welcome to attend any and every liturgy of the Church from beginning to end, the purpose of this solemn dismissal for ongoing instruction and preparation is to underscore in a dramatic manner the fact that catechumens themselves are not yet fully initiated into the Church and its eucharistic communion through baptism.[22]

This practice of solemn dismissal continues throughout the third stage, until baptism.

Rite of Election or Enrollment of Names. This step, usually on the first Sunday of Lent, is presided over by the bishop or his delegate. The catechumens, with their godparents and catechists, determine their readiness for a final period of intense preparation leading to baptism at the Easter vigil. As with the rite of acceptance into the catechumenate, the rite of election takes place after the proclamation of the Word and the homily. The godparents attest to the catechumens' readiness and desire for baptism, and the catechumens are enrolled and their names are inscribed in the book of the elect. After a formal "act of admission or election" and intercessions for the elect, they are dismissed from the assembly to continue their formation. Following this rite, the catechumens are known as "the elect."

Period of Purification and Enlightenment. This period of more intense spiritual preparation ordinarily coincides with Lent. On the third, fourth, and fifth Sundays of Lent, the elect participate in the "scrutinies," rites of prayer and exorcism intended "for self-searching and repentance . . . meant to uncover, then heal all that is weak, defective, or sinful in the hearts of the elect; to bring out, then strengthen all that is upright, strong, and good."[23] A ritual presentation of the Apostles' Creed takes place during the third week of Lent, and a similar ritual presentation of the Lord's Prayer takes place during the fifth week of Lent. On Holy Saturday, in preparation for baptism, which will take place at the vigil held that evening, the elect are expected to pray and fast, and they may also gather for a rite that may include recitation of the Apostles' Creed, the *ephphatha*, and/or choosing a baptismal name.

   Celebration of the Sacraments of Initiation. The sacraments of initiation comprise not only baptism but also confirmation and the first sharing in communion. Baptism includes blessing of the font; renunciation of sin and profession of faith; baptismal washing, preferably by immersion; and "explanatory rites"—which include clothing the candidates with white garments and presenting a lighted candle to them.[24] Confirmation immediately follows baptism. While confirmation has historically been administered by a bishop, the revisers considered the unity of the initiatory rites to be of such importance that in the absence of a bishop, the priest who baptizes is authorized to administer confirmation. The ritual of confirmation includes laying on of hands and prayer for the sevenfold gifts of the Spirit, followed by anointing with chrism.[25] The vigil concludes with the celebration of the Eucharist, during which the "neophytes" receive communion for the first time.

   Period of Postbaptismal Catechesis or Mystagogy. This period begins during the fifty days of Easter, "a time for the community and the neophytes together to grow in deepening their grasp of the paschal mystery and in making it part of their lives through meditation on the Gospel, sharing in the eucharist, and doing the works of charity."[26] The neophytes' experience of the sacraments provides the context for deeper reflection on Scripture and the life of faith. The rituals during this time of mystagogy are the Sunday masses of the Easter season, and a celebration near the end of the season, the Feast of Pentecost, concludes this more intense period of postbaptismal catechesis, or mystagogy. For the next year, until the first anniversary of their initiation, neophytes gather at least monthly for continuing formation.[27] On (or near) the first anniversary of their baptism, the neophytes gather for a final time "to give thanks to God, to share with one another their spiritual experiences, and to renew their commitment."[28]

   As with the 1979 form of the baptismal rite, the participation of the community is an important dimension of the RCIA. It assumes active evangelism by members of the parish for unbaptized adults to be invited into this experience of conversion and formation in the Christian faith. Catechists and other laypersons assist pastors at each stage of formation, explaining the gospel during the precatechumenate, providing catechesis as well as example and support during the catechumenate and the period of purification and enlightenment, and welcoming the neophytes during the period of mystagogy. Sponsors accompany candidates seeking admission to the catechumenate, and godparents are chosen before the candidates' election. The rite of acceptance into the order of catechumens and the rite of enrollment assume the presence of a group of the faithful in addition to the sponsors or godparents. These rites may be celebrated in the context of the Sunday Eucharist. The scrutinies during the period of purification and enlightenment are part of the Sunday liturgies, initiation itself takes place during the public vigil celebration, and mystagogy involves the entire worshiping assembly throughout the Easter season. The very public nature of the RCIA makes possible the renewal of the entire congregation, reminding Christians of the power of their own initiation into the body of Christ.

The Catechumenate in Twenty-first-Century North America

The Rite of Chistian Initiation of Adults has had a significant influence on several North American Protestant churches. Although the worship books introduced during the last quarter of the twentieth century do not include a catechumenate as part of baptism, several churches subsequently provided separate resources with materials for a catechumenate. In 1979 the Episcopal Church's *Book of Occasional Services* introduced rites for the catechumenate along with a brief outline of the process and the principles underlying the catechumenate. During the 1990s the Evangelical Lutheran Church in Canada and the Evangelical Lutheran Church in America both produced similar resources, as did the United Methodist Church.[29] Each of these resources follows the four-stage pattern of the RCIA, with a worship service marking the transition from each stage to the next and rituals that take place during Sunday worship on the third, fourth, and fifth Sundays of Lent. The terms used for the stages and transition rituals vary, and most of the resources do not use the terms "exorcism" and "scrutiny," but the overall form is that of the RCIA. Like the revised baptismal rites of these churches, the materials for the catechumenate are rich with ritual actions such as marking with the sign of the cross and laying on of hands. Like the RCIA, each of these resources stresses the importance of the involvement of the community.

In this age of ecumenical cooperation, Lutherans and Episcopalians in the United States began to work together in the late 1980s to train leaders of congregations that wanted to introduce the catechumenate. This cooperation broadened with the formation of the North American Association for the Catechumenate (NAAC), whose members include Lutherans, Anglicans (including Episcopalians), Methodists, and Presbyterians from the United States and Canada. For several years, NAAC has held annual conferences to support those engaged in catechumenal processes.[30]

Although the RCIA is intended specifically for unbaptized adults, a similar pattern of formation is used to prepare baptized but uncatechized adults for confirmation and first reception of communion and to prepare baptized Christians for reception into full communion with the Roman Catholic Church. This process also includes four stages and transition rites between the stages. Recognizing the different status of these candidates, some rites are renamed, such as "Welcoming the Candidates" and "Calling the Candidates to Continuing Conversion." The final rite, "Reception of Baptized Christians into the Full Communion of the Catholic Church,"includes confirmation and first reception of communion

The texts of the RCIA recommend that the rites for baptized adults not take place at the same liturgies as the rites for the catechumenate. The guidelines of the National Conference of Catholic Bishops point to the potential problems of such an approach:

> It is preferable that reception into full communion not take place at the Easter Vigil lest there be any confusion of such baptized Christians with the candidates for baptism, possible misunderstanding of or even reflection upon the sacrament of baptism celebrated in another Church or ecclesial community, or any perceived triumphalism in the liturgical welcome into the Catholic eucharistic community.[31]

Despite this reservation, an appendix to the American edition of the text for the RCIA provides a series of combined rites that place together unbaptized adults, baptized but uncatechized adults preparing for confirmation and first communion, and baptized adults preparing for reception into full communion with the Roman Catholic Church.[32]

The provision for combined rites reflects the reality that the experiences of those preparing for baptism are often similar to those preparing for confirmation and first communion or for reception into full communion. Individuals in the latter two categories may have lapsed in their membership, or they may be affiliating with a different ecclesial tradition because of an experience of renewed or deepened faith. Changing life circumstances for a baptized person may bring about an experience much like the conversion of an unbaptized adult. The challenge is to balance the sacramental reality of baptism as an unrepeatable experience of incorporation into the body of Christ and the experiential reality of a new conversion through a subsequent encounter with Christ.

After nearly a decade of experience with the catechumenate, the Episcopal Church found that many adults who had already been baptized were participating in the process, including the rites intended for unbaptized persons. In response, guidelines and rites for the "Preparation of Baptized Persons for Reaffirmation of the Baptismal Covenant" were added to *The Book of Occasional Services*. Like the Roman Catholic materials, the initial stage of inquiry concludes with a rite of welcoming, which may take place at any principal Sunday Eucharist. But the second stage concludes, not with a rite on the first Sunday of Lent, but with an "Enrollment for Lenten Preparation" on Ash Wednesday. This rite presents the candidates as examples of continuing conversion, and their service to the congregation includes assisting the presider in imposing ashes on the members of the congregation. The intensive Lenten preparation leads to a "Maundy Thursday Rite of Preparation for the Paschal Holy Days," which includes a rite of reconciliation followed by footwashing. Candidates then reaffirm their baptismal covenant at the Easter vigil, and if the bishop is not present at the vigil, they are later presented to the bishop for laying on of hands, preferably during that same Easter season.[33]

The United Methodist resource *Come to the Waters* includes similar rituals on Ash Wednesday and Maundy Thursday, emphasizing the distinction between unbaptized adults and those who are already baptized. It also adds another category: "searching members," those who are already active participants in the congregation and now want to deepen their faith journey. The text encourages adaptations appropriate to the needs of each searcher; it suggests that while searchers should participate in the same stages of the catechumenate, they should only participate in the final reaffirmation of the baptismal covenant and affirmation of ministry rather than the rites of transition between stages.[34]

The Lutheran texts specify that "every effort should be made not to regard the baptized as though they have not received the sacrament." Despite this cautionary note, separate services for baptized adults are not included. The first ritual for unbaptized adults, "Welcome of Inquirers to the Catechumenate," may include a presentation of the affirmers, followed by marking them with the sign of the cross and blessing them. No parallel provisions are made for the rite of enrollment, but notes on the services for the third, fourth, and fifth Sundays of Lent allow those preparing for Affirmation of Baptism at the Easter vigil to join the unbaptized candidates in the ritual.[35]

In addition to specifying a process and rites for baptized persons preparing for reaffirmation, both the Methodist and Episcopal resources include a parallel process and rites for parents preparing for the baptism of their children. This process may begin during pregnancy or when parents begin adoption procedures. In the Episcopal *Book of Occasional Services,* the first stage is relatively brief and concludes with a blessing of the parents at the beginning of pregnancy. After the birth of the child, the second stage concludes with the Thanksgiving for the Birth or Adoption of a Child.[36] Preparation then continues until the baptism of the child. The Methodist resources mark the transitions between stages with the services of "Welcome of Hearers through the Parents" and "A Service for Calling Children to Baptism." These materials describe the fourth stage, which follows baptism, as an extended period of formation and integration that continues until the person is confirmed in adolescence or early adulthood.[37] One benefit of each of these processes is the presence of a community of support should any difficulty arise in the course of the pregnancy or in the search for a child to adopt.

Conclusion: Christian Initiation and Reaffirmation of Faith in Twenty-first-Century North America

The various approaches to the preparation of baptized persons for rites of reaffirmation of faith (or in the Roman Catholic tradition, confirmation and first communion), as well as the introduction of parallel processes for parents preparing for the baptism of an infant or young child, reflect the complexity of Christian experience in North America. It is not uncommon for a person to be baptized in infancy but to receive no further Christian formation as a child. In a highly mobile society in which consumer values predominate, many Christians feel free to affiliate with a different denomination that better meets their needs at a particular point in their life. Marriage may unite people from different denominational backgrounds, and many of these marriages result in one or both members of the couple switching denominations. Many adults experience career changes, or several changes, in a lifetime, and such change can bring a renewed faith experience.

Recognizing that in the course of a lifetime Christians may have more than one experience of renewed conversion and reawakening to the gospel, many contemporary worship books provide various services of affirmation or reaffirmation. Certainly the primary affirmation of faith following baptism is ongoing devotion to "the apostles' teaching and fellowship, to the breaking of bread and the prayers" (Acts 2:42). But for several centuries Protestant and Anglican churches have also provided a service of confirmation or affirmation in which those baptized as infants profess their faith and are admitted to communion. A new insight of the late twentieth century was the possibility of a repeatable affirmation in response to a variety of circumstances.

A ritualized action of affirming one's faith can underscore renewed Christian commitment in an age often described as "post-Christendom." In this contemporary era, the predominant North American culture (as well as other Western cultures) is indifferent or even hostile to Christian practice and teaching. For example, no longer is Sunday morning set aside for worship; sports, the proliferation of businesses open "24/7," and other forces compete for the attention of Christians. In this context, the extended process of Christian formation through the catechumenate and the parallel processes for persons already baptized can provide an opportunity for in-depth reflection on one's journey of faith in the company other Christians and can foster the development of a strong Christian identity.

Although the revival of the catechumenate is in many ways a response to contemporary contexts, a note of caution is in order. Like much of the liturgical renewal of the late twentieth century, the catechumenate is based on new understandings of ancient worship practices and so may be considered the fruit of liturgical scholarship. However, to the extent that the catechumenate attempts only to reproduce practices from the fourth and fifth centuries, it is little more than an exercise in historical romanticism.

But as noted above, the restoration of the catechumenate in the Roman Catholic Church also drew on missionary experience. Moreover, the ritual texts encourage adaptation to local circumstances and the needs of candidates. For example, in one Texas parish the scrutiny on the fifth Sunday in Lent included a litany that named forces that separate people from God (pain, addictions, unloving parents, and so on), and the congregation chanted in response "Jesus is Lord." Here, the ancient concepts of temptation and sin are phrased in the language of contemporary North American experience.[38]

Adaptations are also evident in the various Anglican and Protestant versions of the catechumenate and their parallel processes. While many of the symbolic actions are retained, the titles and language of the rites are often quite different. Terms such as "exorcism" and "scrutiny" that may be confusing or may even become a barrier are replaced by more common English terms, for example, "affirmation" and "examination of conscience." A congregation in the Episcopal Church adapted the presentation of the Apostles' Creed and the Lord's Prayer to catechumens during Lent by presenting framed copies of the texts to parents preparing for the baptism of their infant children. The public presentation during the Sunday liturgy calls attention to the families preparing for the baptism of a child, and the families experience the rite as a sign of the church's care for their children.

The provision of texts and explanatory material for the rituals offers the possibility of powerful experiences of personal and congregational renewal. But introduction of the catechumenate and parallel processes calls for significant commitment by an entire congregation, not just a select few leaders. A lively, ongoing catechumenate requires unbaptized adults, and such persons are most often introduced to the Christian faith by other Christians. The establishment of a catechumenate thus means a commitment to evangelism. The public nature of these processes further requires a congregation to be involved through prayer, example, and support of candidates. The expectation that candidates will join members of the congregation in a life of Christian service and mission implies that the congregation is already actively engaged in this way of life.

What does the future hold for our practices of Christian formation, initiation, and reaffirmation? Congregations that have made the extensive commitment to the catechumenate have found themselves renewed and transformed as they experience the Holy Spirit at work in the lives of converts to the faith. Congregations that have adopted a fuller use of symbols—such as water, oil, the sign of the cross, laying on of hands, and lighted candles—are deepening their understanding of the profound implications of initiation into the Christian faith and life. Congregations that admit all the baptized, including infants, to communion are being enriched by the insights offered by some of the youngest members of their communities. These renewed practices of

Christian initiation are quite recent, and they are far from universal even in the churches with official texts that support or encourage them. The future of Christian formation, initiation, and reaffirmation is found in the renewal of congregations as they renew their initiatory practices and further refine the ritual texts and supporting materials in response to their experiences with the rites.

6

Ritual and Pastoral Care

William H. Willimon

Though not as skillfully, I, like Robert Webber, have spent much of my scholarly life attempting to bridge the gap between the Free Church evangelical (some would say "low church") tradition and the tradition of the larger church called catholic. Twenty-five years ago, when Bob was issuing his clarion call for evangelicals to recover the catholic tradition—his "Chicago Call"—I was moving from the parish to teach worship and liturgy at a United Methodist theological school. Little did I know when I made that move that I would soon become dependent on Webber's approach to worship matters.

We Wesleyans ought to embody Webber's linkage of the evangelical and the catholic. But teaching my first courses at the seminary, I found that these Free Church evangelical seminarians were suspicious of all things liturgical and fearful that I would make them "high church" and "ritualistic." Their idea of a good Sunday was "when we just get together and praise the Lord." The few "chancel prancers" (Luther's term) among them who resonated to my courses in liturgical theology and history bothered me with their (what seemed to me) rather archaic, antiquarian, and dilettantish approach to the liturgy.

In defense, I created a course called "Worship as Pastoral Care." If I could not get at my students through liturgy, perhaps I could sneak in through the back door by the only subject they seemed to automatically like—pastoral psychology. Beginning in the early 1960s, pastoral care had become all the rage at many Protestant seminaries. My own teacher of pastoral counseling at Yale, James Dittes, was a realist about this pastoral infatuation with his field. While pastors had been pushed out of so many of their former social functions—healing, teaching, community leadership—they were at least still respected as counselors. Dittes theorized that so many pastors were interested in psychology because pastoral counseling was the last socially approved function left for pastors in our contemporary and psychologically dominated society.

The discipline of contemporary pastoral care, I soon found, was at that time deeply suspicious of traditional ritual practice. The discipline had come of age during the 1960s, when there had been a lively critique of institutions and traditional practices as being inherently repressive and limiting to the development of the free and unfettered self-actualizing individual.[1] Pastoral care had become detached from the worshiping community and its rites and was linked more to the discipline of psychology than to the historic practices of the church. What the seminaries called "pastoral care" was usually taught by a psychologist who tended to be influenced more by secular psychotherapy than by the peculiar theological context of the church.[2] For its part, liturgiology was suspicious of pastoral care as a purely anthropological, psychologically dominated practice with only the thinnest theological justification.

I, like Bob Webber, attempted a kind of marriage of the disciplines, or (considering the historic practices of the *cura animarium,* the "care of souls") a remarriage of the two.[3] In my course, I led seminarians to examine worship as a principal means of caring for the congregation, a major resource of pastoral care, a source for deep pastoral insights into the lives of individual believers, and a historic way to care for souls.

This course eventually became a book, one of my most popular, *Worship as Pastoral Care.*[4] Thus began my quarter-century interest in looking at the liturgy through the lens of pastoral care and, in turn, criticizing contemporary pastoral care from the standpoint of the rich care that the church had traditionally offered in its *cura animarium*—the rites, rituals, sacraments, and services of the gathered community.[5] After my effort to be liturgical from the standpoint of the pastoral, I joined with John H. Westerhoff III to demonstrate the educational significance of our liturgical leadership, and the result was *Liturgy and Learning through the Life Cycle.*[6]

In the years since the publication of our book, Protestant clergy have become accustomed to thinking of worship as a richly significant human endeavor, thanks in great part to the efforts of Bob Webber. To be sure, the main purpose of Christian worship is the glorification and enjoyment of God (our "chief end" as described in the Westminster Confession). Yet while we are busy glorifying and enjoying God, God also ministers to us. As God is being revealed to us through our acts of worship, our deepest selves are being revealed as well. Or as the Second Vatican Council put the matter, Christian worship is both the glorification of God and the sanctification of the faithful.[7] As the faithful glorify God, they are being sanctified and formed into the people of God. Our worship says much about the God whom we adore, but it also says much about us.

Ritual as Unavoidable and Helpful

Ritual—patterned, purposeful, predictable behavior—is a component of all Christian worship.[8] Our Puritan forebears, sensing the inadequacies of the conventional worship of the established church, sought to purify worship by removing all "vain and repetitious" aspects of worship. In their view, the ritualized—patterned and predictable—aspects of worship had degenerated into deadening, formalized motions without the prompting of the Spirit and spontaneity of the heart.

Yet we heirs of the Puritans have learned that to merely remove "ritualism" from our worship does not enable us to avoid the pitfalls of inadequate ritualization in worship. Ritual is not only patterned and predictable behavior; it is also purposeful. Ritual does things for us that cannot be done any other way. Perhaps that is why ritual is not only patterned and predictable but also virtually unavoidable. Wherever human beings congregate to do important work, wherever people are asked to cross certain difficult boundaries in life, to move from death to life, alienation to salvation, isolation to community, guilt to forgiveness, silence to speech, there one finds ritual. We cannot live without the predictable, traditional and traditionalized, purposeful acts that enable us to cope, but more than to cope, to explore, to venture forth into new modes of being, to be saved.

Sigmund Freud complimented the Puritans' disdain for ritual with his contention that ritual acts tend toward the pathological. Observation of the private ritualizations of some among the mentally ill convinced Freud that ritual was a means of repressing unresolved personality conflicts, principally obsessive-compulsive disorders. For Freud, the best thing for the excessively ritualized person was psychotherapy designed to break the ritualization, thereby to "free" this person to confront his or her conflicts more honestly.[9]

Fortunately, psychologists like Erik Erickson introduced many of us to an appreciation for the healthy aspects of ritual. Erickson believed that ritual was more than a mechanism for avoidance; it was also a means of confrontation and adaptation. Ritual is a creative means whereby the ego orients itself amid cultural and psychological conflicts. Ritual provides us a safe, predictable environment that gives us somewhere to be, a place where we are given the courage to reflect on our lives and move into new modes of being.[10]

A Quaker meeting, a Billy Graham crusade, a Catholic High Mass, a Campus Crusade praise service—all are heavily ritualized occasions, because meeting and being met by God is too threatening, too against our natural inclination, too potentially transformative to go it alone. Cultural anthropologist Victor Turner noted the positive effect of ritual during certain times of "liminality" within a culture, when members of a community are asked to cross a threshold and to confront certain limits like birth, death, and puberty.[11] Ritual holds our hands during difficult passages, teaches us the words and the moves that enable us to negotiate difficult life moves without being destroyed by them, and tells us what to think and how to act in the presence of the numinous and the holy.

Arnold Van Gennep was the anthropologist who popularized the term "rites of passage," noting the way that ritual helps to provide meaning, structure, and community during times of radical life changes.[12] Much of our ritualized behavior, Van Gennep demonstrated, is not for the purpose of keeping us conservatively fixed in one life location (the Freudian view of ritual), but rather, serves to force us to move forward. Ritual, like rites of passage, enables us to sever one mode of being and move toward another through the predictable movements of separation, ordeal, education, and incorporation. Hippolytus tells us that the third-century church in Rome separated catechumens from their accustomed pagan community and friends so that the catechumens could be given up to three years of educational instruction by the church.[13] The catechumens were allowed to participate with the congregation only through the opening service of the Word, then they were removed for instruction while the baptized received the Eucharist and had prayers. If the catechumens were judged by the leaders of the church to have successfully completed their years of instruction, they were baptized at the first light of Easter morning. Thus, in many of its elements, baptism represents the same elements of any rite of passage. After this set of initation rituals, we have passed from one existence to another. We have become another. Ritual not only secures a world and fixes a place for us to stand; it also prods us toward a new world and offers us a new way to be.[14]

The presence of much ritual at some human gatherings is not necessarily a testimonial to our dull, habituated tendencies, but rather, attests to the challenge of the difficult life transition that is being negotiated at the gathering. Generally speaking, whenever a pastor encounters much ritual behavior, it is not a sign of the stupidity of the behavior, but rather, a sign of its deep importance for the community. I know one pastor who was removed for decreeing that the congregation would no longer have the "processional of the flags," in which fifty American flags were paraded into the church on the Sunday nearest July 4. Another pastor of my acquaintance nearly lost her job when she merely suggested that the annual visit by Santa Claus on the first Sunday of December might be replaced by the lighting of the first candle on the Advent Wreath. Neither of these beloved and staunchly defended rituals were written down anywhere. They did not have to be. These rituals were not merely signs of two congregations that were poorly formed in the historic Christian faith; they were also signs of the deep meaning that was being enacted by the rituals.

In the last five decades, the worship of the church has changed more than it has in the past five hundred years. Many of us pastors have spent much of our ministries doing that which our clerical predecessors never did—tinkering with the liturgy, explaining and preparing people for more robust participation in Sunday worship, renewing and modifying the ritual of the people of God. Much of this innovation and change in ritual has been fruitful, enabling the church to praise God in more faithful ways. Yet experienced pastors learn that they thoughtlessly violate a congregation's beloved rituals at their own peril. A seemingly meaningless congregational ritual that is staunchly defended by the congregation is a sure sign that the congregation finds meaning in a ritual, despite the pastor's lack of understanding of that ritual. Therefore a major aspect of pastoral leadership in our age has been the analysis of a congregation's beloved rituals. This analysis has often been followed by the pastor's attempt to provide the congregation with more adequate ritualization. We heirs of the Puritans have realized that displacing inadequate rituals through our liturgical reform can sometimes lead to even worse rituals. The pastor is the ritual specialist for the congregation, helping God's people find more adequate and faithful means of celebrating the faith through patterned, predictable, meaningful behavior.

Recently, I attended a wedding at a church that I am sure prides itself on its spontaneous, free, and nonritualized approach to the worship of Jesus. Yet when it came time for the marriage ceremony, it was as if they had backed up a truck to the church and unloaded every possible gesture, ceremonial, high-sounding platitude, and maudlin musical sentiment they could think of. The service took forever. Roses were exchanged; "unity candles" were lit; Scripture was read as well as poems; advice was given; mothers were hugged; signs, signals, and gestures were made—all in the interest of uniting Tony and Terry forever in matrimony.

They were right to ritualize such a frightening, risky, and mysterious moment in their lives. Sadly, their church had given them so little guidance and so few resources from the tradition to show them the way and to guide them at this time that they had to assemble and concoct the ritual for their wedding as best they could. As I sat there in the congregation, I felt rather ashamed that the riches and practices of our faith that could have consoled them at this terrifying time were mainly absent, leaving the couple, and the congregation, to fly by the seat of their pants.

So the issue is never, Shall we worship through ritual? but rather, Will the ritual that characterizes our worship be faithful and functional, or not? In our pastoral desire to enable Christian liturgy to be all that it ought to be for the people of God, many of us pastors have found the insights of contemporary ritual studies to be helpful. An example of such insights, arising out of a psychotherapeutic context, is the work on object relations theory by the British child psychotherapist, D. W. Winnicott.

Object Relations Theory and Ritual

Born to a Methodist family in 1896 in Plymouth, England, D. W. Winnicott converted to the Anglican Church as an adolescent at boarding school. Possibly, this move signaled Winnicott's innate fascination with and respect for ritual—a move that might be considered an early theological parallel to Bob Webber's own theological journey. We do not know all of Winnicott's motivations, but we do know that Winnicott became a pediatrician. His work with children and their parents lead him to a career as a child psychotherapist. Specifically, Winnicott became fascinated by the way the children internalize their early relations with objects within their world, particularly the relationship between the child and the mother.

Relationship with various objects enables the developing child to move from complete fusion with the mother toward a personality that is separate from the mother. The child moves from absolute dependence on the mother to relative dependence, said Winnicott, and uses objects to begin to differentiate between inner and outer reality. The principal period for this transition appears to be from the sixth to the eighth month of life and also from the eighteenth to the thirty-sixth month. The self learns to integrate good and bad images of itself, learns to express feelings, and begins to claim wants and needs that are distinct from those of the mother.

Crucial to this development, said Winnicott, is the mother's provision of an optimal environment where the young child is given the freedom to experience some frustration with the world, but not too much, and where the child feels safe to venture forth into the world and begins to view himself as a distinct self. This process of venturing forth and self-definition does not end after the toddler stage, but continues as a constant task of the self throughout life. No self is complete. Earlier dealings with the objects in the world are reactivated under a variety of circumstances and must be renegotiated by the self.

From his observation of babies, Winnicott devised a distinctive and non-Freudian version of psychoanalysis—*object relations theory*. Objects relations theory is best illustrated by an observational tool Winnicott devised called "the spatula game."[15]

In the spatula game, Winnicott would place himself alongside a table, across from a mother with her infant on her knee. He then placed a shining tongue depressor on the table, asking the mother to hold the infant so that if the child wished to handle the depressor, he or she could. Winnicott then observed the child.

Winnicott's observations show that the baby most often begins by placing his hand on the spatula, but at that moment discovers that he must carefully consider how his mother and the doctor will react to the placement of his hand. Some babies immediately withdraw, burying their faces in their mother's blouse. Yet for most, the period of initial hesitation is gradually overcome. The baby becomes so bold as to act on his desires, seize the depressor, and insert it into his mouth for further exploration and delight. The baby's whole physical appearance often changes at this point, showing great self-confidence and pride that this step has been taken and no reprimand has come from doctor or mother. Winnicott found that it was almost impossible to force the child to take the spatula if the child had decided to withdraw from the tempting object. Efforts to insist that the child take the spatula produced, in some instances, screaming and crying.

Repeated observation of this experiment led Winnicott to theorize that desire arises and is best expressed in a secure, safe, and inviting setting, "a holding environment" as he called it. Within the safe "holding environment," the infant feels secure enough to venture forth, gains self-confidence and self-definition in the process, and both discovers the inviting spatula and also has the illusion and delight of having created it. The spatula enters the infant's consciousness, changing it, yet the infant also imbues the spatula with significance. This led to another of Winnicott's seminal observations: We both discover and create reality.

Attempts to force the infant to take the spatula after the infant has decided to withdraw from it lead to distress or to a compliant, passive self whose greatest desire is only to please the figures of authority that surround it. In the face of strong, overbearing external authority, the infant tends to develop a passive mode of acquiescence, in which the child cares for the caregiver's desires rather than her own and becomes overly concerned about the effects of her actions on those authority figures within the environment.

Winnicott expanded these observations of infants to apply to his practice of psychotherapy. The therapist cannot force a patient into new ways of understanding and behavior. Rather, the therapist creates a safe space, that "holding environment," wherein the patient is free, if she summons the courage, to explore new ways of thinking and acting. The therapist must be willing not to judge, must be adept in the creation of a safe space, must encourage playful experimentation with new modes of conceptualizing and understanding the client's situation, and must be willing sometimes to keep silent so that the patient is free from compulsion or compliance.

Winnicott believed we learn about the world by interacting with the world. The world does not force itself on our passive minds, nor is the world merely a projection from our subjective consciousness on to a blank slate. We understand by interaction, through continual negotiation with other people and with the world. Thus, Winnicott could say that the truth is both "created and found."[16]

The rites of the church are the ritualized ways in which we meet and are met by God. In the church, we place the truth of the risen Christ within the grasp of people, but like the infant in the mother's lap, we do so in the context of a relatively safe "holding environment." The church is sometimes criticized for being a too comfortable and placid. We speak in muted tones, the organ plays softly, and a gentle pastor pleasantly reassures us that all is well. While such characterization of the church suggests infidelity to the demanding gospel of Christ, it is also understandable. People must be securely "held" and reassured before they have the confidence to venture forth into more demanding encounters with Christ.

In the liturgy, the demanding, potentially threatening presence of God is within the reach of the congregation, yet rests in the patterned, predictable, reassuring context of the accustomed liturgy. For this presence to become an experience for the worshiper, the worshiper must be free to pull away from the demands of the divine presence, must not be coerced into reception of the message, yet must also be free to engage, grapple with, create, and construct the presence. The presence of God is a gift of God to the church, an experience of the risen Christ. But the presence is also the product of our own striving, devising and grappling with the text. The truth is, as Winnicott contended, "created and found."

In his observation of toddlers, Winnicott also made the discovery of "transitional objects."[17] He noted that various objects are prized by the toddler—a doll, a blanket, or a bedtime ritual. This cherished object becomes a secure, reassuring presence to the child in times of anxiety. Parents learn to carry the object while traveling and to retrieve the object during times of sickness or whenever the child needs comforting reassurance. The object gives the toddler a permitted illusion, an illusion of a powerful presence. The object is an intermediary, a means of negotiating the inner and the outer world. The wise parent honors the object, even though the parent does not have the same feeling for the object as the child does.

A transitional object, theorized Winnicott, gives the child an essential experience of "not me." The child assumes power over the object, affectionately cuddling it one moment, jerking it around and mistreating it in another. The object, paradoxically, seems to give warmth and affection and at the same time elicit feelings of disgust. The object neither arises solely out of the infant's subjectivity nor is it totally outside the toddler's self. It is not a mere hallucination; its identity and value reside within the infant's frame of reference. It is both created and discovered. The object adds to the toddler's world, but the toddler also imbues the object with great significance, which makes the object into something that it would not be without the toddler's meaningful interaction with it. Eventually, the growing child seems to lay the object aside. Winnicott believed that this occurs when the child no longer needs the transitional object to deal with difficult transitions in life.

The "good-enough mother" (Winnicott's famous term) begins by doing all that she can to care for the infant, responding immediately to the infant's every need. Gradually, the wise parent begins to give the infant more room to explore, more opportunities to experience some level of frustration with the environment. The "good-enough mother" understands the importance of not immediately meeting the growing child's every demand. Winnicott redeemed Freud's negative view of "illusion." He showed the necessity and developmental value of some illusionary objects and experiences. Without the initial illusions that are fostered in the infant—the illusion that the infant is omnipotent over the parent, the illusion that there are certain objects in the world that protect and help the infant withstand the threats of the world—the infant would never venture forth to explore the world.

Thus, the infant moves into the world, collaborating in the creation of the world, letting go, and venturing forth from the parentally fostered Eden to interact with the world in ways that are increasingly demanding and risky. Freud saw the child as a hedonist who is constantly being told not to seek and enjoy pleasures. Winnicott saw the child as more of an artist who is constantly interacting with the stuff of life, creating a world that is trustworthy, interesting, and demanding, but manageable.

In the liturgy, we care for people principally by placing the holiness and otherness of God within the range of our people. Certain objects—bread, wine, water—are set beside our people's consciousness and placed within the range of their experience. In the gathered assembly, the congregation is given permission to touch, to taste, to handle, to interact with, and to play with these objects. Winnicott noticed that in promoting an object to the status of a transitional object, the infant necessarily abrogated some omnipotence over it. The newly embellished object, as a transitional object, is granted an objective reality of its own. Similarly, in raising the stature of a chalice to the status of a transitional object, the pastor abrogates a certain degree of power over the object, acknowledging the object's own inherent integrity, freeing the object to speak, to become part of the congregation's experience in ways that are not controlled or contained, not fully defined or delineated by the pastor.

In the relatively safe and secure confines of the liturgy, worship becomes pastoral care. People are given the safe place they need to dare to venture forth into one of the most threatening, and thereby most avoided, experiences in life, namely, the experience of meeting and being met by God. In the liturgy, certain objects become for us transitional objects that enable us to be encountered by God, in the safe confines of the Sunday ritual, in such a way that we have the possibility of being bold enough to risk encounter with God in the world.

A woman of my acquaintance, an every-Sunday participant in our assemblies for worship, was asked in a committee meeting why she was so committed to our congregation's soup kitchen for the poor. She responded, "I meet Jesus, in the broken bread, whenever we worship on Sunday. I meet Jesus, in the broken bread, and broken lives, whenever I serve a meal on Wednesday nights at the kitchen." To my mind, hers is a vivid embodiment of the power of the liturgy to be a transitional object for mature Christian living. In praising God, she was also being cared for in a way that produced Christian maturity. Winnicott's observations are thus, to my mind, a vivid example of the ways in which our own pastoral leadership of the liturgy can be enhanced, informed, and reveal new meaning through the insights of the social sciences' study of ritual and its effects. Using Winnicott as a lens allows us to see the deeper dimensions of the more obvious pastoral acts of worship. Weddings and funerals, for example, can provide Christian symbols that reassure us in times of great stress or need. In our rituals, we are given a safe place to explore the promises of God. This became very evident in the aftermath of the terrorist attacks of September 11, 2001, and the rituals that arose to meet the needs of a nation in grief.

Upon my arrival at one of my congregations, one of my members introduced himself and said, "I'm the one who buys the wine for communion."

This seemed odd to me. Methodists, since the early part of the last century, tend to use grape juice at the Eucharist, although not always. Purchasing wine is not a major congregational expense.

Then the man explained to me, "I'm a recovering alcoholic. When I go to a liquor store and *buy* the wine, then see it placed on the altar, blessed, and given to the church, it's a major way of my overcoming the demons."

Deep pastoral care is being performed through such ritualization.

A Concluding Caveat

All this having been said, a concluding caveat is warranted. Human effects, even the noble effect of good pastoral care, are not the main concerns in the complex of rituals that comprise Christian worship. The purpose of worship is the delightfully purposeless, pointless, nonutilitarian purpose of the glorification and enjoyment of God. We do not gather on Sunday primarily to receive peace and security, courage and conviction. We gather at the summons of the risen Christ who keeps coming back to the very people who betrayed and abandoned him. In participating in the rituals of Christian worship, we do sometimes receive peace, security, courage, conviction, or a host of other virtues. Yet all of the human good that comes from Christian worship is a gracious byproduct of the main good of glorifying God and enjoying God forever. Whenever worship is used for some human good, no matter how good it is, worship is being used and therefore abused. We worship for the love of it, or we do not worship the God who is loved for first having loved us.

This theological warning needs to be sounded in any sociological, psychological assessment of the Christian liturgy. It is a fundamental theological insight that was the beginning and the end of any of Bob Webber's discussions of Christian prayer and praise. In a time when theology seems constantly in danger of degenerating into anthropology, let it be the last word to be said on the relationship of ritual and pastoral care. The primary test of our worship is not psychotherapeutic usefulness, but rather, theological faithfulness. The primary purpose of Christian worship is not something even so noble as the care of our people. The purpose of worship is for people to be in the presence of God. If, in the act of submitting ourselves to that restless, demanding, alluring, and frightening presence, we feel that we have been cared for, then that is good. But that can never be our main purpose for gathering.

We come to God because God, in Jesus Christ, has come to us. That truth is reason enough for the gathering and for the mysterious, richly rewarding, infinitely demanding convocation that is the worship of the people of God.

7

On the Making of Kings and Christians

Worship and Culture Formation

Rodney Clapp

Worship is a waste of time.[1] That is the first thing that must be asserted in any careful discussion of the Christian custom of gathering regularly to praise the God of heaven and earth. For the praise of God is what worship is all about. Like the ethos of Sabbath at its roots, worship is not primarily about productive work. Worship is distorted and even perverted if it is made instrumental, the means to some other end than glorifying and honoring God. Today we can hear a growing chorus of voices saying that regular worship and clean Christian living makes people happier, healthier, and—some would add—wealthier. But if people undertake worship *in order to* become happy and healthy, they are then using God as a means to their own ends. Yet, if worship does not show us that the God met in Israel and in Jesus Christ is not a god to be used, what does it show us? Instrumentalized worship is debased worship, worship reduced to psychological therapy or political-consciousness raising. True and right worship (literally, *orthodoxy*) is first and foremost the service of God and needs no other justification.

That said, Christians do not want to deny that worship has consequences. Worship is a meeting of God and his people, and personhood is made in relationship. The God proclaimed by the church is triune, defined and identified by the Father's fatherhood of the Son, the Son's sonship to the Father, and the Spirit's being and empowerment through both. Even God knows himself in relationship. How much the more so, then, for dependent, contingent creatures made in God's image? Since orthodox Christian worship is not an escape from this creaturely sociality, but is indeed the gathering and very constitution of a people and a culture of God, we can expect it to have effects on the people gathered. Worship is first and last the service of God, but exactly as such, it ought to make people who worship more ready and able to serve God in all the days of their lives—not just for a few hours on Sunday morning.

That indeed has been the expectation of the church from its earliest days. The third-century church father Cyprian, for instance, asserted that "it is of small account to be baptized and to receive the eucharist unless one profit by it both in deeds and works."[2] Hugh of St. Victor would later say, "Sacraments are known to have been instituted for three reasons: on account of humiliation, on account of instruction, on account of exercise"—that is, to help Christians become humble, learn the faith, and live by it.[3] At least two developments in the twentieth century (continuing into the twenty-first century) have reawakened in the church the potential of worship's formative capacities. One development is the liturgical renewal movement, which emphasized the participation of all worshipers (not just the clergy) in the action of worship and insisted that worship (specifically, the Eucharist) makes the church—and so, makes Christians.[4] A second development is the recovery of virtue ethics, or the necessarily social formation of excellent character, by the Catholic philosopher Alasdair MacIntyre and, most influentially in theological circles, by Stanley Hauerwas.[5]

These two related developments have, in fact, spread to such an extent and taken root so deeply that in some circles there are extreme, unrealistic expectations of Christian worship and ritual in general. Catherine Bell, a scholar of ritual, understandably complains that some writers now think ritual, all by itself, can end war and bring justice on earth.[6] On a more commonplace level, there are those, especially those in Free Church (so-called nonliturgical) traditions, who sometimes protest the emphasis on worship. After all, they say, corporate worship occurs for only two or three hours a week; can we really believe it has much of an effect on changing the minds, behaviors, and attitudes of even the most faithful worshipers?

I want to set forth the case that liturgy is formative of the church and of Christians, to suggest what plausible and actual formative effects liturgy has, and finally to explore how liturgy might even more powerfully make the church a distinctive culture and its members more faithful Christians.

Rituals Make the Man, the Woman—and the Culture

I necessarily must base my argument in explicitly theological warrants, but I will begin in the more generalized terms of anthropology and sociology. We can observe that ritual has, intuitively if not self-consciously, been important to human cultures across time and around the world. For their survival and prospering, humans are dependent on inculturation to a degree far surpassing other animals. Other animals are born with instinctual equipment that largely determines their behavior. From dogs hunting for food to salmon returning to mating stations, there is an *inbuilt* "programming" that enables survival and propagation of the species. Human infants, by comparison, are unusually poor in instinct. Consequently, they are unusually dependent on other humans for their survival and for their formation as persons. It is from culture, and not from instinct, that the human animal learns to build everything from campfires to skyscrapers. Culture is that congeries of stories and practices that grants humans identity and gives them a vision of the world and of the purposes of life. It is not without reason, then, that the etymology of the word *culture* links it to our agricultural and botanical word *cultivation.* Culture cultivates persons. Without this cultivation, people would not be the persons they become. Try, for instance, to imagine George Washington with any developed or thick identity apart from America, or Joseph Stalin without any recourse to Russia and Marxist Communism. We now identify Washington and Stalin by the projects they devoted their lives to, by the causes that they assigned great worth.

Mention of devotion and worth points us to another etymological linkage of *culture*—the closely related word *cultus.* The ritual worship of a people is its *cultus,* and this ritual is embedded in what a people most profoundly value, the highest worth to which they grant their deepest devotion. Broadly speaking, rituals are repetitive, formalized, symbol-laden ceremonies. They repeatedly bring a people back to its founding stories or myths; they are performed with learned and elaborate manners, gestures, and words; and they are marked with visual, verbal, and other symbols that encapsulate or point to the culture's highest hopes, ideals, and exemplars. Thus have all cultures sensed the importance of ritual in making a person a part of a culture.

In that regard, I can return to my examples of George Washington and Joseph Stalin. Each, of course, had his own history and was "made" by cultures that preceded him. In turn, each played significant roles in creating new cultures, defining respectively the culture of the United States and the United Soviet Socialist Republic. In the United States, Independence Day parades and picnics hearken back to the founding stories of Washington and his revolutionary cohorts. Fireworks reenact the young nation's wars. Other rites punctuate the Fourth of July and spill beyond it as well: schoolchildren learn and recite the Pledge of Allegiance, baseball and football fans ritualistically sing and honor the national anthem before beginning their games. Such rites can seem especially important when cultural cohesion and formation appears to be in any question. Historian Eric Hobsbawm notes that it was in the late nineteenth century, with the huge influx of immigrants, when it was acutely recognized that "Americans had to be made."[7] Immigrants were not only urged to adopt American rites already in place, but the Pledge of Allegiance itself, and its daily recitation, originated in the 1890s. "The Star-Spangled Banner" was written in 1814 and was officially made the national anthem in 1931.[8]

The USSR was possibly even more self-conscious and intentional about developing rituals that inculturated and made Russians (and others) into Soviet citizens. Rites and ritual systems were "designed and revised in government offices by various scholar-bureaucrats for the explicit purpose of social control and political indoctrination."[9] The anniversary of the Great October Socialist Revolution and other commemorative holidays were annually celebrated. Ritual anthems were written and instituted. Initiation ceremonies were designed for youth groups and the workplace. Personality cults were developed around Stalin and Lenin. Marriage ceremonies were revamped to be non-Christian and to declare the family "the most important cell of our State."[10]

I mention such examples since they are familiar and nonexotic, and because they demonstrate the perdurance of ritual even in countries as determinedly modern as the United States and as designedly nonreligious as the USSR. Those who would found or sustain cultures seem intuitively or expressly to recognize the importance of ritual in doing so. "Rite" or "ritual" can have echoes of quaintness to the modern and postmodern ear and can sound remotely like something left to (supposedly) benighted "natives" and (again, supposedly) to a more religious and less enlightened past. But in fact, it appears no culture or polity can do without ritual. This, of course, says nothing about the degree of success or effectiveness particular rituals will have in making and sustaining a culture. Some holidays and rites take, and others don't. At the least, there may be one or more competing *cultus* attracting a population's attention. And rituals may be misconstrued or ignored. But the pervasiveness and persistence of ritual does indicate, I think, that there can be no culture without a *cultus*. Some or another kind of ritualistic practice may not be a sufficient condition for the functioning of a culture, but it seems to be a necessary condition.[11] Not for nothing, then, do various cultural movements in our day devise and practice their own rituals—from Kwanza in the African-American community, to feminist rites of passage for menstruating girls, to the insecurely masculine adherents of the men's movement retreating into the woods with sweat huts and drums.

J. L. Austin and his speech act theory may add philosophical ratification to these historical and sociological observations.[12] Austin and his followers reminded us that much speech is performative—that some speech *does* something—accomplishes and creates realities. He called such talk illocutionary, and it shows up frequently in rituals. The marriage vow, for instance, is illocutionary. It does not simply talk about or represent marriage: the bride's and the groom's mutual statements of "I do" and the minister's acknowledgement are the very act of marriage. These statements, in their ritual context, actually *perform* the wedding and make the couple wife and husband. Likewise, political rites are illocutionary: the king is made king by his coronation. Or, for a recent and nonmonarchical example, consider the U.S. presidential election of 2000. In the frayed civil fabric of contemporary America, voting is certainly the premier—if not the only—significant ritual act left to citizenship. Balloting, in a democracy, is intended as an illocutionary kind of "speech." The people speak, the votes are counted, and through this ritual action a new president is made. The ritual's effectiveness, here as in general, depends on whether or not it is properly and legitimately performed. And in this case, in the state of Florida, the legitimacy and proper conduct of the ritual was debatable. Were some voters really speaking for Pat Buchanan with their voting gestures, or did they intend Al Gore? Were some voters improperly excluded from ritual participation? These and other messy points of contention left the country without a next president for several weeks. Finally it was resolved, to the satisfaction of some and dissatisfaction of others, that the people had spoken for George W. Bush. Most of the country, shaken, but eager to reaffirm one of its few remaining civic rituals, rushed to ratify Bush's presidency.

This was an instance of the importance of ritual in sustaining a culture and, more specifically, a polity. Ritual not only recognizes husbands and wives, or kings and presidents, but it makes them. When there is doubt about the legitimacy or proper conduct of the ritual, there is doubt about nothing less than the actual existence of a particular marriage or presidency. Ritual illocutionary speech acts appear ineluctably at the center of a culture's polity and institution of family. In this regard, my earlier remark about ritualistic practice as a necessary condition for the *functioning* of culture is too weak. Ritualistic practice is indeed necessary for the very *creation* and *constitution* of a culture.

Social Science and the Effects of Worship

The church did not need speech act theory to tell it that ritual constitutes a culture. The church has, in fact, long seen its own culture made and sustained in and through the liturgy. But before I depart from modern "secular" scholarship and turn more directly to the theological grounding of the church's rituals, the social sciences can give us one further assist. Sociologists and pollsters have in the past two decades done a number of studies to determine whether or not the behavior and beliefs of people are affected by their worship. What have they found?

Robin Gill has scrutinized scores of studies done mostly in the United Kingdom and Australia. Most of his 263-page book is devoted to detailed recitation of statistics culled from the studies. He finds belief in church doctrine consistently correlated to the frequency of church attendance. In one 1993 British poll, for instance, 80 percent of those who were weekly worshipers affirmed belief in a personal God, while 71 percent of those attending once a month did; 85 percent of weekly worshipers believed that Jesus was God as well as man, while 77 percent of the fortnightly worshipers did; 95 percent of the weeklies affirmed Jesus' resurrection, and 79 percent of the fortnightlies did; 70 percent of the weeklies saw the Bible as the "complete Word of God," while 41 percent of the fortnightlies did; and so on. The weekly worshipers were also significantly more likely to read the Bible daily (33 percent to the fortnightlies' 7 percent) and pray every day (80 percent as compared to 30 percent).[13]

Other studies indicate the behavioral differences extend beyond strictly devotional practices. A poll repeated across Europe in the 1980s showed 28 percent of weekly churchgoing Catholics and 12 percent of nonchurchgoing Catholics involved in volunteer work. Among Protestants, 58 percent of the weekly churchgoers were involved in volunteer work, while only 10 percent of Protestant nonchurchgoers were.[14] Nor did behavioral differences disappear when allowances were made for volunteer or social involvement beyond the purview of church activities. Regular churchgoers, for example, were more likely to be involved in an environmental group than nonchurchgoers.[15] Overall, Gill concludes that British "churchgoers have, in addition to their distinctive theistic and christocentric beliefs, a strong sense of moral order and concern for other people. They are . . . more likely than others to be involved in voluntary service and to see overseas charitable giving as important. They are more hesitant about euthanasia and capital punishment and more concerned about the family and civic order than other people."[16]

Gill quickly adds that "none of these differences is absolute." People who long ago stopped going to church may still profess belief in Jesus Christ as the Son of God, and certainly nonchurchgoers are involved in voluntary social services. But there are differences: The "distinctiveness" of churchgoers is "relative" but "real."[17]

Comparable results are found on the other side of the Atlantic. Political scientist Robert Putnam, surveying a raft of studies, concludes that churchgoers in the United States are "substantially more likely to be involved in secular organizations, vote and participate politically in other ways, and to have deeper informal social connections." Among other results, Putnam specifies that about 75 to 80 percent of church members give to charity, as compared to 55 to 60 percent of nonmembers; and 50 to 60 percent of members volunteer, compared to 30 to 35 percent of nonmembers.[18] Social psychologist David Myers notes similar figures and adds that U.S. adolescents who attend church are, in comparison to nonattenders, "much less likely to become delinquent, to engage in promiscuous sex, and to abuse drugs and alcohol." He cites one study that showed "church attendance is a 'substantial' predictor of inner-city black males escaping poverty, drugs, and crime." Yet another study found that 63 percent of all U.S. parents of adoptive children were weekly worshipers. In a statement that echoes the wisdom of the ancient church maxim *lex orandi, lex credendi* ("the rule of prayer is the rule of belief"), Myers writes, "One of social psychology's premier lessons is that we are as likely to act ourselves into a way of thinking as to think ourselves into action."[19]

Of course, none of these studies—nor all of them together—show that regular worship always or automatically makes people into wondrous Christians. It can hardly be cause for celebration that, for instance, up to one-quarter of U.S. church members fail to give to charity. (And even those who give often do not give generously, according to other surveys.)[20] Nor do any studies, so far as I can tell, try to sort out the effects of corporate worship specifically from those of other church practices—and surely Christian beliefs and behaviors are reinforced through potlucks as well as through the Eucharist. Still, corporate worship is the major practice in which "churchgoers" or "attenders" regularly engage. And if Christians, true to the teachings of the church, persist in selfish, hateful, and other sinful behavior, these studies give us grounds to think regular participation in the liturgy makes them less selfish and hateful than they would be otherwise.[21] In the terms of the modern social sciences, worship does appear to make a "relative" but "real" difference in the way people live and believe.

Classical Christian Worship: Call and Response

We have seen that ritualistic practice is pervasive across history and all known cultures, that ritual is necessary to make and sustain cultures, and that social science seems to indicate worship has a real formative effect on worshipers. But where is God in all this? Indeed, all of the above can be said without reference to the peculiar God met in Israel and in Jesus Christ. Anthropologists and sociologists look across a range of human rituals and, for good or ill, try to assume a practical atheism in their study. At best, they "bracket" the question of whether or not any god or gods actually act through or in rituals. But a Christian account of worship and its formative potential can hardly afford to stop there, because stopping there can only instrumentalize worship. Instrumentalized worship says worship is valuable because it makes for better, more orderly citizens—and if there really is a god somewhere behind worship, isn't it nice that this god so neatly serves our purposes? But the God of Scripture and of the church's tradition is not at the mercy of human whim and, if anything, is more apt to disrupt than prop up complacent and powerful cultures.

In a properly Christian account of liturgy and its effectiveness, then, we cannot bracket God or even simply leave room for God at the end of our account. By Christian account we must start with God because God started with us. Yahweh first sought out Abraham, and called him from his comfort and security in Haran to Canaan, for the establishment of a "great nation" (Gen. 11:31–12:3). Likewise, Moses, the fugitive from Egyptian justice, was called by Yahweh back to the land of Egypt. The enslaved Israelites were led, despite their recurring reluctance, out of slavery and into freedom. It is no different for Gentiles who, lost without hope to our own designs and desires, were brought by Christ into "the commonwealth of Israel" and only so were made party to Yahweh's "covenants of promise" (Eph. 2:12). The Christian (and before that, the Jewish) confession is not that people discover in themselves— as some sort of innate human quality—the incentive, energy, and resources to achieve salvation and fulfillment. On the contrary, the unwavering witness of the biblical tradition is that people left to their own designs or natural endowments remain lost, blind, adrift, and ultimately, always bewildered. Furthermore, people simply left to their own designs cannot know true justice and peace and so cannot establish genuine community or polity.[22] So in the biblical tradition God acts first, and through God's Spirit people respond. Thus, whatever its good intentions, the Campus Crusade evangelistic crusade with "I found it" bumper stickers and billboards had the classical Christian profession exactly backwards. Ex-slave merchant John Newton was more on the mark with his jubilant recognition, "I once was lost, but now am found." We do not find Yahweh; Yahweh seeks and finds us.

Accordingly, throughout history and right on into postmodernity, Christian liturgy, like good jazz or gospel music, has always been structured on call and response. God calls; we respond. It is our response to God's historical acts in Israel and through Jesus Christ that gathers us to worship. Thus the liturgy— in Scripture readings, preaching, and the Eucharist—elaborately and repeatedly looks back to founding events of Israel and the church. Robert Webber is characteristically lucid on this count. "In worship," he writes, "we retell and act out a story." Preeminently, of course, the story we retell and act out is the story of Christ's life, death, and resurrection. As Webber puts it, "Because worship is the enactment of an event, the organization of worship is not left to the whim of creative people or community consensus [as with a club or interest or affinity group]. Rather, it is rooted in the historic meeting that has already taken place between God and man." By retelling and reenacting the event of Christ's life, death, and resurrection, "worship proclaims the meaning of the original event and confronts the worshiper with the claim of God over his or her life." All this means that "the overriding concern of worship is not simply the recreation of the event, but a personal meeting with God. On one side the emphasis is on God who has acted; on the other side the emphasis is on human responding. In this way 'something happens' in worship: God and His people meet."[23]

We can delve further into this divine-human meeting by focusing on a particular liturgical practice, the Eucharist. The institution narrative, shared across all wings of the church, recall's Jesus' words introducing and hosting the holy meal: "Take, eat: This is my Body, which is given for you. Do this for the remembrance of me."[24] In some Protestant traditions, especially in the train of the modern emphasis on individualistic subjectivity, this "remembrance" can be read in a rather pale and diluted fashion. That is, it becomes simply the individual communicant's memory of Christ's Last Supper and sacrifice on the cross. Surely subjective memory is an important aspect of the rite, but the classical Christian tradition maintains that much more is happening at the Eucharist. Indeed, in this tradition Christ is actually present in and through the Eucharist. As Herbert Vorgrimler wrote, in the sacrament "the divine Spirit uses this human action as a means and a way by which to make Jesus Christ, with his historically unique saving activity, memorially, really, and actually present. . . . It is the Spirit of God who takes the initiative and supports the whole event, causing the effects in human persons."[25]

We are helped to keep God's initiative actions (rather than human subjective response) in the foreground by noting that our English word *remembrance* is derived from the Greek biblical term *anamnesis*. *Anamnesis* is much more than the psychological recall of past occurrences. As the profound student of liturgy Dom Gregory Dix explained, "In the Scriptures both of the Old and New Testament, *anamnesis* and the cognate verb have the sense of 're-calling' or 're-presenting' before God an event in the past, so that it becomes *here and now operative in its effects*."[26]

Plumbing the depths of Dix's statement requires remarking that this re-calling or re-presenting is done "before God." That is, it is not only the human participants in the liturgy who are reminded to bring out of memory Jesus Christ's sacrifice and victory. God, too—or really, first and foremost—is "reminded." So it has always been in the history of Israel and the church. In the second chapter of Exodus, for example, God hears the groaning and cries of his enslaved people and then remembers his covenant with Abraham, Isaac, and Jacob. It is then that God acts to resume the initiative of the covenant he made with the Israelites' forefathers. Or consider the common Israelite prayer form, as instanced in Psalm 25:7: "According to your steadfast love remember me, for your goodness' sake, O LORD!" In the Old Testament, God's remembering is not merely or even primarily an isolated or insulated event within God's "psyche" (if we could so speak). Instead, as Robert Jenson writes, this remembering "occurs precisely as [God's] hearing of Israel's cries and as his answering prayer." When a human being remembers, Jenson goes on, the remembering is itself a present act. "When it is God who remembers, his answer creates what it mentions, as do all his addresses."[27] God creates the heavens and the earth by fiat, by mere utterance (illocutionary speech at its most radical!). Christ is also fittingly designated as God's utterance or Word, God's performative and salvific address of broken creation. The performative power of divine speech was rightly discerned by the centurion who petitioned the Lord on his sick servant's behalf: "Only speak the word, and my servant will be healed" (Matt. 8:8). Following this pattern, in the Eucharist we remember the Son to the Father, and by the Spirit the past event of salvation is made a present event in our gathering. Thus God and God's people meet.[28]

Given this meeting, we should ordinarily expect subjective responses on behalf of communicants at the Eucharist. The response is important and is in fact the actual unfolding, formative work of the Eucharist. Yet we know human nature. At times I approach the Eucharist tired or distracted or bored. Often (thank God), my spirit is moved at Eucharist and another step of healing is taken or new energy is given for the resolve to be changed more and more into a Christ-bearer. But not always, by any means. On those occasions when my spirit is not moved, has God not acted, or has Christ failed to be present—at least to me? The classical tradition respects individual intentionality in worship, but when I participate in a legitimate Eucharist, I participate as part of a *community* that God has constituted and resolved to meet. So when at Eucharist my attention wanders or I nurse resentment and "my mind is elsewhere," it is better to say I have failed to be present than it is to say God was absent to the entire gathering.

This objective, formative, effective sacramental presence is evidenced repeatedly in New Testament eucharistic accounts. Remembering that all the New Testament texts were written after sacramental practices were instituted and ongoing, it is illuminating to revisit eucharistic incidents and observe their objective effects. In John's Gospel, Jesus declares at the Last Supper that the one to whom he hands a piece of bread will betray him. Then he dips the bread and hands it to Judas. When Judas takes the bread, Satan enters "into him" (John 13:27). That is, whatever Judas's subjective state at the moment, Jesus' words and ritualistic act occasion Judas's overwhelming by evil. More famously, two disciples meet the resurrected Lord on the road to Emmaus but do not recognize him. He walks some distance with them, doing a bit of peripatetic Bible study, yet they remain ignorant of his identity. It is only at dinner, when the risen Christ takes bread, blesses and breaks it, and gives it to them, that their "eyes [are] opened" and they recognize their host as the beloved Jesus (Luke 24:30–31). Here, despite subjective states of (we might suppose) weariness and wariness, a eucharistic performance enables the disciples to recognize Jesus' presence. Finally, consider Paul's assertion that hasty, inconsiderate, and careless conduct in the Eucharist in the Corinthian community has brought on some the all too objective conditions of weakness, illness, and even death (1 Cor. 11:27–33). It is a fearful thing: God may visit our worship even when we really don't want him to.

It is, then, the real presence of Jesus Christ, the objective visitation of God, the Spirit's making alive of past events, that most fundamentally affect and form (and reform) worshipers. In worship we are again and again drawn into the living, dynamic re-presentation of Jesus' past. So in reenactment we are made more like the Son by the graceful and gracing God. We carry the failures and triumphs of our own stories into Jesus' story and must continually revise them to more nearly fit his character and the plotline that leads to a cross. Even our future is drawn into Jesus' past, as at Eucharist we are made bold that the resurrection now lying behind Jesus lies assuredly ahead for us.

Christ has died.
Christ is risen.
Christ will come again.

Is the World Really Changed?

We have seen that there is, in theological terms and in the terms of the modern social sciences, evidence that worship does change worshipers. In general, and to a degree, liturgy affects the behaviors and beliefs of those who regularly participate in it. But even a cursory reading of newspapers and religious periodicals (not to mention Paul's first letter to the Corinthians) demonstrates that regular worshipers remain capable of lying, embezzlement, national chauvinism and war, pettiness, adultery, murder, robbery, rape, cheating, bigotry, genocide, and just about every other sin known to humanity. While most of our misbehavior is not interesting enough to make headlines, no one who has been a part of a church can remain unaware of a gap between Christian aspirations and Christian realities. So what hinders worship from more thoroughly forming and reforming worshipers' lives?

My first and most important response to this question includes the epoch or cultural setting in which we now live, but is not unique to it. Our age is encompassed by the entire stretch of history that spans from Jesus Christ's resurrection until his (still awaited) parousia. Really, the question of whether or how much Christians are changed cuts much deeper than liturgy. The Christian confession is that Christ's death and resurrection has changed the world and even the cosmos. The apostolic witness is that Christ's work has reconciled humanity to God, brought together Jews and Gentiles (the greatest and most radical social division the New Testament writers could imagine), begun the renewal of what modernity has called nature, and defeated the powers of sin and death. Yet grievous and manifold evidence of separation from God, social division, nature's ruination, and the ongoing presence of sin and death all remain. Was Christ's death, then, in vain, and his resurrection illusory, or at least, ineffectual?

The church's response is that we awkwardly live in the time between the times—in between Christ's authentically world-changing resurrection and his yet awaited parousia, with the consummation of all the work begun by his inauguration of the kingdom of God on earth. The powers of death and sin really have been defeated; a new age has broken into our tired old age. But those powers, though vanquished, remain on the field until the consummation of Christ's reign. As Hendrik Berkhof summarized it, "The Powers are already unmasked and disarmed [as we are informed in Colossians 2], and shall be imminently defeated. 'Already' and 'not yet' are the poles of the tension that dominates the entire New Testament proclamation. For faith is no contradiction, any more than it was contradictory for us in the Netherlands during the 'hunger winter' (1944–45) that the Nazis, defeated, were still oppressing us."[29] Thus, the church, in its worship and life witnesses to a past fact (Christ has died and has defeated the powers by his death), a present experience (Christ *is* risen), and a future hope (Christ will come again).[30]

To some real and significant degree, Christians are formed by worship and by the culture of the church. But the church itself is pulled between the new age and the old age that will drag on until Christ comes again. So the church and its members inhabit both ages and remain marred by sin. In addition, the church's members in this time between the times belong not only to the polity of the church but also to competing polities and cultural structures. Thus, they are inevitably formed to some degree not only by the church but also by nationalisms, economic systems, various cultural enthusiasms and fashions, technological matrixes, and so forth. The church struggles for the undivided loyalty of its members, and its faithful members struggle to be loyal. The faithful want to be determinatively formed by the church's liturgy and other practices. But until the consummation of the kingdom Christ inaugurated, there will be at least some degree of divided loyalty. And the liturgy will be hindered and challenged in the formation of Christians.

Other Hindrances: Expressivism and Spectacle

Thus, today's church faces the hindrances and challenges typical to Christian formation in all historical epochs. We can, however, observe some hindrances to the liturgy's formative effectiveness that are more peculiar to our own time.

Until (roughly) the eighteenth century, the church was perceived as a public body—in the language we have often resorted to in this chapter, a polity.[31] In medieval Europe, for instance, cities were gridded or laid out in the shape of a cross, with the cathedral at the center. Church bells not only rang the liturgical hours but, in doing so, "told time" for all the inhabitants of the town. The Christian calendar ordered each year. Even monarchs respected at least the possibility of church discipline and were crowned in Christian liturgical proceedings.

Without occupying this degree (or exact kind) of political power, the earliest church also saw itself as a polity. The pre-Constantinian church could have avoided Roman persecution by suing for status as a *cultus privatus,* or "private cult," dedicated to the purely personal spirituality and otherworldly salvation of its members. But the God who gathered and constituted the church was known as the God of the universe, the real king of all nations. Christ's advent and work had changed history and society. Thus, the church could not be itself— could not be a public, deliberative body pursuing a common good revealed in Jesus Christ—if it understood and (de)structured itself as a mere interest or affinity group. The earliest Christians, then, quite intentionally designated their gathering an "*ekklesia* of God," which in contemporary terms could be translated as what New Englanders might call "a town meeting of God."[32]

It was after the advent of modernity that the church was privatized and so "depoliticized." The sense of the church as a communal and traditional authority was, to say the least, downplayed. Christian spirituality was individualized, and religion in general was rendered a personal interest. As Catherine Bell notes, in this context "the liberal Protestant theologian Paul Tillich defined religion as that which is of 'ultimate concern' to a person. In other words, religion does not define the nature of human beings, human beings define the nature of religion."[33]

Since liturgical rites were, and are, at the center of the church's existence, Christian ritual was inevitably affected. Modernity confined ritual to sacred "symbolic activity" set decisively apart from the practical conduct of everyday, and what we now call "secular," life.[34] In this setting liturgy falls under heavy pressure to be instrumentalized to cater to the privatized spiritualities of churchgoers. A premium is put on altering or reinventing church rituals so that they will serve individual emotional fulfillment. Christians can no longer tend to see themselves constituted as Christians by their induction into the church, but instead, see themselves initially and fundamentally as (somehow) Christians apart from the church. The church can then be nothing but an interest or affinity group: rather than it constituting Christians, individual Christians now assemble to constitute the church, to reinforce and *express* their faith in a crowd. Indeed, the liturgy is made not so much a culture-constituting and formative practice as an expressive ceremony. Bell aptly summarizes: In the modern reinterpretation,

> ritual is primarily a medium of expression, a special type of language suited to what it is there to express, namely, internal spiritual-emotional resources tied to our true identities but frequently unknown and undeveloped. Ritual expression of these internal dimensions will unleash their healing power for the self and others. This is not ritual as time-honored or heavenly ordained worship by which the transcendent collapses the gulf between the human and the divine, on the one hand, and the human world dispenses its responsibilities to the heavenly one, on the other. The new paradigm is directed more inward than outward, apt to define community and society in terms of the self rather than the self in terms of the community.[35]

Modern (and postmodern) liturgy, then, is inclined to be instrumentalized—and instrumentalized to human ends. Rather than the liturgy constituting and forming Christians, met in worship by a God whose "ways are not our ways" re-presented in the sacraments, liturgy is often warped to simply express and celebrate "our ways." Given this, how could liturgy's power to form Christians be anything but hindered?

So we might reasonably expect liturgy to be more formative if we retrain ourselves to take the liturgy on its own, classical Christian terms. In and through liturgy, Jesus Christ is objectively re-presented and is really, actively present. In liturgy we express ourselves, but only in response to a living and initiating God who first sought us—and who is not yet done with us.

A frequent consequence of instrumentalizing worship, especially in our age of mass media, is that worship is made into spectacle. Churchgoers come to church expecting to be entertained, just as they were entertained by a movie brimming with special effects the night before. Surely spectacle and entertainment can have formative effects, but they will be flattened and diluted. To take a non-Christian example, Bell relates a Japanese incident from the 1989 state funeral of Emperor Hirohito. The ceremony was staged especially for television (that is, rendered a spectacle), and crowds lining the street to honor the funeral procession were shocked and disappointed when the line of limousines sped by in a matter of seconds. One witness said, "We who had gone out into the streets were much like the 'live studio audiences' put together for television shows. . . . We were, in fact, part of the spectacle, live props for the television-viewing audience."[36]

With or without television cameras, when worship is reduced to spectacle, worshipers are reduced from participants to spectators. And as social psychologist David Myers indicates, participation intensifies the formative power of an activity. It is one thing to watch worship as a detached (or merely amused) observer. It is another thing to enter into it fully—body, mind, and spirit—expecting to be met by God and re-called and remade as a member of the body of Christ.

A final, and related, hindrance to liturgical formation in our age bears mentioning. Mass society and mass communication has greatly increased the number of ritualistic practices bearing down on communities. Too often the church and its members fail to recognize competing rituals or ritualizations that shape our lives. Advanced capitalistic consumerism surely stands as one of the most powerful formational systems in our time, and perhaps throughout history. Compulsive shopping, a constant barrage of ads, buying on credit, and symbolic systems of dress and transportation should be acknowledged as ritualizations that promote consumerism as a way of life.[37] For instance, credit card companies now teach our children that securing their first credit card is a premier rite of passage, a sign that in a world ruled by the almightly market, adulthood has been achieved. A church confident in its own rituals will claim their power and boldly recognize and confront alternative, incongruent ritualizations, demonstrating among other things that human beings were created ultimately to be worshipers, not consumers. To such prospects, may all the people make that most robust of performative utterances: Amen. So be it.

8

Rich Treasure in Jars of Clay

Christian Graduate Theological Education
in a Postmodern Context

Mary E. Hess

The September 10, 2001, issue of *America* reported that "there are more than 300 professional Catholic lay ministry formation programs in the United States, with a combined enrollment of more than 35,000—about 10 times the number of seminarians in post-college studies and 13 times the number of men in deacon formation programs."[1] Around the time I read that article I was part of a forum at Luther Seminary in St. Paul, Minnesota, in which one participant noted that "as many people are entering public leadership in the ELCA [Evangelical Lutheran Church of America] through nonseminary, nonjuridical routes, as are entering each year from all eight ELCA seminaries combined."[2] This latter statement is more anecdotal than statistically verifiable, but it still highlights a trend similar to the one occurring in Catholic contexts.

What are the consequences of these trends? And what should those of us who care about and tend to graduate theological education—particularly in seminaries—do about these trends? I believe that the postmodern trends in our wider culture are at the heart of this shift, and while for some these numbers bespeak crisis, we ought instead to consider them a sign of ferment and opportunity. I would like to propose quite a simple definition of postmodernism, namely, that this is an era in which there is widespread rejection of claims to absolute knowledge, an era in which we engage most institutions with significant skepticism and concern about the ways in which languages of "power over" permeate our social and political spaces, and an era in which we greet "difference" with more openness, and even celebration, than was once the case.[3] Perhaps these themes sound abstruse, but I hope to make clear both

123

what I mean by these phrases and how I believe they are shaping the context in which we teach and learn.

Let us begin by considering a "trio of triads" that I find useful for reflecting on education practices before moving on to examine two important challenges that graduate theological education faces in our current contexts.

A Trio of Triads

Each semester as I teach my introductory course in Christian education, we begin with what I call a "trio of triads." These groups of three educational concepts follow us through the term and allow us to consider a whole host of issues in Christian faith nurtured from a common yet flexible perspective. Here, too, they are useful for charting a course through the bumpy waters of the postmodern excursion. The first triad I work with is very basic: Any learning event always rests on three elements—the context in which the learning is taking place, the people involved, and the purpose for which they have gathered (context, people, purpose).

The statistics with which I began this chapter suggest that at least one of these elements has shifted dramatically in the last few decades—the context in which graduate theological education takes place. People entering public religious leadership are no longer streaming through the doors of traditional seminaries. Preparation for this kind of religious leadership (that is, nonordained leadership) is increasingly taking place in contexts that are only loosely linked, if linked at all, to traditional institutions of theological education. Churches are "growing" youth leaders within their midsts, utilizing the expertise of their congregants who are trained for other institutions (such as businesses and nonprofit organizations), or identifying very specialized forms of ministry (such as music ministry) that draw people from "secular" institutions.

There are many reasons behind this shift, but one of the most obvious is linked to a second element of this triad: people. Most seminaries were established to serve the needs of those preparing for ordained ministry at a time when people generally came to a sense of their call early in their lives. Most such students knew by the time they left college, if not high school, that they wanted to prepare to enter ordained ministry. They were most often young, male, and able to participate in a process of ministerial education that involved long stretches of residence on a campus interspersed with periods of intense practicum in a local parish. Seminary education was built around the needs of such students, and to some lingering extent it still is. Yet today the majority of students responding to a call to ordained leadership no longer fit this description. The *Fact Book on Theological Education* put out by the Association of Theological Schools (ATS) notes that across all ATS schools, "more than fifty percent (51.95 percent) of the total head count enrollment was 35 years or older. . . ." Women now account for 34.91 percent of the total enrollment across ATS schools, even though they are precluded from participating in some programs. At Luther Seminary our classes are now almost evenly divided in terms of gender.[4]

With this shift in both the people who are entering theological education and the immediate context in which it is taking place comes the third element of my triad: purpose. The reasons for which students enter graduate theological education no longer carry the uniformity of purpose that "becoming a pastor" once implied. Certainly many students enter seminary with precisely that goal in mind, but many others are preparing for other kinds of ministries or are at the beginning of a longer faith journey in which seminary is simply the first step in deepening their spiritual awareness and religious commitments.

Context, people, purpose. In introducing this triad, I used the notion of context very simply, but, as with any of these terms, there are both broad and deep elements contained within it. *Context* is a word that is increasingly used in theological education, but often with more than one meaning. At its root, the word has to do with "the interrelated conditions in which something exists or occurs."[5] We may speak of "contextual education" when referring to the parts of a seminary degree that require a student to work within a parish setting for a year before graduating. Yet we also talk about "reading the context" in various kinds of theologies, particularly those that have feminist or liberationist roots to them. I use the word *context* to closely parallel in some ways another oft-used word, *culture.*

Culture can be defined as all those activities that allow someone to give meaning to, draw meaning from, and derive meaning within a specific location. When we consider the shifts that are underway in graduate theological education at the moment, we have to take into account the ways the larger contexts in which our institutions are embedded are shifting, and here the word *culture* is particularly helpful. It is not just our student body that has changed; it is also the myriad cultural contexts surrounding and permeating our institutions that have changed.

I teach at a large Lutheran (ELCA) institution in the upper Midwest, although I myself am a Roman Catholic layperson. Even two decades ago it was possible for students and faculty at this institution to rely on the culture surrounding the seminary to prepare students for entrance into theological study. "Christendom" might be a term that is no longer in much use, but just twenty years ago it was perhaps still descriptive of a certain kind of Lutheran reality in the northern reaches of midwestern America. We could count on our entering students to be familiar with the Bible, to have an understanding of their identity as Lutherans, and to be comfortable with basic worship practices. Our task as a seminary was to help students deepen these understandings and commitments and reflect critically on them.

Now we find ourselves at a different starting point. Many of our students have little if any familiarity with Scripture texts, Lutheran confessions, or the rhythms of Lutheran worship. In part this is because some of them are not Lutheran! But in part, it is also because those who are Lutheran were not deeply immersed in Christian education as children and may have come with college degrees in apparently unrelated fields (accounting, physical education, and so on).

Even this degree of unfamiliarity would not pose the kind of challenge we are facing if it were accompanied by thorough grounding in religious culture, ease of use and fluency with print discourses, and an ability to self-consciously reflect on personal experience. Instead, we have students who are fluent in digital technologies, with ritual experiences shaped by television and film and reflective patterns shaped more by sympathetic identification than by philosophical argument.[6] In such a shifting culture, it becomes increasingly clear how context, people, and purpose come together and how influential they are within educational contexts. Certainly our earliest Christian educational leadership— such as Paul's correspondence to the scattered churches—demonstrates an exquisite sensitivity to context and to the purposes for which one gathers in a Christian community.

If learning experiences are fundamentally shaped by people, purpose, and context, then seminary educators need to take note of the dramatic changes occurring in our midst. Many of us, trained in the rigorous print-based searches of scholarly pursuit, are uncomfortable with these changes and are more challenged than affirmed by them. We worry about the coherence of thought taking place around us, we struggle to tend our own disciplines at the same time we ponder how to make them relevant to students who have no interest in scholarly endeavors, and we sometimes fall into the quagmire of assuming that our own experiences—particularly in worship—are normative.

So what are we to do? If considering the triad of context, people, and purpose presents us with these challenges, perhaps the next triad—cognitive, affective, and psychomotor—can help us to address them. This triad utilizes terms that are drawn primarily from psychological disciplines. For my students, I sometimes begin by suggesting that a *modified* version of this triad—ideas, feelings, and actions—might make more sense to them. The key to this triad, however, lies in the recognition that learning always takes place in multiple ways. While in any given learning environment we might intentionally focus on one of these processes, the other two are involved as well.

During the time when seminary education took place within a more homogenous cultural context, and seminary students shared more in common than their differences, teachers did not have to attend quite so carefully to this tripartite learning model. Feelings and actions—the affective and the psychomotor—were a language that shared similar terms and were built into shared assumptions. A male teacher putting a friendly arm around the shoulder of a young male student in the context of exploring the unease generated by a historical-critical approach to a biblical text could be "read" as supporting that student's struggle and encouraging the student's pursuit of truth. In our current context, the same action could be read quite differently—and in multiple ways. Nonverbal gestural sign systems, what many of us call "body language," differ among genders and between cultural locations. Now we must be more aware of them, more intentionally reflective of how we engage them, and more thoughtful of their multiple interpretations.[7]

Rather than being another problem, however, this is an enormous opportunity. The wider cultural contexts we inhabit, particularly those of the digitally mediated, globalized society that is increasingly the United States, are contexts in which nonverbal gestural sign systems are in a rich and abundant array of usage. As Adán Medrano and others have argued, we approach digital media in ways more akin to ritual practice than to print-oriented practice.[8] This suggests that the kinds of traditions we represent, the meaning-making databases we tend, if you will, have never been more necessary than they are now. It also opens up vast new arenas for scholarly pursuit of fundamentally important questions. Finally, it provides a framework in which we can approach with a greater degree of respect and openness the students who enter our contexts, because we can be intentionally thoughtful about all of the levels on which their learning is occurring.

There is one final triad in my "trio," and that is a group that Elliott Eisner first identified: the "explicit, the implicit, and the null curriculum."[9] Here again, I sometimes simplify these terms for my students, talking instead about those things we "intentionally" seek to teach, those things students learn "incidentally," and those things that are taught and learned because we do not address them directly, what some have called "unacknowledged learning."

When combined with the previous triad, this group is particularly helpful in identifying some of the opportunities present in the challenges we face in current contexts of graduate theological education. Consider, for instance, the ways in which students may be highly adept at "sympathetic identification" through their socialization in media culture, but quite unfamiliar with basic philosophical argumentation. Because liturgy in particular is such a multidimensional, experiential discipline, it becomes a helpful test case for this triad. For example, a teacher who begins a course by expecting students to do brief philosophical essays as a way to demonstrate their grasp of liturgical theology may find outside her door a line of students complaining about the irrelevance of such an assignment.

The teacher in this example intentionally designed an assignment to support students' critical reflection on a crucial element of any pastor's practice. The students, however, span the gamut from those who plan to be pastors, to those who are simply fulfilling a curriculum requirement on their way to doctoral studies. For the first group, the assignment strikes them on the implicit or incidental level as a "misread" of their needs in the course, and if their emotions are engaged in opposition to the teacher, it becomes a serious problem to support their learning much of anything in that context. For the second group, brief essays may seem like a trivial hoop to jump through rather than a space in which to explore important theological issues. For both groups, the "feeling" level of the assignment sends an incidental message that the teacher does not respect them and does not understand their context. They may be spurred to any number of actions, possibly including outright hostility or disengagement from the course in all but the most passive mode.

On the other hand, a teacher could design the early part of a worship course with sufficient attention to the embodied nature of liturgy—perhaps requiring students to experience multiple forms of worship in various churches or asking them to be "visitors" in another tradition—and later require students to engage those experiences in a descriptive essay, then a more critical essay, and finally a philosophical essay that uses concepts drawn from liturgical theology to explore their experiences. In this scenario the students are being supported by first being invited into an experience, then asked to describe it in narrative form, then asked to reflect on it more deeply, and finally asked to explore that experience with a full complement of theological terms to draw on.

I can already hear the concerns my colleagues might raise: If we do all that, how can we possibly accomplish all we need to in a course? Isn't it important to challenge students and require them to live up to expectations, rather than to "dumb down" our approaches? How can we possibly design such assignments to meet the diverse needs of all our students?

Let me take each of these objections in turn. First, as to the concern about coverage of material, there is significant research from the last decade that suggests that students learn more when presented with less.[10] That might seem counterintuitive, but consider the ways in which scholarly work often proceeds. A question begins to occur to you, and you ask yourself what your response to that question might be. If no answer emerges, your next response might be to ask a friend or colleague what their "take" on it would be, or you might go to a presentation at a conference or look for an article that deals with the general topic. Only after fussing around with it for a while do you begin to refine your questions, and then, and probably only then, you are able to turn to more focused and philosophical texts to help you structure your response.

It is almost a truism of adult education now that adult learners need to be supported into self-initiating inquiry. Another way to think about this would be to use Parker Palmer's description of the "grace of great things." His argument is that we teach more by going deeply, even if narrowly, then we do by going broadly but staying near the surface.[11] Our students live in an information-rich, even information-saturated, environment. It is far more important for us to help them develop information-accessing abilities, information-critiquing abilities, and information-integrating abilities than it is to transfer content to them. So, as one of my friends often puts it, we need "just in time" learning rather than "just in case" learning.

The second objection my colleagues might raise is the concern about challenging students rather than lowering content standards. This is an important objection, because educational scholarship also points repeatedly to the necessity of asking students to reach up rather than not requiring enough of them. The key here, however, is linked to the triad of ideas, feelings, and actions along with the "explicit, implicit, and null." Far too often we make extraordinarily challenging assignments without recognizing how hard they are, let alone providing sufficient support to meet their challenges.

A case in point: We, as scholars and as representatives of historically grounded religious communities, often have personal histories of deep and prolonged experiences of worship that are complex, diverse in character, and richly meaningful. We come to teach worship with these experiences in our background, often with the assumption that our students will trust our knowledge and experience enough to accept our guidance as to what they need to know and how to go about learning it. Our students, on the other hand, often come from quite impoverished experiences of worship, perhaps having only one or at best two or three kinds of worship to draw upon. Many of our students find various other kinds of ritual—attending a film with friends, engaging in sporting events, activism—at least as, if not more, profoundly engaging as church worship.[12] They praise God and reconcile themselves with God in a range of ways we may only dimly fathom and for which we may have little respect.

Thus, they enter a worship classroom with some distrust, if not open suspicion, of the ability of a professor in an academic institution to speak to their ritual experiences with any knowledge or utility. When we teach from our background experiences and assume that they are shared, on an implicit level we are already sending the wrong messages. If we then refuse to engage our students' questions—particularly those that have to do with digital media or various forms of music (both of which are issues of deep and constitutive importance to many students)—we teach through the "null" curriculum that we do not respect these experiences and, consequently, do not respect our students. It is thus a deeply challenging assignment we give to our students—to come into our classrooms and meet us more than halfway; to submerge their own experiences, intuitions, and instincts; to submerge the better part of their experiential resonances; and in turn to accept our claims and definitions as binding.

That is an extraordinarily challenging task, and it teaches a number of lessons I believe we do not want to teach. On the other hand, if we can invite our students' experiences into our classrooms with sufficient hospitality and respect, we may be able to develop a shared language that could support them in coming to a deeper recognition of the shared riches of liturgical tradition, for instance, and the necessity of evaluating our emotional or experiential resonances against the hew and grain of our tradition. My argument here is that we as teachers need to be aware of the "clay" with which we are encasing the riches of tradition. We must also be aware of the treasures our students may be unearthing if we could only collaborate with them.

The third objection my hypothetical colleagues might raise grows out of a deep concern for teaching in ways that have coherence and respect for students. Indeed, how can we teach in such a way as to meet the needs of all the diverse students in our classrooms? This is an important issue, and there is no simple answer. It is our task as teachers to provide coherence and substance for our students and to respect them in their diversity. These two goals can be in conflict. The tension between the two can be so strong that we may retreat into a standardized curriculum that does not fit anyone well but that at least has the virtue of being standardized. Or the tension can lead us to be "good enough" teachers, putting together materials that meet the needs of most of the students, most of the time. This has been the position I have tried to take in my own teaching. But ultimately, we must also take into account what Palmer calls the "grace of great things." He argues that

> We invite *diversity* into our community not because it is politically correct but because diverse viewpoints are demanded by the manifold mysteries of great things. We embrace *ambiguity* not because we are confused or indecisive but because we understand the inadequacy of our concepts to embrace the vastness of great things. We welcome *creative conflict* not because we are angry or hostile but because conflict is required to correct our biases and prejudices about the nature of great things. We practice *honesty* not only because we owe it to one another but because to lie about what we have seen would be to betray the truth of great things. We experience *humility* not because we have fought and lost but because humility is the only lens through which great things can be seen—and once we have seen them, humility is the only posture possible. We become *free* men and women through education not because we have privileged information but because tyranny in any form can be overcome only by invoking the grace of great things.[13]

One of the benefits of focusing on the "grace of great things" and the practices that go along with it is that it can free us as teachers to experience the humility of being in the presence of God. I am not the primary teacher in any learning environment; the Holy Spirit is.

Toward that end, I work to develop frameworks for learning events that are as flexible and choice driven as possible. In the beginning of any class, for instance, requiring students to develop their own learning goals in relation to the stated goals of a course helps to alert the teacher to ways in which the design of the course might need to be modified, or to individual students who might need extra support. Developing a syllabus that has a menu of assignment options can be one element of such flexibility, giving students the ability to choose assignments that match their intelligences and their learning styles, not to mention their diverse purposes in coming to seminary. Asking students to fill out brief half sheets after a lecture, in which they must list one thing they have learned and one thing about which they still have questions, can make even highly scripted lectures an interactive process over time. These kinds of choices can increase the difficulty of a course because many students have been socialized into being passive learners. Yet the earlier they can be supported into taking charge of their own learning, the earlier it is possible to effect convergence along all the curricula (explicit, implicit, and null).

The trio of triads can in the end be defined as (1) the primary elements: context, people, purpose; (2) the learning domains: cognitive, affective, psychomotor; and (3) types of curricula: explicit, implicit, null. Each of these lenses helps point to some of the challenges we face in Christian higher education. But these are, in some ways, only lenses through which to view the difficulties. There are two profound challenges facing Christian higher education that we have only briefly touched on, and it is to these challenges that I now turn.

Thinking through Others

The first of the two challenges has to do with the ways in which we are essentially working "across cultures" in our teaching and learning. There are many ways to speak of this challenge—and many who have done so. In this chapter I will address only one such cross-cultural work, which regards the division of the print-based academy and the mass-mediated popular culture context outside of it. I have written at length in other contexts about this divide, but I believe that one of the frameworks by which I have engaged this divide—Richard Shweder's—bears repeating.[14]

Shweder, a cultural anthropologist, has developed a four-part typology for the ways in which anthropologists "think through others." His framework suggests they do so by thinking by means of the other, getting the other straight, deconstructing and going beyond the other, and witnessing in the context of engagement with the other. Each of these strategies follows upon the other, and so it is worth taking them each in turn. "Thinking by means of the other" has to do with engaging some aspect of the "other" as a means to learn more about ourselves.

> Thinking through others in the first sense is to recognize the other as a specialist or expert on some aspect of human experience, whose reflective consciousness and systems of representations and discourse can be used to reveal hidden dimensions of our selves.[15]

Shweder's first mode requires an honest acknowledgement of the ways in which the "other"—and here I am suggesting academic culture in relation to mass-mediated popular culture as "other"—can indeed be expert in some way.

Faculty at graduate theological institutions are familiar with thinking of ourselves as "experts" in various kinds of discourse and study that can reveal hidden dimensions of thought and reality. But how often do we acknowledge that popular mass-mediated culture might also have resources to bring to this task? Certainly our students are expected to recognize and grant authority to our expertise, but how often do we acknowledge our students' fluency in the discourses of popular culture? There are rare professors who hire students to write web pages for them, for instance, or to serve as participant observers in ethnographic observations of youth culture. But even here, we, the faculty, hold the defining and controlling expertise.

Yet it is in media culture—no more evident than in the recent months since September 11, 2001—that the most relevant questions of faith are being debated. It is within digital media (a category that includes television, film, radio, and the Internet) that decisions are being made on questions of crucial communal importance. The divide between an academic religious culture and a digitally mediated culture was perhaps no more evident than in the three major rituals of grief and healing after September 11—the service in the U.S. national cathedral and the multichannel televised fundraising event put together by Tom Hanks and other Hollywood superstars. For many, if not most, Americans, it was the second event that was watched, talked about, and emotionally resonant. Our digital media clearly holds some kind of expertise that reveals hitherto hidden dimensions of who we are and who we want to be as a people. The last, the memorial service at Yankee Stadium, was presided over by Oprah Winfrey, arguably the high priestess of our media culture.

Shweder's second mode of thinking through others is something he terms "getting the other straight," by which he means "providing a systematic account of the internal logic of the intentional world constructed by the other. The aim is a rational reconstruction of indigenous belief, desire, and practice."[16] This mode of inquiry has so much in common with historical-critical biblical practice as to require no explanation here. Yet it is precisely this commonality—and the tendency to use historical-critical interpretive tools in isolation and thus send the implicit message of biblical "otherness"—that is most challenging to many of our students, since the conclusion they draw from using historical-critical tools can be that the Bible is a thoughtworld so different from ours as to be accessible only through the application of specialized tools. This same message is often sent, again unintentionally, by Bible studies structured in small groups of laypeople circled around an expert pastor who holds forth on the correct interpretation of a text.

Another example of this mode might be the way we seek in teaching worship to provide a "systematic account of the intentional world constructed," not in this case by the "other," but rather by us, in community. Media-studies scholars have over the last two decades shifted their understanding of how mass media operate, from a model that might be called "instrumental" to one that is far more open to the expressive reception of media. No longer are media producers viewed as determining solely the meaning of any "texts" channeled through digital media; they are seen rather as only one partner in a complicated dance of the creation of meaning. One analogy these scholars have used to describe the ways in which we engage media is that of ritual. In this analogy, people engage digital media as a resource in meaning making, using a set of practices that seek to shape time and location in engaging various digital media. We can "get lost," for instance, on the web, emerging hours later with no sense of time having passed. We listen to a background version of the radio, seeking to hear other people make sense of the day's events while we make dinner or finish our commute.

How often do worship faculty ask students to think about the ritual implications of their media practices? This is an important question, perhaps no more so than now, when worship faculty are increasingly being asked to reflect on the use of digital media within worship. In what ways do our students' socialization within media culture shape the discourses and patterns of practice we seek to facilitate within worship? It is just as important for us to be able to give a "systematic account of the intentional world constructed" by digital media as it is for our students to be able to do so of the world we seek to name and proclaim through worship.

Shweder's third mode of thinking through others, at least from an anthropological point of view, involves "going beyond the other." Many educators would identify this mode as "critical reflection," which indeed has a lot in common with Shweder's description:

> It is a third sense, for it properly comes later, after we have already appreciated what the intentional world of the other powerfully reveals and illuminates, from its special point of view. "Thinking through others" is, in its totality, an act of criticism and liberation, as well as discovery.[17]

It is this third mode that I believe we as teachers are most anxious to support our students in "getting." Yet it is Shweder's assertion—and mine as well—that this is properly achieved only after first moving through "thinking by means of the other" and "getting the other straight." Earlier I pointed to some of the problems that can occur when teachers ignore the affective and psychomotor components of learning, or when we refuse to consider the implicit or null curricula embedded in our teaching. These are the same dilemmas that emerge when teachers move too quickly to "going beyond others." We face an enormous opportunity in the postmodern context if we can bring our analytical and creative minds to bear on the issues that appear before us, on the questions that our students bring to us. But this opportunity contains within it an abyss of difficulty if we move too quickly to the critique of digital media, for instance, without first considering digital media from within their own frameworks of meaning. Similarly, we can invite our students into shared ritual leadership, or we can refuse to respect their own learning and contexts and simply try to transfer our own understandings to them. The latter stance will drive more people out of the church than it will invite in.

Yet there is an important step here, as Shweder acknowledges, a step that can be deeply respectful—that of moving to think beyond digital culture. This step requires us to think beyond and through institutional religious culture as well. Sociologists point to the deep skepticism members of the Gen-X community have toward institutions. Often that skepticism is expressed primarily toward religious institutions rather than media institutions. Perhaps we could respectfully invite young leaders within Gen X into religious institutions, thus in some ways bringing their criticism "inside," while at the same time encouraging them to turn their critical lenses onto media institutions.

Shweder's fourth mode of thinking through others is "witnessing in the context of engagement with the other":

> In this fourth sense of "thinking through others," the process of representing the other goes hand in hand with a process of portraying one's own self as part of the process of representing the other, thereby encouraging an open-ended self-reflexive dialogic turn of mind.[18]

This last mode of engaging the "other" is the mode with which we in religious institutions have the least experience. Far too often we engage in conversations across differences—whether ecumenically or in interfaith dialogue—from the arrogant position of having the truth rather than from the humble position of confessing that the Holy Spirit is ever at work in the world, continuing to reveal God to us. Again, if the months since September 11, 2001, have taught us anything, I would hope we have begun to learn that supporting religious identity formation that is too rigid has the effect of creating terrorists rather than of bringing us to our knees in awe of all that God has created among us.

Perhaps the clearest example of the way in which we as theological educators "witness in the context of engagement with the other" can be found in the ways we as teachers embody the deep humility of a teacher who is drawn to teaching because she is drawn to learning. As much as Martin Luther fought to keep hold of critical reason in relation to Scripture, it was also he who most liberated Scripture from the tyranny of an elite educated class of interpreters. Bible studies that are open circles of inquiry, shaped by the evaluative criteria of a historically grounded tradition but open to the emerging questions and life experiences of contemporary readers, exemplify this "open-ended, self-reflexive dialogic turn of mind."

The End of Education

The final challenge I find deeply embedded in the examples used at the beginning of this chapter is the third leg of the first triad—that of purpose. What is the "end" of graduate theological education?

Up until 1994, Luther Seminary's mission statement read:

> Luther Northwestern educates men and women to serve the mission of the gospel of Jesus Christ. Congregations and ministries throughout the church rely upon this seminary for well qualified and committed pastors, teachers, and leaders. The church and the public look to Luther Northwestern as a center of Lutheran theological reflection.

Now it reads: "Luther Seminary educates leaders for Christian communities: called and sent by the Holy Spirit, to witness to salvation through Jesus Christ, and to serve in God's world." There is an evolution here, as well as clear implications for our work together as faculty, students, and staff. This shift reflects an intentional broadening of our institutional vocation and our sense that public leadership in the church takes more forms now than it did in previous decades.

Hanan Alexander writes that "education is not about acquiring just any knowledge, but that which is worthwhile; and to judge the worth of something requires a vision of the good."[19] Part of what is sustainable and exciting about graduate theological education in our contemporary context is that we have a vision of the good—perhaps in shorthand form, this vision would be "the reign of God." But we need to translate this vision, or at the very least embed it, within our understanding of the "good" in relation to our vision of theological education.

For many decades graduate theological education has been strongly shaped by the dynamics of scholarly guilds, by the shape and construction of higher education more broadly construed, and even to a certain extent by the rubrics of "scientific positivism" afloat in the larger cultural spaces. It is difficult to find a way to move within those forces with sufficient clarity and vigor. What would a curriculum look like that has at its heart "educating leaders . . . called and sent . . ."?

Alexander notes that "the purpose of learning is to enhance one's moral insight, not increase one's material worth; to become better at *living well* or *practicing a valued craft*, not at *earning a living*. Professionals who graduate from educational institutions require not merely *practical skill* but also *purposes for which to practice*."[20] At the heart of the dilemmas we face in graduate theological education is the articulation of the "purposes for which to practice," purposes that must be sufficiently compelling and resonant to students who are socialized in digital media culture.[21]

On the face of it, I can not conceive of a more compelling educational "end" than Luther Seminary's current mission statement. But I also know that many students find it difficult to figure out what is meant by "witnessing to salvation," particularly if we intend to do so "in God's world"—which extends beyond the walls of the local church. A generation of people socialized within a mass-mediated popular culture, in which explicitly theological language was most often represented as belonging only to a few vehement fundamentalists, must now work to find ways to reclaim explicitly theological language that has resonance with their own experiences and that speaks within their own contexts.

The opportunity here is vast and can be recognized even in the commercial success that puts books such as Kathleen Norris' *Amazing Grace* or Roberta Bondi's *Memories of God* on the local megabookstore shelves. People are hungry for language and experiences, beliefs and commitments, that are deeply rooted in historically grounded religious communities. For that hunger to be fed, however, people also rightly seek respect for their own positions.

Which brings us back to the statistics with which I began this chapter: "currently there are more than 300 professional Catholic lay ministry programs in the United States with a combined enrollment of more than 35,000—about 10 times the number of seminarians in post-college studies, and 13 times the number of men in deacon formation programs."[22] I also noted my colleague's anecdotal reflection that "as many people are entering public leadership in the ELCA through non-seminary, non-juridical routes, as are entering each year from all eight ELCA seminaries combined." These statistics point both to the willingness of people to enter public leadership in their communities of faith *and* to their refusal to participate in graduate programs that do not respect who they are and the contexts in which these programs are embedded.

How can we take seriously each of the legs of the "trio of triads" I pointed out earlier in this chapter? How can seminaries in particular, but Christian higher education more generally, participate in bringing our enormous resources to the task of equipping and sending leaders for Christian communities? Alexander discusses Lee Shulman's core set of competencies that "spiritual pedagogues" require:

> Subject-neutral critical thinking skills that transcend disciplines and traditions, the subject-specific thinking of their own ethical tradition and of relevant cognitive traditions, familiarity with at least one empirical discipline that teaches the fallibility of its results, and appreciation for aesthetic forms of representation that celebrate creativity and hope. They also need what Shulman calls "pedagogic content knowledge"—intuitions learned from experience about enabling others to inquire as well as the inquiry skills themselves.[23]

Several years ago, we at Luther Seminary undertook a major revision of our curriculum, a revision spurred in large measure by our growing recognition that the contexts around us were changing and that the students coming to school were changing. I offer a description of our efforts not as a prescription for any other institution, but as an example of the way one institution has tried to support such competencies. It should also be noted that I work from a description of our ideal practice, which is lived out with various degrees of commitment in daily life.

To begin with, we decided to move away from "departments" that focused on particular disciplines and instead formed just three "divisions" of our faculty: Bible, history and theology, and leadership. These divisions also parallel, in some ways, a threefold movement in our curriculum: learning the story, interpreting and confessing, and leading in mission.

It is too simple to say that each division has responsibility for one of these movements—Bible for learning the story, for instance—since there are elements of each movement in all three divisions. But it is true that the key emphasis within the Bible division has been on deep engagement with sacred text, and that within our history and theology division, significant time and effort is given to helping our students trace how our communities have interpreted and confessed the faith—and continue to do so today. Our leadership division, which is made up of what in the past might have been the "arts of ministry" faculty (religious education, homiletics, pastoral care, worship, and so on), is now engaged in a vibrant conversation about what "leadership" means in a community of faith. How can we speak of collaborative leadership, for instance, and what does it mean to work with ideas around embodied and performative practice?

Let me examine in turn each one of Shulman's competencies. First, "subject-neutral critical thinking skills that transcend disciplines and traditions." As Shweder notes, before one can "think beyond the other," one must first get inside the other's position, understand its core logics, experience its central emotions, live within its commitments. At Luther we support the development of critical thinking skills by working with students to learn the basic "scales," so to speak, of the tradition they will soon play improvisationally. We still require our M.Div. students, for instance, to take both biblical Greek and biblical Hebrew. These languages are then taken up into various Bible, theology, and leadership courses in ways that help students parse the central grammars of our tradition sufficiently deeply so as to be able to play with its margins and extend its translations. In this way, the skills these students learn are brought to bear on various disciplines within Christian higher education.

We also work with more than the cognitive, particularly in our requirement that students participate in Discipleship, a core set of courses that provide small-group Bible studies as a way to reflect theologically on their daily experiences. We require that all students participate in cross-cultural immersion experiences. This latter requirement grows out of an understanding that critical thinking requires a grasp greater than one's own context. Finally, we have worked for the past decade on establishing a master's program in Islamic Studies at Luther. This program supports students who want to concentrate in that area and is also a rich resource in the wider curriculum for supporting students' thinking across traditions. I am not arguing that all seminaries should do the same, but I *am* suggesting that it is crucial that our students, who are called from and will be sent to communities of faith in a pluralistic world, have familiarity with respectfully engaging in ecumenical and interfaith dialogues.

The second competency Shulman says students need is "subject-specific thinking of their own ethical tradition and of relevant cognitive traditions." One entire movement of Luther Seminary's present educational strategy is the "interpreting and confessing" strand. This component of our curriculum seeks to develop within our students a deep appreciation for, and a concomitant ability to confess within, their tradition's core faith witness. Many of the courses in this strand are quite similar to courses in ethics and history at other institutions. But our worship course is situated in this strand as well, and our senior biblical theology course is an IC (interpreting and confessing) course. These courses require students to work at the level of feelings and actions as well as that of ideas. The courses also regularly draw on leaders from outside the the curriculum as teachers, or at least as featured guests on a particular topic.

Shulman's third competency is "familiarity with at least one empirical discipline that teaches the fallibility of its results." This particular goal is perhaps one we have struggled with the most. Currently our curriculum includes a class at the beginning of each student's course of study entitled "Reading the Audiences." This course brings sociological theories, particularly in the areas of demographics and cultural studies, to the task of congregational study. Students are challenged to describe in numerical terms the community in which a specific church is located, with presentational charts that utilize spreadsheets and other more quantitative software. Many of our students find this course particularly challenging and resist the idea that such empirical work could have anything at all to do with proclaiming God's Word. Yet a central issue in understanding statistics, demography, and other such empirical disciplines is learning how to critique and modify unstated assumptions. Such work teaches, as Shulman notes, "the fallibility of results" and is thus crucial to nurturing the deep humility that must always be at the heart of any Christian confessional stance.

"Appreciation for aesthetic forms of representation that celebrate creativity and hope" is the fourth of Shulman's competencies. This competency is thoroughly embedded in Luther Seminary's explicit curriculum through worship courses that study architecture, Bible courses that utilize images as interpretive tools, preaching and rhetoric classes that work with poetry and other forms of literature, but it is also present in our "implicit" curriculum. Daily chapel, for instance, is an important, if yet implicit, part of Luther's curriculum, and we strive to have this central worship experience draw on a multitude of aesthetic forms and frameworks. Music varies from elegant Bach choruses accompanied by full organ to more spare and informal praise bands. The cross is represented in a multitude of ways, from the large bronze crucifix permanently installed in our smaller chapel, to the Taizé painted crucifix that was temporarily in our larger chapel, to representations of the cross in a myriad of other media. We are also beginning to experiment more directly with digital media and electronic representations.

Shulman's final competency is "pedagogic content knowledge"—intuitions learned from experience about enabling others to inquire as well as the inquiry skills themselves. This is by far the most difficult of the goals we have set. How do we support our students in conscious and intentional reflection on their patterns of inquiry? How do we help them move beyond their own *self-knowledge* into learning from experience in supporting others? We do not yet have full answers to these questions, but our central intuition is that this kind of work can and must spread beyond the usual classrooms of a seminary. Already we are beginning to build relationships with churches, parachurch organizations, and other kinds of community institutions in which religious leadership flourishes. We have always had a "contextual education" component to our curriculum, but recently we have been working to ensure that our entire curriculum reflects "learning congregational leadership in context."

As I have noted, when the context around us is one of continual and rapid change, our educational leadership must be flexible, outward oriented, and deeply connected to the communities from which our students are called and to which they will be sent.

Hanan Alexander writes:

> Our very lives and those of our communities must become the intensive spiritual hothouses that summer camps represent. I call this *organic community* because there is a natural flow of complementary and mutually reinforcing ideas and ideals, study and practice, from the home to the neighborhood, the school to the synagogue, the youth group and summer camp to the cultural center and the social welfare organization. Communal norms can only be transmitted when the study, practice, and celebration of goodness is valued as highly by parents, grandparents, aunts, uncles, and neighbors as it is expected to be valued by their children.[24]

Although Alexander is writing in a Jewish context, I believe his words are equally compelling in a Christian context. We know the powerful impact Christian summer camps have on people. We can work toward a similar organic community that supports graduate theological education. Why is this important? Because in the broader cultural climate we face a context in which "reasoning by sympathetic identification" and learning embedded in practice is far more common than philosophical argument. Evangelism now does not look like a well-reasoned argument as to why Jesus Christ is our Savior. Evangelism now looks like many different things: the music of U2, the melodrama *West Wing* on network television, WWJD bracelets, and Bill Moyers on television. None of these examples are controlled by, or even promoted by, historically grounded, institutionally shaped communities of faith. In the last five years there has been an explosion of energy in using the Internet to communicate faith, and hundreds of thousands of sites have emerged with all sorts of information—accurate as well as highly misleading or even false—on religion. When we attempt to build the "transition community" (to use Bruffee's phrase[25]) that higher education can be, we must be mindful of the socialization our students have already encountered, and we must speak in the languages with which they are most familiar if we are to have any hope of teaching them any other languages. We must also ensure that that community does not end at the seminary walls and that the leaders we are educating continue to educate us.

Paul once wrote: "But we have this treasure in clay jars, so that it may be made clear that this extraordinary power belongs to God and does not come from us" (2 Cor. 4:7).[26] In a postmodern context those of us who tend to graduate theological education must, at a minimum, practice a deep respect for the meaning making going on beyond our walls and continue to be open to all of the ways in which the Holy Spirit continues to work within and among us. Only by doing so will we be able to support all those who are "called and sent by the Holy Spirit, to witness to salvation through Jesus Christ and to serve in God's world."

9

Promises and Problems of a Multiethnic Church

Kathy Black

Multiethnic churches are an emerging reality in cities and small towns across the country. These churches add an exciting and challenging component to the fabric of Christianity. Congregations that are comprised of members from different ethnic backgrounds come in various shapes and sizes.[1]

One model of the multiethnic church is when two or more ethnic congregations share the same church facilities. One congregation usually owns the facilities, and the other congregation(s) is a "nesting" church. For example, a Vietnamese congregation is given or rents space from a Euro-American congregation, or a Spanish congregation is given or rents space from an African-American congregation. In this model, the two congregations are separate; they simply share a space. The congregations may worship together from time to time, and there may be occasional joint fellowship activities, but the interaction between the two diverse groups of people is minimal. Both cultural and linguistic factors make this an appropriate arrangement for each congregation.

A second model of the multiethnic church is similar to this one except the pastoral leadership and administrative duties are housed under one umbrella. There is one budget for all the ministries. This is a multiethnic congregation that has several language ministries within one constituted church. There is one congregation with two or more pastors or pastoral leaders who take responsibility for a particular ethnic constituency within the congregation. For example, a large downtown church may have four pastors—a Korean pastor, a Filipino pastor, a Hispanic pastor, and a Euro-American pastor. While it is one congregation, the various ethnic ministries have their own worship, educational programs, and fellowship activities. Occasionally the whole congregation meets together for worship, outreach, and fellowship. This model allows for more interaction, joint planning, and oversight for the one congregation, but also honors the cultural and linguistic needs of the various constituencies.

A third model of the multiethnic church is represented by those congregations in which people of various ethnicities are a part of every aspect of a church's life and ministry. The people from different ethnic backgrounds don't separate for worship or fellowship or education. The church community is multiethnic. For example, one-third of a historically Euro-American congregation is Filipino, or one-quarter of an African-American congregation is made up of people from Africa and the Caribbean.

In some situations, the multiethnic nature of the congregation has been intentionally sought out. Church leaders made decisions that fostered outreach and evangelism among a diverse population. In many instances, however, these multiethnic congregations just "happened" over time. The ethnic backgrounds of the neighborhood surrounding the church changed, and one new family started coming to the church, then invited their friends and extended family members, and over time the church became multiethnic.

Within this model of the multiethnic church, there are many approaches that can be taken. Assimilation and often assimilationism are common responses. Assimilation, defined as "the process by which a person or persons acquire the social and psychological characteristics of a group,"[2] is necessary to some degree for anyone trying to become an active member of a particular group. In the United States, those who are from other cultures and nations need to assimilate—at least somewhat—to survive. For example, immigrants choose to join an English language ministry in order to facilitate their acquisition of the English language. For congregations that are having a difficult time dealing with the changing neighborhood, the influx of people into their congregation who they deem to be "other," assimilation is often the most immediate response. An implicit message is often conveyed: "You are welcome, but we are not changing our ways of being and doing to accommodate you."

Assimilationism, on the other hand, is an attitude that forces people to reject their own ethnic consciousness in order to adhere to the core principles and behaviors of the dominant group. In multiethnic congregations, assimilationist messages can be sent to newcomers: "Anyone can come into the life of this congregation as long as you fit into or learn to adapt to and accept the existing ways of being within this congregation. Stop being who you are and become like us, and all will be well." This often means assimilating to the music, preaching, and prayer styles of the congregation's worship, the perceived acceptable way to teach and discipline children, the traditional patterns of raising money, the acceptable way of relating to one another and to the pastor as a person in authority, and so on.

There is another approach, however, an approach that values what each ethnicity brings to the faith community. It is a model of reciprocal assimilation.

In this model the message is, "Yes, we want you to learn our ways of being and doing and praying, but we also want to learn your ways of being and doing and praying. Together then, we can create a new way of being a church that integrates elements from the various cultures present." I call this a culturally conscious congregation—one that takes seriously the various ethnicities and cultures represented in the congregation. Rather than the newcomers assimilating into the culture of the existing congregation, a third culture is created out of the blending of the various ethnicities present. People share across cultures how they worship, how they pray, how and what they sing, and what educational experiences and fellowship activities bring them together as a Christian community. The myriad forms of the church's life and ministry are reconceptualized according to the diversity present. It is this model of the multiethnic church that I want to focus on in this chapter.

The Promises of the Multiethnic Church

Living into the Pentecost Vision

There are many exciting possibilities within a multiethnic congregation. The vision that is presented to us at Pentecost—that of people from various countries speaking a multitude of languages, all sharing in the good news of God's love for us through the life of Jesus—has the potential of being lived out in our day and time. By the end of chapter 2 of the book of Acts (vv. 44–47),

> All who believed were together and had all things in common; they would sell their possessions and goods and distribute the proceeds to all, as any had need. Day by day, as they spent much time together in the temple, they broke bread at home [or from house to house] and ate their food with glad and generous hearts, praising God and having the goodwill of all the people.

This vision of Christian community may still seem utopian to some. In many multiethnic congregations, however, this text is foundational to their understanding of who they are as a diverse community of believers. The people may speak in various languages, yet they work hard at communicating the good news of Jesus Christ to one another. They also work toward sharing their gifts and goods with one another. "With glad and generous hearts," they eat the foods of different cultures that nourish people's bodies and souls, and they collectively praise God. "Having the goodwill of all the people" in mind allows congregations to work together toward creating a faith community where diversity is valued and even celebrated.

This is not to say that creating this kind of community is an easy task; it certainly is not. But the biblical witness and the Pentecost vision inspires congregations to hold this image as a goal toward which to strive.

Creating a Multicultural Microcosm

Multiethnic congregations also provide a microcosm of our multicultural society and world. If a multicultural community cannot be created in small, congregational microcosms, how can we expect people to get along in diverse contexts in the secular world? Some people join multiethnic congregations because they work in a multiethnic environment, they work out in multiethnic health clubs, their kids go to schools that are multiethnic, their daughter's soccer team is multiethnic, their son's karate classes are multiethnic. Our society is increasingly multiethnic. Many people want to worship in a multiethnic church as well.

Many recent immigrants to this country prefer to assimilate (to whatever degree they deem necessary) by learning the ways of being in this country through a Christian context.[3] They want to know what values, attitudes, and behaviors Christians hold in this country. For those of the dominant culture, it often feels safer to learn the skills that are necessary for navigating in diverse secular contexts in a Christian environment as well. How can we expect the society at large to be able to respect difference, and even celebrate difference, if diverse members of one Christian congregation cannot? How can we expect people in the secular world to negotiate and mediate cultural difference in a humane, nonviolent way if it cannot be done in the multiethnic church?

The multiethnic church becomes a Christian training ground for children, youth, and adults to learn how to live in a multiethnic, multicultural society.

Reciprocal Sharing of One's Faith

The multiethnic congregation provides wonderful opportunities for people to learn from each other and to share the deep resources of their faith. Learning new ways to pray, new songs to sing, new practices of spirituality, new rituals to mark life's rites of passage, and new symbols of the faith breaks open numerous possibilities for our spiritual growth. Articulating our personal faith for another forces us to dig deep into the sources of spirituality that sustain us for the great and often difficult journey of life. Not only do we learn more about ourselves and our own culture, we also learn about other expressions of faith and about other cultures and languages, which can be a truly fascinating journey in and of itself.[4]

Respecting Difference

Multiethnic congregations provide the opportunity for people to learn how to respect those who think differently, act differently, and even believe differently. We can learn how to agree to disagree and still be in community with one another. We experience firsthand what it means to stand in solidarity with a person whose life circumstances overlap very little with our own. For example, we support the sister or brother in Christ who is suffering because of a war in their home country and the absence of contact with loved ones. When one member suffers, we all suffer. When one rejoices, we all rejoice. But being in solidarity with another also means being willing to sing the song that most deeply touches the other's heart and even to sing it in the language that speaks to the depths of his or her soul, even though the song or the language does not initially have much, if any, meaning for us personally.

Respecting difference means being open to change. To embrace the other means welcoming the other's contribution to the structure and content of the church's programs, worship life, educational ministries, and fellowship activities. Respecting difference means recognizing that compromise is a given reality and that negotiating across differences must be handled with care so that power dynamics don't continually oppress the marginalized among us. The multiethnic church provides opportunities and guidance on how to respect, and even love, those who are different from us.

Cacophony Rather Than Unison

Multiethnic congregations help us learn how to live with a cacophony of voices and practices and music rather than an assumed unison. In multiethnic congregations some may be singing in Spanish while others are singing in English. Those from Southeast Asia may stand for prayers, while others choose to sit. Some may verbalize their agreement (or disagreement, as the case may be) to what the pastor is saying during the sermon, while others sit quietly and listen intently. Some may wave their hands and move their bodies to the rhythms of the congregation's songs, while others sing with their feet firmly planted on the floor.

In multiethnic congregations we learn to live with ambiguity and cacophony rather than unison. While it may sound chaotic, it is not. There is a *unity* expressed in and through the diverse community, even though the notion of *unison* is replaced with cacophony. Cacophony respects and values the spiritualities and faith journeys of oneself and of the other and gives people the freedom to express that faith in ways that foster their relationship with God in the context of the worshiping community.[5]

The Problems of the Multiethnic Church

Lack of Shared Story

One of the problems in the multiethnic church is the strong possibility of the lack of a "shared story." In liturgical traditions such as Roman Catholic and Episcopalian parishes, the prayer book or liturgy is held in common across cultures and provides a shared story for the diverse congregation. But in many Protestant congregations no shared cultural story, no shared national story, no shared denominational story, and no shared liturgical story exists.

Even the biblical story has been interpreted through diverse cultural and theological lenses as well as through different languages. When the prologue to the Gospel of John is translated into Spanish as "In the beginning was '*el verbo*'" (the verb) rather than "*la palabra*" (the word), it has a major impact on one's understanding of who Jesus is and what he is about. Likewise, there are some languages that do not have the word *resurrection* in their vocabulary. Resurrection, then, is interpreted into words that the language does have—words that may convey one or more aspects of *resurrection,* but that may also have nuances that we don't have in the English language, or that may not have been present in the original Greek.

The lack of a shared story challenges the congregation to discover which religious vocabulary, theological concepts, and liturgical practices they do have in common. It is important for people to share their different perspectives in order to learn from one another and to begin to develop a new shared story out of the stories present in the midst of the multiethnic congregation.

The most public manifestation of a lack of shared story is in the act of worship. Some people come from cultures in which the body is the vehicle of the presence of God. Worship is a time to celebrate, to dance, to move to the rhythms of music. Music is accompanied by rattles or shakers and drums that give voice to the heartbeat of the community. Prayer emerges from the depth of their beings as people feel led by the Spirit.

People from yet other cultures may approach the worship space with a sense of awe and mystery. Worship is a time for quiet reflection and meditation. The printed prayers that have been passed down to us through the ages, or prayers that have recently been written, are read in unison by the worshiping community. Some people come from traditions that stand for prayer, others from traditions that sit for prayer, and still others who kneel for prayer.

In some cultures, worship has not begun until there has been a "call to worship" from a Psalm text. In other cultures, an opening prayer, a musical introit, or a responsive greeting calls the congregation to worship; still others begin with a litany of songs and choruses. People from some cultures expect the sermon to last thirty to forty-five minutes, while in other cultures fifteen to twenty minutes is plenty.

Because of this lack of a shared liturgical story, much conversation needs to take place, with the expectation that compromise and negotiating across difference is a given in multiethnic contexts. The congregation must learn how to value the experiences of the other, learn from the other, and work toward a new style of worship that is unique to that particular diverse community of people. The lack of a common story does not have to be a barrier for long. The people present in the multiethnic congregation can create a new shared story that is unique to their faith community.

Authority Issues

In Euro-American culture today, many factors have come into play that challenge authority on various fronts: the authority of the pastor, the authority of the Bible, the authority of the sermon. A democratic society values (at least in theory) the participation of all in the community. In the past thirty to forty years there has been a movement away from hierarchy and vested authority. Many pastors want to be viewed as one of the congregation—set aside for the responsibilities of their office but not because of some unique spiritual qualifications. Partially, this emerged out of the feminist movement and the increase in women being ordained. Women devalued hierarchy and authority "over" others. And women were not automatically granted authority by virtue of their education and ordination. Authority was something that had to be earned through the authenticity of being in relationship with the members of the congregation. In addition, postmodern philosophies have emerged in recent decades that continue to challenge universal truth claims and external authority granted because of one's education or position. In dealing with issues of truth, the question is no longer "What is true?" but "Whose truth?" We live in a postmodern world where pluralism is a given. No longer can the white, Western males of society determine what is universally true for everyone. More and more, people value the "truths" that are brought to the community from different ethnicities, cultures, genders, and generational affiliations.

In the Euro-American church context, this challenge to authority has manifested in several ways:

1. The traditional "herald" model of preaching has been given over to pastoral, storyteller, and witness models of preaching. The pastor no longer wants to be the herald—"the voice of God"—for the community. The pastor is human and has given up that preaching "authority." The preacher can witness to her or his own faith journey and experiences but cannot necessarily assume that this is true for everyone. Or authority for the minister comes in being the pastor and counselor for the congregation—the healer and comforter. Or the pastor is the storyteller—the one who draws people into the story of the Bible, the story of the faith community, the story of the symbols of the church.[6]

2. Sermon talk-back times became popular, in which people could (and would) critique the pastor's sermon. Since the pastor is no longer "the voice of God," the sermon could be critiqued. And since the pastor no longer had sole authority in matters of the Bible, laypeople could also

be a part of the interpretation of the biblical text and its application for the faith community.

3. Many pastors have chosen not to preach behind the pulpit anymore. The pulpit as a symbol of the authority of the preacher has become a barrier between the pastor and the people rather than the conduit where the people meet the Word of God through the preacher. When the pulpit is seen as a barrier to the people, preachers move out and among the congregation to be more present to them—to create or reinforce the perception that the pastor is just one of them. The sermon then becomes more of a conversation with the people than a proclamation of the "word" of God.

4. Increasingly, worship is being designed (and even written) by a group of laity in consultation with the pastor. No longer are the structure, content, and design of the worship service at the sole discretion of the pastor. The design of worship is becoming more of a democratic and collective process that involves the input of the laity, both in the planning process and in leading worship (for example, lay liturgists).

But in many other cultures in this country, the authority of the pastor is still unquestioned. The pastor is the herald—"the voice of God"—and people take very seriously what the pastor says and calls the congregation to do. Sermon talk-back times are inappropriate because one does not critique what is considered a sacred speech act. The pulpit is still a sacred place—the place where the Word of God encounters the world through the being of the preacher. It is expected that proclamation will take place, not just conversation. And it is the pastor's decision as to the structure, content, and design of the worship service.

These opposing expectations around issues of authority and the role of the preacher in worship can cause tension, even conflict, within the congregation. These expectations need to be addressed openly so that people can come to understand one another and why they hold the beliefs they do.

Understandings of Time

Another aspect of a multiethnic congregation that creates tension is how people relate to *time*. Cultures vary in their understanding of time, but most fall within one of two categories: monochronic time or polychronic time. Most Euro-Americans understand time to be monochronic; time is linear. We schedule our calendars so we move from one appointment or task to another. Time is an entity that can be wasted, killed, spent, lost, made up, or saved. And "time is money." We deeply value time and consider it rude to impose or intrude on another's time. Because time is linear and we talk with one person or one group at a time, it is also considered rude to interrupt. Your (linear) turn will come.

When worship starts at 11:00 A.M., or a meeting starts at 7:30 P.M., most Euro-Americans at least try to be "on time."

Other cultures, however, operate on polychronic time. This understanding of time is more cyclical. Time is not an entity. One can't lose time or gain time. Time is not a valued commodity. Relationships and the community are more important than schedules and appointments. Rather than sitting in an office and taking one appointment after another with the door closed, people are involved in several things with several people at one time. It is acceptable to intrude on another's time or to interrupt because no value judgment is placed on these actions. Time is not linear. Fostering community relationships is what is valued most highly.

Worship, therefore, begins when the community has gathered, greeted one another, and is "ready" and in sync with one another. Worship ends when the people have exhausted their praise and thanksgiving and lament and are full of the Spirit. When worship begins and when it ends has nothing to do with the hands on a clock. In multiethnic congregations that were historically Euro-American, however, the chimes often strike the hour and worship begins whether the community is present or not. Others may arrive ten, twenty, or even thirty minutes late. People who operate from a monochronic time perspective often judge these latecomers as being rude for arriving late. Conversation needs to take place so that we understand the cultural differences that relate to time.[7]

Personal Interaction Behaviors

The ways in which we have been taught to relate to one another are culturally determined. These behaviors are so ingrained in us that we don't think about them or question them. We not only consider them the norm but believe they are universally held. However, they are not universally true for every culture.

Greetings. For example, how one *greets* another person varies from culture to culture. What is appropriate? A hug, a bow, a handshake, a kiss on the cheek, a kiss on each cheek? Is the greeting only appropriate between two women, or two men, or between a man and a woman? Does the meaning of the greeting change if it is exchanged between persons of different ages or different statuses, or is a different greeting required in these cases?

People from Korean, Japanese, or Chinese cultures may bow to the pastor in greeting, but it may not be appropriate for the pastor to bow (at least not too low) when greeting a layperson because of the perceived difference in authority and status between the pastor and a layperson. Cambodians often greet each other by placing their hands in a "praying hands" posture and raising their hands so that the thumbs are touching the nose or forehead area and giving a slight nod of the head. Filipinos may greet the pastor with *mano pa*. This is a gesture of respect performed by taking the pastor's hand and touching the back of his hand to the Filipino's forehead.

Rather than being awkward about greeting others from different cultures because one is not sure what is appropriate, it *could* be a fun and exciting process to learn the greetings used around the world. Doing this would require that a spirit of openness to other cultures be created, nurtured, and expanded within our congregations.

Naming. How we *name* one another is also culturally determined. In Euro-American culture, it has become increasingly common for people to use first names with one another. This is another attempt to break down hierarchies and issues of authority. Titles not only seem too formal, but there is a belief that the use of first names creates a sense of intimacy and a knowledge of the other that is sought in relationships. Using titles between adults is often felt to create a sense of distance in the relationship.

But in other cultures, the use of one's first name is a sign of disrespect. First names are reserved for family and a few close friends. In many cultures this practice is related to status and hierarchy within the social order. One would never call an older person or a person of higher status by his or her first name. In the multiethnic church community, however, tensions can arise when calling persons by their titles and last names is motivated by a yearning to get to know the other better but is received by the other as distancing. And calling persons by their first names as a way of deepening the relationship may be received as disrespect. For the diverse community to coalesce, these differences need to be discussed and dealt with.

Eye Contact. Direct eye contact and open body language is valued within the Euro-American culture. In often unconscious ways, we "read" a person's body language and make certain assumptions, even judgments, based on our ingrained cultural definitions of the meaning of direct eye contact versus indirect eye contact, open body language versus closed body language. If someone won't look us in the eyes, we might decide that the person is indecisive, evasive, even shifty or dishonest. When we want to determine if someone is "telling us the truth," we often say, "Look me in the eyes." We believe that direct eye contact can give us knowledge about another in ways that foster a relationship.

In other cultures, however, direct eye contact is often considered rude. Not making direct eye contact is a sign of respect for the other, a respect that builds the relationship. Knowing what is appropriate and inappropriate for each culture represented within the congregation and working through some of these issues goes a long way toward creating community.

Personal Space. How close we stand to another when in conversation is determined by our cultural definitions of what we consider *safe personal space.* In the Euro-American culture, people usually stand two to three feet from the person or persons with whom they are talking. When a person stands too close, we get nervous or even scared. We feel as if our personal space is being invaded and we may become fearful. Usually, we just take a step or two away until we have created safe personal space that is comfortable for us. On the other hand, if a person stands far away from us, we wonder if the person is actually interested in having a conversation or if the person is trying to distance himself or herself from the relationship.

In some cultures, however, safe personal space is only one foot away, and in other cultures it is five feet away. If someone tries to talk to us and is only a foot from our face, we may think the person is pushy or getting too personal, or we may become afraid for our own safety. And if someone tries to talk to us and is standing five feet away from us, we may get closer and closer, forcing the other to retreat. We make value judgments about people who do not conform to our own definitions of safe personal space. Understanding cultural differences on this matter can help alleviate the confusion that can arise when a person from one culture tries to develop a relationship with a person from another culture.

Indirect Speech. The use of indirect speech, or what is sometimes called "the relational yes," is one of the most difficult personal interaction behaviors that people from the Euro-American culture confront in cross-cultural contexts. On the whole, Euro-Americans prefer direct speech—tell it like it is, be up front about it, be honest, tell the truth. But think of indirect speech as "the little white lie" that is also part of the Euro-American culture. Certainly outright lies are told for personal gain. But the little white lie is used to protect the feelings of another or to protect a relationship. Someone you love comes home with a new haircut and is all excited about her new look. "How do you like my new haircut?" she asks. The truth is, you hate it, but you respond, "It looks great." It's just a little white lie to avoid hurt feelings and, ultimately, to protect the relationship itself. Those within the same culture can often recognize "the little white lie" for what it is.

Indirect speech is also used in other cultures to protect relationships. For instance, the pastor asks a person from another culture if he will be present at the board meeting next week. The person says yes but knows that he will be out of town on business at that time. The relationship between the person and the pastor is so important that the person doesn't want to disappoint the pastor, hurt the pastor's feelings, or create any tension in the relationship. So, the person says yes to protect the relationship at the time of the request, and this act takes precedence over the future date and time when the parties will not be physically present to one another. Avoiding or protecting the disappointment of the person when the request is made and the two parties are face to face is more important than the disappointment that might be felt when the person doesn't show up later on. People within the same culture can "read" this form of indirect speech, and there are no hurt feelings. But indirect speech is difficult to learn across cultures and can cause congregations to stop asking certain people to serve on committees or participate in other activities when they use this "relational yes" and are misunderstood.[8]

Benediction

There is no doubt that multiethnic congregations pose challenges—even problems—that must be dealt with. But I truly believe that the promises of the culturally conscious multiethnic church provide a vision of God's kingdom on earth—a community not based on hierarchical kingship, but a community of God based on treating one another as kin, as children of God.[9] Too often we exist within our own ethnocentric universe and are unaware of the ways God acts in and through people from other cultures. We become limited in our understanding of God, limited in our experience of God, and limited in the ways God can use us in the world.

Multiethnic congregations reinforce the Pentecost vision for us today and provide hope for our society and our world. Such congregations not only show us that people from diverse backgrounds and cultures not only can exist side by side despite their differences, but that they can grow into loving, faith-filled, and faithful communities. They empower people across cultures to work toward common goals that will build up the community rather than divide and conquer it with tensions created by fostering hatred and suspicion. Multiethnic congregations encourage us to share with one another and to learn from one another the many and diverse ways that people experience God and give honor and praise to God.

May the blessings of God rest upon culturally conscious multiethnic congregations so that they may be a blessing and a source of hope to the Christian church at large.

10

Denominations
in the New Century

Gilson A. C. Waldkoenig

In the family that is the body of Christ, denominations are the middle children. New movements, upstart congregations, and sects are the younger children. They hold promise for the future, keep twilight years at bay, and defy the dead weight of institutionalization. Church traditions, on the other hand, are the elder children of the Christian family. The Roman Catholic and Orthodox Churches seem as if they will carry on the traditions and not be swept away by youthful binges and ephemeral distractions. What they lack in innovation, they make up for in elderly legitimacy.

Being the middle children, denominations—modern compromises between church traditions and sectarian forms of the church—lack both the full credibility of the older church traditions and the exuberant freshness of the young. Denominations are the form of the church that nobody ever wanted. While church traditions seem to be divinely ordained, and while newer movements exude decisiveness and contextual relevance, no one ever sat down and said, "You know, we really need a form of the church that is stultifyingly bureaucratic yet lacking in any theological or social authority, precedence, or meaning."

In their unwantedness, denominations have lived with a constant refrain that predicts their imminent demise. In their origins as national churches transplanted on colonial shores and as newly empowered sectarian movements freed of legal restraints and persecutions, the denominations rarely acknowledged that they were one among many. Most denominations carried on the false consciousness of being the one true church, even though countervailing evidence was right before their eyes. Although denominations became a major outlet for the powerful forces of American volunteerism, organizational impulses, and the enthusiasm of modernization, they were ever the thing everyone wanted to get past as quickly as possible. Some Protestant groups have molted denominational forms at an astonishing pace.[1]

But the denominations come from good families, so to speak, and so they have usually been well fed and protected despite their basic unwantedness. A "denomination" is literally, after all, a name under the larger name of Christian. It might be worth sustaining as a stage in the evolution to better things—at least that is what they were to the Progressives of the early twentieth century. Just as Protestants have put a great deal of energy and resources into making and sustaining denominations, so too, a good deal has gone into merging and closing old denominations. Denominations are the classic "second sons," destined not to inherit the family business and lacking the great freedom and promise of the younger, ones but tagging along as a part of the Christian household anyway.

In the beginning of the third millennium, denominations are rising and declining all around, but denominationalism is as strong as it has ever been. Just when a growing congregation thinks it is succeeding in being truly "non-denominational," the inevitable procedures of organizational existence bring about denominational forms. Meanwhile, just when an old-line denomination rises above its latent sectarianism and joins in wider communion, rifts within its ranks threaten to create two denominations where there was recently one. The situation is ironic and is challenging to the integrity of individual ministers and gathered communities of believers.

In this chapter I will describe the phenomenon of denominations as a modern and postmodern American form of religious organization. I will then frame the practical implications for individual ministers and for believing communities who seek to live their traditions faithfully amid the denominational landscape.

Disintegrative Tendencies

It is as if there is an invisible force throughout American history that generally works against Christians trying to unite in organizational networks. Once upon a time, Americans were recognized for their willingness to join in voluntary associations. But when it came to religion, such voluntarism found robust expression only at the congregational level, where it abounded. Efforts to organize Americans into larger networks were halting and the few successes anomalous.

Take as an example the efforts of Count Nicholas von Zinzendorf in the eighteenth century. He was the German benefactor of refugee Hussites from Moravia. A Lutheran by training and confession, Zinzendorf saw little division between the original Protestants, as it were, and his Lutheran Pietism. German Lutheran officials in his native Saxony disagreed and censured Zinzendorf. But the Count came to North America, far from Saxon officials, eager to enact his vision for uniting all German-speaking Protestants into one pious church. Zinzendorf served as a Lutheran pastor, as well as a Moravian bishop, until he withdrew from the territorial challenge of one Henry Melchior Muhlenberg.

Muhlenberg was friendly to other pious Protestants, including Presbyterian Gilbert Tennant and English-speaking revivalist George Whitefield. But his vision of church was, in practical terms, a replication of the territorial and confessional church of his German home. He carried a party spirit against Zinzendorf and the Moravians from his training school at Halle and reported back to his supporting officials upon successfully ousting Zinzendorf from the Lutheran congregation in Philadelphia that he then controlled. Muhlenberg's later efforts were to gather a Pennsylvania ministerium, the protodenominational organization of American Lutheranism. He assisted German Reformed churches, but appealed to their European consistories to send a leader rather than try to meld German-speaking cousins into one church as Zinzendorf did. The experience of Zinzendorf and Muhlenberg was a precursor to the persistent differentiation between religious groups in America that would contribute to a church form later named the "denomination."[2]

A Function of Modernity and Postmodernity

Prior to the modern world of the past two to three centuries, there were no denominations. Christianity existed in three basic sociological forms: the local congregation, the monastery, and the networks that transcended and linked congregations and monastic communities. The networks followed first regional and then political patterns. The church became associated with the empires and later with the nation-states of Europe. The term "establishment" refers to the more or less hegemonic position of the church in the law and the culture.

With the colonizing powers, the established churches came to North America, but a plurality of colonial churches and increasing separation of church and state contributed to *dis*establishment, which is now normative. The root of denominationalism lies in colonial pluralism. Quaker Pennsylvania, for example, welcomed all Christian sects to an environment of free exercise of religion, but the Puritan establishment in Massachusetts and Connecticut lasted into the first third of the nineteenth century. Different traditions from Europe— from sectarian and Free Churches to displaced national churches—continued in recognizable continuity with their European forms as long as regional, ethnic, or socioeconomic cadres could sustain them. Thus German-speaking Mennonites who lived intentionally on rural farms sustained their distinctive subgroup of Christianity over the centuries, and Presbyterians could maintain a fairly well-differentiated existence in the mid-Atlantic apart from their Puritan cousins to the north.

Scholars of American religion have noticed the invisible social scaffolding that has upheld in the North American environment the variant traditions from Europe. Gerald Brauer wrote on regional differences, for example, and Martin Marty identified ethnicity as the "skeleton of American religion." As long as communities of people were identifiably separated by region or tribe, distinctive religious traditions would persist.[3]

Sidney Mead insightfully interpreted the displacement of the state churches from Europe. In contrast to an American religion of Enlightenment deism, such as Thomas Jefferson held, Mead saw the confessional and sectarian Christians as unadapted holdovers from Europe. He likened the establishment types to cows that ingest an indigestible plant while grazing: they can't pass it and can't regurgitate it, and so they die. So, argued Mead, do the old traditions try to live an established existence in a disestablished environment. Lacking the sword of the state behind them and facing assimilation and modernization to the fore, eventually the old traditions must meld into a new American Christianity or die out.[4]

The first American church historian, Phillip Schaff, also predicted a gradual melding of traditions into one American Protestant Church, although he envisioned its being more orthodox than rationalistic. The meld has not happened to date, however. Unorthodox or orthodox, traditional or enlightened, it matters not; American Christians have a difficult time forming organized networks. The primary reasons for this have been social differences.

In a classic work called *The Social Sources of Denominationalism,* H. Richard Niebuhr pointed out in 1929 that each denomination in North America owed its separate existence to socioeconomic, ethnic, and racial differences as much as to distinctive theological positions.[5] Niebuhr built on the sociological perspective of Ernst Troeltsch, who had developed a typology of church and sect that helped to explain the ironies of European Protestant and Catholic belief and behavior.[6] Niebuhr posited the denomination between church and sect, clearly identifying that it was social determinants that prevented sects from retaining their cultic identities and energies.

After *Social Sources,* Niebuhr wrote an interpretation of the risings and declines of American religious movements in which the providence of God through history underlay the social determination of religious movements. *The Kingdom of God in America* reckoned the limits of denominational groups to be a tool in the hands of God for the continual renewal of American Christianity.[7] Just when one movement became encrusted in organizational weight, a new one would rise to express the fresh work of the Holy Spirit. Hence, Niebuhr showed that the will of the divine was in some way more fundamental than the determinism of social causes. However, the historical-theological perspective of *The Kingdom of God* implied that when denominations persist beyond their energetic phases of fresh mission, they are no longer in the vanguard of the progress of the kingdom of God in America. Indeed, they are probably deadweight to missional advancement according to the tenor of Niebuhr's book.

Choice and Conflict

Other scholars have focused not so much on the development or plight of the denominations as entities but have instead simply chronicled the continual conflict and choice in American religious history. Whereas the scholars mentioned above noticed the shadow of an "evangelical establishment" in the vacuum created by disestablishment, Jon Butler gathered evidence that North Americans never were as "churched" as the quasiestablishment theories would imply. Butler called religious activity in the eighteenth and nineteenth centuries an attempt to "Christianize" a populace that was basically heterodox and disorganized religiously.[8]

In a different vein, but with equal emphasis on free choice, sociologists Roger Finke and Rodney Stark demonstrated in *The Churching of America* that the "free market" of religious choice has continually produced more and more congregations, even though certain types of congregations and their denominations decline.[9] The most significant fact for Finke and Stark is the continual birthing of local religious communities. Denominations, in turn, are secondary phenomena. These analysts do not entertain the wider ecclesiological or theological implications of the persistent weakness of transcongregational networks in the modern and postmodern environments. They seek neither Niebuhr's providence nor Mead's enlightened religion in their study.

A danger lies on the horizon of the free-choice landscape: the creep of individualism may ultimately undermine local gatherings as it has transcongregational networking. At this point the thesis of Robert Putnam in *Bowling Alone* would indicate that just as national churches lost their hold early in modernity, local congregations are now being undermined.[10] Nancy Ammerman has offered some countervailing evidence of how postmodern people still congregate: on Wednesday nights and over coffee rather than in choirs and pews at 11 A.M. on Sundays.[11] Nevertheless, the Putnam evidence, along with major assessments by Robert Bellah, Amatai Etzioni, and other communitarians, would indicate that denominationalism will decline in tandem with more locally organized group encounters.[12]

Along with choice, continual conflict and change in American religion works against denominationalism. At the local level, every parish pastor knows that any given parishioner can "walk" at any time—and several frequently do. The ties to denominations are looser, and so the walk is easier. Not only overt conflict but also milder clashes of traditions and worldviews regularly cause the shifting of members from one denominational stripe to another. A marriage, a divorce, or a move to a new community can easily dislodge an individual or a nuclear family unit from a venerable tradition to an upstart independent church, or vice versa. On the ragged edges of declining ethnicity or regionalism, and in the wake of mobility and increasing social status, the coherence of denominations is threatened.

Denominational Tendencies

Even with the overriding influences of individual autonomy, conflict, and change, there are instances of protodenominationalism amid the independent churches and choice-oriented congregations. Calvary Chapel in Costa Mesa, California, started during the "Jesus Freak" days of the 1970s as a decidedly anti-institutional movement geared for the individualist. Today it has daughter congregations in several cities, and its pastors and churches report to, and seek direction from, Calvary. Such is protodenominational activity, in which lie lines of authority, flow of resources, and institutional accountability.[13]

There are other instances of rising denominationalism among nondenominational churches. Willow Creek, the quintessential megachurch of the 1990s, offers a leadership school every summer that rivals the programs of the best seminaries. Working on seminary-like activities and shaping new leaders are typically denominational activities. Other independent ministries have grown to become media empires. With the structure of modern corporations but infused by charismatic authority, such religious organizations are miniature denominations unto themselves. Protodenominational activity fits the long-recognized theory of the drift from sect to church. There is a movement, albeit a reluctant one, away from the sect type toward the church type every time a Free-Church movement experiences any degree of institutionalization.

Even beneath the conflicting rhetoric of American religion and society, there is not only relatively peaceful coexistence of differing groups but also interesting alliances in common causes. Martin Marty has often pointed out the web of practical convergences between rhetorical enemies in modern and post-modern society.[14] Hence, anti-Catholic evangelicals put their dogma aside to march in antiabortion rallies with Catholics, and anti-Semitism gets hushed when Christians and Jewish Zionists advocate together U.S. support for the state of Israel. The roots of the reasons are radically different, but the practical positions convergent. While such convergences will not form denominations across radically different traditions, it does indicate that when certain issues are at stake, new networks can emerge.

In the future, new denominational lines will likely form along the fault lines of major public issues, just as they have in the past. In *The Restructuring of American Religion*, Robert Wuthnow produced a detailed chronicle of the postwar convergence of liberals with liberals and conservatives with conservatives across denominational lines.[15] Prayer in schools, symbols in public spaces, policy on abortion, sexual orientations, ecology, or a number of other public issues have the potential to split and reform denominations.

Denominational developments have been associated with political events at least as often as with religious or theological causes. A revolution against an English king brought anticlerical fervor with it, so that Methodism and Baptists grew at the expense of the Church of England and parallel established traditions. The Civil War divided northern and southern Presbyterians, as it did several other denominations. The social revolutions of the twentieth century, most notably in civil rights, gender roles, and environmental protection, have spawned breakaway sects or distinctive minorities from the mainline denominations. In most cases, a thin veneer of biblical or theological disagreement is distended over the various "culture wars."

Such was the case when the Lutheran Church Missouri Synod splintered into two denominations in the 1970s. Biblical literalism and repristination of seventeenth-century theologies were on the banners of the conservatives as they ousted perceived liberals, but the deep social changes of American society were the real dividers of the once ethnically and socioeconomically homogenous denomination. True to Niebuhr's *Social Sources,* when Lutherans left the countryside and became modern suburbanites, they developed subtly different canopies of meaning and interpretation. The conservative position was as modernized sociologically as was the liberal position. New social sources created two new Lutheran denominations, although one retained the name of the predecessor body. Southern Baptists similarly split some two decades later, amid the suburbanization, increasing population, and rising wealth of the American South.[16]

Progressives among the mainstream Protestants at the beginning of the twentieth century dreamed of mergers of denominations and the creation of an efficient Protestant organization. With impetus from shared experiences in world missions, and bankrolled by the likes of John Rockefeller and other philanthropic believers, Protestants set to work in collaborative organizations such as the Young Men's Christian Association, the Interchurch World Movement, the Federal Council of Churches in Christ, and later, the National Council of Churches in Christ. The twentieth century saw only one organic merger across mainline denominational traditions, however. In the 1950s the United Church of Christ merged the Congregational and German Reformed denominations. Elsewhere, mergers internal to the various traditions were the rule. Many Methodist and Wesleyan groups united, Presbyterians consolidated, and Lutherans worked themselves into two major and several minor denominational bodies.

At century's end a pan-Protestant Commission on Church Union continued among mainstream Protestants, but with no organic merger in sight. The closest some came was a series of "full communion" agreements; these were declarations of full acceptance of one another's ministries that made no attempt at church union. The Evangelical Lutheran Church in America (ELCA) was in the middle of a web of such agreements. By century's end the ELCA had entered into full communion with the Presbyterian Church in the United States, the Reformed Church in America, the United Church of Christ, the Moravian Church (Zinzendorf and Muhlenberg reconciled!), and the Episcopal Church in the United States. The other Protestant bodies were not accepted into full communion with the Episcopal Church, but they had inched closer through Lutheran intermediation. Meanwhile, the ELCA joined world Lutheranism in an agreement with the Roman Catholic Church on the doctrine of justification by faith. Few Lutherans returned to Rome, but the central doctrine of the Reformation was now understood in a pluralistic way so that Catholic and Lutheran emphases could coexist on a foundation of shared beliefs.

Full communion agreements are the formal and theological side of ecumenism. A conciliar style of ecumenism also had long roots among American Christians, based on cooperation in common outreach causes. Protestants made common cause in social ministries, political advocacy, campus ministries, and so forth. In a number of local settings, cross-denominational ministries were working well. Cooperative parishes, for example—area mission strategies that were composed of congregations from different denominational traditions— served well in rural and urban settings. The full communion agreements signaled the interchangeability of the ministers and sacramental practices of the denominations. These steps would remove the last barriers against close cooperative strategies.

Implications for Clergy and Religious Leaders

In the early 1960s, *Time* magazine featured on its cover the leader of the Lutheran Church in America. The somewhat liberal, somewhat conservative branch of American Lutheranism stood in the middle of many possible ecumenical relationships. This would bring Protestants together, it was thought, and would mend ties between Protestants and Catholics because of its own combination of Catholic and Protestant traits. Sociologists of religion observed the rapprochement of sectarian and churchly ways in the ecumenical movement of the mid-twentieth century, and the LCA Lutherans looked to some like the poster children for eventual religious unification in America.

Some three decades later, the Evangelical Lutheran Church in America, the successor denomination to the LCA, fulfilled only in part the midcentury predictions. It entered full communion agreements with several denominations and a doctrinal truce with Roman Catholicism. But ironically, it was further apart than ever from its Lutheran cousin in America, the Lutheran Church–Missouri Synod. It teetered on the brink of division over stances on major societal developments such as plurality of sexual orientations. Locally, it was united for cooperative mission with other Christians, but most local pastors and congregants stayed in mental orbit with denominational headquarters, be that a happy or a complaining relationship.

The population in seminaries tells a different story, however. At the beginning of the twenty-first century, more seminaries are training candidates for denominations other than their own than ever before, according to the Association of Theological Schools. Only Lutheran and Episcopal schools have remained predominantly homogeneous. Thus, the population of those entering the ministry is finally taking on the profile of the rank and file of the last four decades of American church life.

In the same three decades from the sixties through the nineties, the plurality of the larger American religious scene both increased and received greater recognition from mainstream scholars and religious leaders. Christian ecumenical unity still lagged, but there were the high-profile convergences like the Lutheran example. The greatest amount of church growth, however, was among independent churches and newer denominations rather than among the historic bodies that groped to overcome ancient divides. At the same time that overt agreements emerged within historic denominations, strong ideological fissures threatened to pull them apart.

The future of particular denominations is questionable at the beginning of the twenty-first century. But this very tenuousness and the developmental realities of denominations are confirmation of the continuing strength of the phenomenon we call denominationalism. Hence, while particular denominations migrate between birth and death, denominationalism is in the full, robust, adult phase of its life as a basic condition of religion in American life.

An important component in the full communion agreements mentioned earlier is that ELCA clergy are to be interchangeable with the clergy of the partner churches. This means that any given graduating senior from an ELCA seminary today is faced with the real possibility that she or he will be called at some point in her or his ministry to serve one or more congregations of the Presbyterian, Reformed, United Church of Christ, Moravian, or Episcopal traditions. It could mean as little as a "side gig" of supply preaching at a very small congregation that can't afford a full-time clergy person. Such was already a common practice among many denominations, but now the Lutheran would celebrate communion in the Reformed or Episcopal liturgy as well as preach and lead prayer.

However, the new agreement could mean much more: a full call to a congregation in one of the partner denominations, or a shared call between Lutheran and full-communion-partner churches. The practical implications of interchangeability of clergy go far beyond transfer into the symbolic world of the various traditions of theology and liturgy. When one considers the vast network of subtle cues associated with a particular congregation in a particular tradition, a Lutheran is at a profound disadvantage in trying to lead, say, a

Presbyterian congregation, and vice versa. Those who glibly dismiss the weight of theological and church traditions overlook the vast consequences that ignorance of such traditions can cause in working with particular communities formed in those traditions.

At the same time, local church life, worship practices, Christian education, and methods of service and outreach are changing dramatically. The typical seminary graduate will find herself or himself engaging in day-to-day routines very different from those of the previous generation of pastoral leaders. Absolutely everything is under debate and changing. For example, in a world of e-mail and voice mail, pastors debate the value of house visitation. Amid the sanitized and economized funeral industry, it is now possible for a pastor to preserve a "day off" by scheduling a funeral one day later than the family requests. With outpatient surgery and other wizardry of the medical industry, the old bedside confession and prayer lacks a place and a time.

The individual minister facing the future, and the local religious community forced to adapt to changing social conditions, may find some sage instruction in the historical background of American denominationalism as a particularly modern, and now postmodern, form of religious organization. The church has been here before, so to speak, and has lived through a variety of expressions in the nether land between sect and church types. Hence, the first practical implication for the present moment is to avoid panic and overblown predictions of total collapse or total transformative renewal for the church and its ministries.

Beyond that starting point, the overall goal for the public church today, in sociological terms, is to become both more churchly and more sectarian: to aspire to the independent legitimacy of the church type but with the energy and relevance of the sect type. Individuals and local communities may take the following practical steps in the direction of a churchly and evangelical posture.

1. Prepare in a specific tradition, but with readiness to adapt and change. The lessons of the past show that one cannot be generally nondenominational and stay out of the inevitable definition of one's ministry, community, or movement in relationship to the rest of postmodern society. On the other hand, if one is specific in belonging to a particular tradition but conversational in approach to others and society, one can engage initial ecumenical relationships and incrementally find more expansive ecumenical relations grounded in shared concerns and needs. Once grounded in a historic tradition, one is then free to explore the rich traditions of neighbors as well as to evolve in one's own identity within a living tradition. Such organic growth in tradition and the conversation of traditions is an antidote to the captivity to social sources and the relativistic process of becoming just one more denomination.

2. Avoid conformity to the social sources of denominationalism. Although social sources are inescapable and everyone must emerge from some local cultural circumstances, it is not necessary to let the church be totally passive toward its ethnic, racial, and socioeconomic origins in society. Take steps to cross those barriers and to grow in the creative Spirit of a God who is not bound by human social sources. Cross-cultural steps strengthen both the churchly legitimacy and sectarian energy of Christianity.

3. Avoid conforming to the political sources of denominationalism. Don't allow the church to be the chaplain to national or global political regimes. Take steps to cross political barriers: make friends with defined enemies and advocate justice for the poor and oppressed. These efforts will strengthen both the churchly legitimacy and sectarian energy of Christianity and will complement the similar cross-cultural steps called for in step two.

4. Catechize, catechize, catechize! In the postmodern world the enemy is not so much ignorance as it is misunderstanding. There is widespread misunderstanding of traditions of culture and religion, even while many have some knowledge, interest, and respect for religious traditions. There is a need for deeper study and formation. Give attention to rites of passage and to the learning stages of all age groups. Work consciously against the postmodern tide of huge amounts of surface information on many things, and go for deep information and formation in historic traditions.

5. Worship, pray, and sing. The traditions of worship, prayer, and song in Christianity are rich and robust. They come from many different social sources and can therefore be extremely helpful in our efforts not to be captive to the social sources of religion. New worship forms, prayers, and songs are natural, but they hold no guarantee that they will be anything but captive to their social sources. Only the variety of sources from the many different social settings of Christianity can break the hold of contemporary social sources. Thus, the historic forms of worship, prayer, and song are essential to the sociological health and critical prophetic edge of Christianity.

Denominations as a sociological form of overt organization will be with Christians (and those of other faiths) in the foreseeable postmodern future. Whatever one's theological assessment of the denominational form, it is possible to make the most of the benefits and opportunities while still preserving traditions or even growing them. It is possible to keep aspects of churchliness and sectarian fire alight even while being denominational in a de facto way. The history of denominations and denominationalism in modernity shows that much, and it is reasonable to expect that the foreseeable future of postmodernity will present a similar stage for the overt organizational life of Christianity in its evangelical, mainline, and Catholic forms.

11

Visual Christianity

"The Peril of Pleasure and the Value of the Experience"

Robert K. Johnston

Ours is a visual culture—an image-driven culture. It is also an increasingly post-Christian culture. "Calvinism" is no longer recognized by many in our society as a theological system but, according to *New York* magazine, is the name given to a fashion trend initiated by the clothing designer Calvin Klein. The logos we commit ourselves to is not the *logos* of John 1:1, but the Nike emblem (a swoosh) and Ralph Lauren's polo player.[1] There are many reasons for the increasing abandonment of the Christian *logos* to various icons of popular culture. Some would charge that we have, as a society and as a church, simply become intellectually lazy. But this is too simple an explanation (and probably a largely mistaken one). It fails to take into account the societal shift in our communication paradigm from that of "word" to that of "image" and the new manner in which our intellect increasingly engages reality.

The *logos* the Protestant church presents (particularly the churches that Calvin himself helped found in the Reformation) has become chiefly a cerebral proclamation to be heard rather than seen, something that is more "logical" than visceral. That is, the divine *logos* is no longer visually understood as "flesh." (John. 1:14). The rationality of the Christian *logos* can be articulated clearly through discourse and dogma, but in an increasingly visual culture, people find such unadorned propositionalism unconvincing and even boring. The exodus from our churches, though lamentable, is predictable.

The poet Edwin Muir wrote:

The Word made flesh is here made word again,
A word made word in flourish and arrogant crook.
See there King Calvin with his iron pen,

And God three angry letters in a book,
And there the logical hook
On which the mystery is impaled and bent
Into an ideological argument.[2]

Granting poetic license, here is a word-picture, an image, of what too many Protestant churches look like today to too many outsiders (and to an increasing number of insiders). We have a mystery that has been impaled and bent into an ideology. We have failed to recognize the full implications of what John wrote: "the Word [*logos*] became flesh and lived among us," and we saw his glory, a glory full of grace and truth. (John 1:14) What the eye saw has been reduced to what the ear can hear, and many in our culture, particularly those who are younger, have responded with a yawn. If you doubt this, ask yourself whether it was a movie you saw or a sermon that you heard that last engaged you in discussion with a Gen Xer (or even anyone under fifty, for that matter).

Our movement from a print culture to an image culture has been escalating at an astounding pace. Since 1975 we now have personal computers, CDs, video stores, home video games, the Internet, video cameras, CD-ROMs, and the list keeps growing. Our "family rooms" are now "entertainment centers." We no longer ask our friends what books they have read for fear of embarrassing them, but instead ask what movies they have seen. We have the TV on at home eight hours a day on average (with work and sleep subtracted, this means nearly all the time). One study even found that when children between the ages of four and six were asked whether they liked television or their fathers better, 54 percent of those sampled chose TV![3] Mitchell Stephens chronicles these changes in his book *The Rise of the Image, the Fall of the Word* (1998), while at the same time suggesting that we are just at the beginning of this communications revolution.[4] The transition will be as far-reaching as those earlier shifts from an oral to a written culture, and from a written to a print culture.

We in the church know this revolution is happening. Yet we agonize whether or how we should be adapting to it. Our religious expressions remain more Gnostic; we aren't sure we want the material, at least not in our worship. A guitar is often the most we can muster as we seek to be contemporary—music somehow seems safer. Tom Beaudoin, in his book *Virtual Faith: The Irreverent Spiritual Quest of Generation X,* writes of his experience with church as a Gen Xer: ". . . Churches seemed laughably out of touch; they had hopelessly droll music, antediluvian technology, retrograde social teaching, and hostile or indifferent attitudes toward popular culture."[5]

Protestants think there is a connection between "spirit," "breath," "sounds," and "words." Don't words, not things, mediate the Spirit's presence to us? The screenwriter and director Paul Schrader, a Calvinist by birth and upbringing, adapted Elmore Leonard's story *Touch* (1997) for the screen. The movie tells the story of a former Franciscan missionary to South America who has been given the gift of the stigmata (the marks of Christ's wounds). Though he has left the church, this man is able to heal people by touching them. At one point in the movie, a woman friend offers to do the hero's laundry, only to wonder if it's okay to put stigmatic blood through the wash.[6] Here in graphic parable, is the struggle many Calvinists (and most other Protestants) currently face. Having compartmentalized word (Word) and image, and having linked "Spirit" with words, can we now change and put what is holy in direct contact with the stuff of life?

The question we face today is not whether the visual arts are both educational and entertaining. We know they are, for they are breathed full of life. Rather, the question is whether they should have a place in our worship of the transcendent God, a God who has given us the words of Scripture, but who has also revealed himself both in creation and redemption.

Lessons from the Past

Any essay written in honor of Bob Webber would be deficient if it didn't turn to learn from the history of the church. Webber, along with a very few others, needs to be thanked for helping evangelicals like myself take seriously the wisdom of the saints who have gone before us. The form of our visual art has changed, given the creation of moving images some one hundred years ago. But the issues that the church faced in the past with regard to the use of images are largely the same issues that we face today. And the answers given are often the same answers, however unconscious we are of their original sources.

It is for this reason that I have subtitled this chapter using a phrase from Augustine's *Confessions*: "I vacillate between the peril of pleasure and the value of the experience."[7] Augustine is referring to the use of popular melodies in church music, but his reaction could easily have been to that of video, had there been such a medium in his day. Here is the quandary that the church still wrestles with as it wonders about the use of the arts in its worship. Jeffrey Pugh has suggested, "Ask any person in the culture of Christianity about their understanding of God, evil, sin, even sex, and that person will most often answer with the categories and language that Augustine fashioned."[8] I suspect Pugh is largely correct, at least for Protestants, though I would defer to the judgment of Bob Webber on this. With regard to the place of the sensual in worship, Pugh is certainly right in his assessment. As Augustine reflected on his post-conversion life, he considered how the "lust of the flesh" had ensnared him. He felt he was continually tempted by the five senses—the touch of a woman's body, the taste of food and drink, the smell of (he couldn't come up with any specifics here), the sound of music, and the sight of beautiful objects. All these threatened to displace God from the center of his life. Augustine struggled with how to simultaneously love the created good and the Creator of it.[9]

The quotation that I have used comes from book ten of *Confessions,* where Augustine vacillates between approving hymns that used popular tunes (as Ambrose had used in his church in Milan) and fearing that such sensual pleasures would ensnare the soul and prevent its true assent to God. The words of the songs were most important to Augustine, he said, and he feared the mere "gratification of my flesh" through the music. Yet Augustine acknowledged the great benefit that music in worship had been to him. He wrote, "when I remember the tears I shed, moved by the song of the Church in the early days of my new faith: and again when I see that I am moved not by the singing but by the things that are sung—when they are sung with a clear voice and proper modulation—I recognize once more the usefulness of this practice." [10] Augustine's argument can be summarized as follows: (1) He fears the use of popular, pagan culture in worship; (2) he knows he must emphasize God's transcendence; (3) he is committed to the primacy of the Word and words; yet (4) he recognizes that as a younger Christian, the sensuality of the arts (music in this case) had helped him worship; (5) the arts still help him experience more fully the words; although (6) he fears being trapped by the pleasure of the sensual for its own sake. And so Augustine waffled. He concluded that he was led more to endorse the custom of popular hymnody, "while not advocating an irrevocable position."

Not all who came after Augustine in the centuries that followed would admit to feeling both sides of the tension between sacred and sensual or be so tentative. The iconoclastic controversies have proven some of the most contentious in the history of the church. But the basic issue has remained the same. How do we worship a God who is other than us, a God who has chosen nonetheless to be a part of us? In particular, what place do our senses have in this endeavor? As with other theological controversies, the issue would have subsided long ago if there were not multiple sides to the question.

What, then, might we learn from this longstanding controversy?

The Pedagogical Function of Visual Art

It was Gregory the Great (d. 604) who called religious art the *Biblia pauperum,* the Bible of the poor. Art could serve as a picture book for the illiterate. The church fathers typically agreed, seeing pictures as helpful for lay devotion. Even one of the most outspoken critics of images, Bernard of Clairvaux, writing in the twelfth century, recognized the usefulness of images to teach the uneducated, though he opposed their presence in monasteries where monks had left all the beautiful things of the world behind for Christ's sake. Surely they did not need images to enhance their understanding and excite their internal devotion. Others of the fathers disagreed, however. Gregory of Nyssa (d. 386) wrote with deep feeling about a religious picture that had moved him to devotion. So too, Thomas Aquinas argued for the proper use of images. Others jus-

tified the use of image as an aid to memory. There was thus a baseline established in the church. Despite the fear that images could drag the soul down,
that the sensual could be a distraction to the spiritual in worship, there was a
recognition that the visual could be a pedagogical aid, helping the devoted to
learn. By aiding both affection and memory, the visual could foster greater
understanding.

Even in the Reformation, in which abuse of the visual caused many of the
Reformers to reject the use of all visual representations in worship, Martin
Luther resisted such iconoclasm and continued to hold to a utilitarian view of
the visual arts. Recognizing that people are created as image makers, that we
think in pictures and thus need pictures, Luther confessed that he himself could
not hear the Passion narrative "without forming mental images of it in my
heart." He then concluded, "If it is not a sin but good to have the image of
Christ in my heart, why should it be a sin to have it in my eyes?"[11] And practicing what he preached, Luther sometimes made use of a crucifix in his own
personal devotions.

The best illustration of the visual's pedagogical significance in Luther's theology is his use of religious art to illustrate his German edition of the Bible. Luther
believed that it was not just the person who was inherently given to visualiza-
tion. The Bible itself used visual examples to reinforce its teaching, particularly the parables of Jesus. Thus, Luther personally selected the themes for the
woodcuts that illustrated his German Bible. He expressed concern to those
printing the edition that the prints be more than decoration, and he chose
scenes that were theologically significant that would thus enhance the reader's
understanding of the biblical message. In doing this, Luther was affirming the
tradition of *Biblia pauperum,* even identifying with it himself. There had been
at least fifteen illustrated German vernacular Bibles before his own. Luther
would add another.

On a number of occasions Luther argued that children and simple folk are
"more effectively moved to retain divine history through pictures and parables
than through bare word or doctrine."[12] He even commented, "What harm
would it do if someone had all the most important stories in the whole Scripture portrayed one after another in a little book, which would be called a lay-
man's Bible?"[13] (Here one might recall the African slaves in the movie *Amistad*
who could not read the text of the Bible they had been given but got the heart
of the biblical message through the illustrations in the text.) Many would say
that Luther was arguing the obvious. Certainly he was choosing to continue a
tradition within the church that had been practiced for centuries. But as we
will see, the recognition of visual representations was anything but obvious for
many of Luther's Protestant contemporaries. Nonetheless, Luther recognized
that "external images, parables, and signs are good and useful: they illustrate a
thing so that it can be grasped and retained."[14] Moreover, Luther argued, "the
attention of the common man is aroused by illustrations and examples more

readily than by profound disputations. . . . He prefers a painted picture to a well-written book."[15] If such a conclusion was open to dispute in Luther's day, it will hardly be challenged in the visual culture of today.

Andrew Greeley, the Catholic sociologist, has observed that in Renaissance art, the Madonnas often displayed baby Jesus' penis and testicles to the onlooker. Similarly, he is almost always presented to the Magi stark naked. This was not an attempt by the artists to be salacious, but to demonstrate Christ's full humanity even as the Son of God. Greeley then raises the issue we are addressing here: the relative importance for the ordinary person of narrative and image over doctrine and dogma. Greeley writes, "The Christmas crib is popular Catholicism; the Decrees of Chalcedon are high Catholicism. . . . Anyone who thinks *homoiosios* is more important to ordinary folk than the Madonna and her child [stark naked!] is incurably prosaic—besides being wrong!"[16] Greeley goes on to say that both forms of Catholicism have their place. He is not arguing for the abandonment of the word (nor am I) but for the parallel recognition of the image. It is the Madonna and child, not only Chalcedon, that has taught Christology to Roman Catholics for generations.

Or to give a Protestant example, Nicholas von Zinzendorf was touring Europe, as was customary for a young man of the upper class in the eighteenth century. In a museum in Dusseldorf he found himself transfixed by an image of Christ—scourged, bound, and crowned with thorns. The painting was entitled *Ecce Homo (Behold the Man)*. The artist, Domenico Feti, had added the inscription: "This I have done for you, but what have you done for me?" Zinzendorf related that he understood the meaning of the Christ event for the first time. As a result, Zinzendorf went on to found a pietistic movement, the Moravians, whose emphasis on missionary work, service, and personal spirituality continues to have a worldwide impact. It was not word divorced from image. Neither was the aesthetic opposed to the ethical, or the spiritual opposed to the physical. There was a holism to the gospel that made the truth alive.

If the pedagogical usefulness of visual images can be so easily documented, why haven't Protestants outside the Lutheran tradition tended to see it? There are of course multiple factors, but three stand out: (1) a deficient theological understanding of the human that owes more to Greek thought than to Scripture, (2) an ecclesial context in which the visual threatened to overwhelm the church's worship, and (3) a particular (mis)reading of the Bible, especially the Ten Commandments.

The first reason has to do with the dominant understanding of human nature that was held at the time of the Reformation. Again, Augustine provides a starting point with his Neoplatonic split between the body and the spirit. It is the body that threatens to drag you down; it is the spirit that lets you ascend to God. When the isolation of the Father in his transcendence is grafted onto this Greek anthropology, the visual will have difficulty finding a place in one's worship. Certainly the sensual will have no place. At best, the use of the visual arts will be thought a begrudging accommodation to educate the illiterate (or as in the Eastern church, will be stylized so as not to be sensual, but heavenly). The visual can lead by the hand, to use an illustration from Calvin, as tutors lead children. But the visual was also thought to provide an immature knowledge that one should grow beyond.

The Reformed theologians learned their dualistic anthropology, and with it their suspicion of images, from those like the Renaissance humanist Erasmus. Erasmus believed that images tended to elevate the physical, while the religious life was primarily spiritual. He wrote, "The spirit needs nothing from the body." And again, "You honor a likeness of Christ's face that has been crudely shaped out of rock or wood, or else daubed in paint: much more to be honored is that likeness of His mind which, by the working of the Holy Spirit, has been portrayed in the words of the Gospels." Erasmus even quoted John 4:24, "Those who worship him must worship in spirit and in truth."[17]

John 4:24 was the text all the Reformers made reference to in their discussion of worship, one that when read literal(istical)ly seemed to give a clear and practical mandate. It was Zwingli, having read Erasmus and at times echoing his arguments, who made the strongest use of this text.[18] Explicating the apostle's words, he argued, "He [John] says that God is a Spirit, whence also that those who will worship him can or should do so in no more just a manner than by consecrating their mind to him."[19] Faith, thought Zwingli, was "utterly unrelated to anything involving sensation." The silent Spirit moves in the inner person and is not aided by music (sound), incense (smell), ritual (theater), or image (sight). Thus, when he entered the central church in Zurich after the destruction of all of its art, Zwingli could declare the newly whitewashed walls to be "positively luminous."[20]

A second reason that the visual was so often opposed by the Reformers had to do with the rampant abuse of religious images in the church during the time leading up to the Reformation. In other words, the theology of the Reformers that we read on the subject of visual art in worship is driven by polemical concerns. The religious art of the day sometimes depicted apocryphal themes, mixing fact and fiction. Other art contradicted doctrine, as with many of the pictorial representations of the Trinity. And still other religious art confused the sacred and the secular, as when members of the Medici family became the wise men from the East.[21] Moreover, art was often given by patrons of the church as a "good work," a means of currying favor with God. And though church theologians might try to distinguish between "veneration" (*dulia*) and "adoration" (*latria*) in the laity's use of visual portrayals of Christ and the saints, in fact, veneration was leading to the practice of idolatry. Even idolaters, said Calvin, regard their idols as "visible signs of an invisible God." God is for them "something else than wood or stones." But they become dependent on the images and can no longer imagine God's presence without them. This is what was happening in the churches of the day, as Calvin recognized.[22]

Lastly, to the philosophical and contextual arguments, must be added the biblical. (The Reformers would, in fact, have placed the biblical first, not understanding the extent to which Platonic thought and abusive visual practices provided the lens through which they read their Bibles.) To support their opposition to the use of visual imagery in worship, the Reformers turned to Scripture itself—in particular, to the commandment prohibiting idols (graven images). The Roman Catholic Church (and Luther who did not follow the other Reformation theologians at this point) had understood the prohibition against idols in Exodus 20:4 as an appositive, a repetition of the opening statement, "you shall have no other gods before me" (Ex. 20:3). These verses together made up the first commandment. Zwingli and Calvin, however, in order to emphasize the ban against images in worship, split the two verses, making the prohibition "you shall not make for yourself an idol" (v. 4) into an independent injunction, the second commandment.[23] It was not just the pagan use of idols that was being opposed (the first commandment) but also the church's wrongful use of images (the second commandment). As Charles Hodge was to say some centuries later, "Idolatry consists not only in the worship of false gods, but also in the worship of the true God by images."[24] God has accommodated himself to human capacity through the Word (and by extension, words), not the *Imago Dei* (and by extension, images). The biblical prohibition against all images in worship even alluded to the created order of Genesis 1 and 2. To make an image was to seek to be the Creator, not a creature. It was to use our *Imago* wrongly. One had only to recall the biblical narratives of the golden calf and of Hezekiah's destruction of the bronze serpent on a pole to see that images in worship are to be prohibited.

What can be said with regard to these arguments that still, however unconsciously, shape much of Protestant worship today? Isn't the spiritual noncorporeal and the physical seductive? Doesn't the abuse of images still constitute a danger? Doesn't the Bible condemn all idolatry? The Reformers' arguments have lost much of their force today (for reasons given below). When such arguments appear forcefully, as in James Packer's best-selling explication of the Christian faith, *Knowing God,* they produce more questions and quandary from readers than insight. But though a rigorous theological justification for not using visual images in the church is no longer mounted, the residual effect of the Reformers' rhetoric is still with us. We, as Protestants, continue to shy away from the visual in our worship.

Risking the same criticism that I have given—that I read the Bible through the lenses of my context and its understanding of what constitutes the human (and surely this is true)—let me begin a response to the Reformer's theology of the visual in worship by turning to the Bible. Here is the cornerstone for Protestants, at least for evangelical Protestants. The biblical argument is so simple as to be missed in the heat of the debate. Put plainly, the "second" commandment against idols ("You shall not make for yourself an idol. . . . You shall not bow down to them or worship them." [Ex. 20:4–5]) has to do with *idol-atry*, not with the *visual* per se. To claim that banners in the church or video projections, bas relief or paintings, or even sculpture itself (for what else is a cross?) is what the second commandment is referring to, and is thus a form of idolatry, is eisegesis—that is, faulty interpretation. It also belies common sense. The biblical injunction is against idol, not image.

Hezekiah broke into pieces the serpent Moses had made (2 Kings 18:4), for Israelites were making offerings to it in the belief that something magical would happen. It was the abusive practice of idolatry that Hezekiah opposed. Turning to our contemporary situation, there is little if any danger of visual art, even at its best, being so confused in Protestant worship today. It is a different type of offering altogether that is made to pay for the expense of banner production or video rental.

Turning to John 4, this text is not attempting to spell out a dualism of body and spirit. Jesus is instead contrasting the natural with the supernatural, water from the well with the living water that he represents. In fact, Jesus ends this discussion with the Samaritan woman by revealing to her that he, himself, is the Messiah. In a quite literal way, the spiritual will be understood in and through the flesh. The biblical paradigm that unites body and spirit is most clearly seen in the description of Jesus' bodily resurrection (cf. Jesus saying to Thomas, "Put your finger here and see my hands. Reach out your hand and put it in my side." John 20:27). But this holistic portrayal of what it is to be human begins in Genesis, where we are described as being dust and breath (Gen. 2:7). As the song says, you can't have one without the other. The reason Augustine found that popular music enhanced his understanding of the word in worship has to do with the holistic nature of the human. We learn best when we are fully engaged, body and spirit.

And lastly, though a context might again arise when there is rampant misuse of religious images and subsequent theological confusion, this is not the situation in the Protestant church in the West today. Though we are becoming an image-driven culture, Protestant Christianity remains image poor in its worship. Protestants have developed a cottage industry of material objects of faith outside the worship context (from fish logos on the back of automobiles to WWJD bracelets for children). Perhaps these are an attempted compensation for the absence of visual images in our worship. But in the church, Protestants have ventured little beyond the praise band and the instructional sermon. As a result, the church service (apart from the music) remains a cerebral enterprise. One indication of this is the widespread practice in evangelical church services of labeling our singing "worship," as if the rest is something else (the sermon is sometimes, in fact, labeled "teaching," not "proclamation").

The issue facing the Protestant church today is whether it is willing to respond to our wider image-driven culture by engaging the whole person in worship, not only in words and music but through the visual arts in all its vitality. Or is the perceived threat to faith, given the power of the sensual experience, still off-putting, so that the church is willing to settle for less? Must not our faith be incarnate, expressed within and conversant with the vitalities of life? We know the visual is pedagogically useful from our own experiences outside the church. Some of us even have begun to experiment within our churches out of necessity or frustration. But our implicit theology of worship is too often still located in the debates of the sixteenth century, so our endeavors prove paltry and puny. Like Augustine, we are trapped in indecision, unable to embrace in our worship the vitality of life that a visual culture presents, for fear of somehow profaning the gospel.

The Sacramental Function of Visual Art

It is important to ask, as we have with the pedagogical question, whether images might have illustrative, artistic, and/or experiential significance that can aid our understanding of the gospel in our worship. But this question cannot be isolated from a second and corollary concern, one that the church has also wrestled with throughout its history. Can visual imagery in worship have sacramental meaning as well? Can religious art in worship move beyond the discursive and didactic, and if so, how is this accomplished? If the pedagogical question has especially been the concern of Protestants, this sacramental concern has been more the focus among the Orthodox and the Roman Catholics.

The Eastern Church

In September of 787 A.D. the Seventh Ecumenical Council met in Nicea to deal with the issue of iconoclasm. Nicea II, as it has come to be called, was in part a response to political pressure from the state, as emperors jostled for power and prestige. It was also a response to the real risk of superstition and idolatry, as practical devotion to the icons did not match the careful distinctions of the theologians. And thirdly, the church needed to respond to the persecution of monks and other martyrs who continued the "proper" use of icons in their worship despite the declared iconoclastic position of the Council at Hieria in 754 A.D. Using the theology of John of Damascus (ca. 652–750) as its undergirding, the bishops voted to retain the church's tradition of using painted images to facilitate worship.

The bishops based their theological judgment on an understanding of the incarnation. "Since God has now been seen in the flesh and been received among us human beings," wrote John of Damascus, "I represent what is visible in God."[25] That is, icons, did not attempt to depict an image of the invisible God, something the Old Testament law prohibits, but rather were a type of the form that the invisible God took in the incarnation. Moreover, when Christians venerate icons, they do not worship these two-dimensional images. Rather, the images remind them of the icons' prototypes, and thus, foster one's love and devotion of God. Even when the worshiper seems to be expressing devotion by kissing the icons, "the honour rendered to the image goes to its prototype," the Council argued, "and the person who venerates an icon venerates the person represented by it."[26]

A good icon, one might say, asks the viewer to ignore it and visualize through the mind the reality behind it, to "see" that which it is representing. The icon is meant to be a spiritual window between earth and heaven through which the worshiper contemplates heavenly beings and is able to establish a spiritual link with them.[27] Such icons do not seek the naturalism of a portrait, nor are they aiming at a physical likeness. The humanity that the artist seeks to represent in the icon is one that has been transformed and transfigured with heavenly glory. (It is for this reason that only the faithful are judged suitable to paint icons, and a few of the best icon painters have even been honored as saints.) Using images, gestures, and symbols that have been handed down through the centuries, the painter seeks to express objectively an eschatological reality. To assist the viewer's contemplation, the figure is presented in such a way that the light seems heavenly, filling the entire painting as if it were coming through the painting from the back. And the golden background of the icon is suggestive of a heavenly aura.

Although the physical presence of the icon is necessary, it is always unto something else. As viewers express their veneration, they find illumination and are brought into communion with the personal presence of the divine, wherein they find themselves being transformed into the divine likeness. This process of ongoing illumination, communion, and transformation is described by the Orthodox as *theosis,* or deification. We are not to understand this as a clumsy restatement of pantheism, but as a mystical union with God the Creator as we become one with the divine, even in our distinctiveness. There is a strong rational component to this process, for the icon is "art under the discipline of the content of the message."[28] (In fact, the process of creating an icon is even understood as "writing" an icon, not "painting" it.) Symbols are texts to be studied. The experience of viewing an icon is not visceral, but one that seeks to engage the mind and, through the mind, the heart. Iconography is ultimately in the service of piety.

Bishop Ambrosius finds support in his tradition for comparing the iconic picture to the word. He writes, "According to Basil the Great, 'that which the word communicates by sound, the painting shows silently by representation.'"[29] This correlation of divine word and icon is instructive for those of us in the Protestant church, as Alain Blancy recognizes:

> The icon . . . has a dynamic which suits the Protestant. It fulfills a function, almost a ministry. It is word made manifest; it is the effective vehicle of a mes-

sage. . . . It is discourse even more than it is image. . . . As the Word exists only when proclaimed and the sacrament when administered, so that the Gospel can be made present and effective through them, so too the icon is there only to ful- fill its purpose—to call forth and produce the communication and commun- ion of believers with their Lord.[30]

This description, though brief, should be indication enough that with Ortho- dox iconography, we are dealing with a very narrow but suggestive expression of the visual arts, one that seeks a different reality. There are similar limitations in the Orthodox argument as were encountered in the discussion of icons by the Reformed theologians. In both, we find the influence of a Platonic dual- ism that can be traced back to Augustine, one that falsely bifurcates body and spirit, dust and breath, the physical and the spiritual. In the Orthodox dis- cussion of icons, there is a suspicion of the bodily, as worshipers are encour- aged to ascend to the heavenly. The mandated two-dimensionality of the icon is further indication of this deprecation of the physicality of the time-space continuum in which we live. Iconic portrayals are to be of a transfigured human- ity. Even the saints are portrayed as "saints," that is, those who have been rec- ognized for their spiritual states.

Despite these visual limitations, the creation of an art form among the Orthodox that is sacramental in intent extends our discussion in creative ways beyond the pedagogical focus of the Reformers. As Emilio Castro recognized in his commemoration of the twelve hundredth anniversary of Nicea II, "the icon in itself has no pretensions. A good icon invites us, or obliges us, to for- get it and to see the reality beyond." Writing as the General Secretary of the World Council of Churches, Castro suggested that with the icon, we have an art form whose aim is to be neither instructive nor magical, but spiritual.[31] If Castro had been a Catholic and not a Latin American Methodist, he might even have said sacramental.

The Western Church

The issue that remains for our consideration is whether the sacramentality that the visual provides can be conceived more broadly than in the highly styl- ized and cerebral iconography of the Eastern Orthodox Church. Here, the Roman Catholic Church has answered in the affirmative, though not without its own struggles. A movie like *Chocolat,* which was nominated for best pic- ture at the 2001 Oscars, presents in fable form something of the struggle. Can even chocolate be a sacramental, something that helps one see beyond it to a supernatural grace that it embodies? Or is Lenten denial the path to sainthood? For the Roman Catholic, the answer has been that there is not only a *via neg- ativa* but a *via positiva* as well. The austerity of Lent is to be followed by the celebration of Easter's new life, a celebration that can even include *chocolat.*

Andrew Greeley, in his provocative book *The Catholic Imagination,* expresses his appreciation to a colleague at the University of Chicago, David Tracy, for his discussion in the *Analogical Imagination.* Greeley summarizes Tracy's argument as follows:

> Tracy noted that the classic works of Catholic theologians and artists tend to emphasize the presence of God in the world, while the classic works of Protestant theologians tend to emphasize the absence of God from the world. The Catholic writers stress the nearness of God to His creation, the Protestant writers the distance between God and His creation; the Protestants emphasize the risk of superstition and idolatry, the Catholics the danger of a creation in which God is only marginally present. Or, to put the matter in different terms, Catholics tend to accentuate the immanence of God, Protestants the transcendence of God.[32]

Both Greeley and Tracy are quick to emphasize that God is both transcendent and immanent. Thus both propensities are justifiable and need each other. There is no attempt at Catholic hegemony here.

Without denying the theological importance of stressing God's transcendence, and while continuing to understand the word as a fitting vehicle for the Word—that is, without denying the Protestant imagination its place—it is nonetheless the Catholic imagination that holds particular promise for the visual renewal of Protestant worship. Here is a theological perspective, rooted in God's immanence, that allows for the expression of a robust visual Christianity, one that has the possibility of connecting with our contemporary sensibilities.

There is no focus more characteristically Catholic or more central to Catholic identity than the principle of sacramentality, states Richard McBrien in his monumental study *Catholicism.*[33] In its narrower form, this principle refers to the seven sacraments that mark the forgiveness of one's sins and reconciliation with God, as well as important milestones in life. But within the Catholic tradition there has also always been a variety of "sacramentals"—other material objects like candles, holy water, pictures, and sculpture—through which the faithful sense God's presence. Protestants find the use of such materials almost synonymous with superstition. (And they can be. I am writing this from Malaga, Spain, where the popular piety surrounding the processions of *Semana Santa* [Holy Week] seems, even to the Spanish, largely a mixture of magic and superstition.) But in language we have already heard in the quite different context of our discussion of icons, the Jesuit Richard Blake comments, "Catholics tend to see beyond the object or gesture to the supernatural reality it represents."[34] While the Orthodox have limited their sacramental representations to two-dimensional, stylized, cerebral, nonsensual paintings that are meant to move the viewer heavenward, Catholics understand God to be in the stuff of life and ask us to locate him down here. No wonder, for example, that the Catholic

Church filled its sanctuaries with all forms of art and architecture during the age of the baroque, while the quintessential Protestant art form remained the cantatas of Bach.

One needs, however, to extend this notion of sacramentality still wider than the artistic expressions of the church or even the sacramentals of church life. A completely secular reality may also mediate to us spiritual reality. In the Catholic Church, we encounter God not only in and through Christ who meets us in the sacrament, or even through the church and its liturgies, symbols, sacramentals, and practices, but also through that which exists outside and beyond the church. This sense of sacramentality has been described as God being "present everywhere, the invisible in the visible, within us and within the whole created order."[35] It is not, as we are reminded in the film *Chocolat*, that the Catholic tradition hasn't also had its *via negativa*—the monastic is surely the equivalent of Zwingli's whitewashed walls. It is rather that there has also been a *via positiva*, a willingness to see God as present and active in the material world.

From this startlingly expansive notion of the Creator's presence in and through creature and creation, we can make two observations, one theoretical and the other practical. First, the "sacramental" can be equated with what David Tracy labels the "analogical" and Andrew Greeley the "metaphorical." That is, it is okay for the woman in Schrader's screenplay *Touch* to put stigmatic blood through the wash, for the whole of creation is metaphorically God's showplace. Objects, events, and people involved in ordinary life can, by analogy, make God present to us—or more precisely, can become the occasion for God to make himself present to us. To exclude such metaphorical possibility is to exclude the transcendent God from being present with us, for his ways are not our ways and his thoughts are not our thoughts. Everything in creature and creation can serve to mediate the metaphorical presence of the divine. In Andrew Greeley's words, the Catholic imagination "views the world and all that is in it as enchanted, haunted by the Holy Spirit and the presence of grace."[36]

Practically, this commitment to God's presence through the Spirit in the physicality of life has meant that Catholics have been more willing than Protestants to make use of pagan practices and metaphors, baptizing them with Christian meaning. It was Pope Gregory who long ago instructed Augustine of Canterbury (another Augustine!) not to destroy the temples of the Angles (Anglos), whom he was evangelizing on the British Isles. Augustine had feared making use of the Angles' pagan practices. Pope Gregory wrote with instructions to destroy only their idols. The shrines, he said, should be reconsecrated to the service of the true God. Similarly, he instructed Augustine to let the Angles slaughter animals, as was their practice, but to have them now do it for their own food and in praise of God. Augustine of Canterbury followed the Pope's instruction, and so today we celebrate "Easter," which comes from the feast of

Eostre, the Anglo-Saxon goddess of the dawn, of new life, and of spring. The symbols of her fertility were lilies, rabbits, and eggs![37] Here was a visual culture worth redeeming, one even capable of symbolizing Jesus' resurrection.

Applying the Lessons from the Past

Our reflection on the use of the material in worship, and thus of the possibility of a more visual Christianity, has led to our consideration of the pedagogical and sacramental functions of visual art in the worship life of the church. In conclusion, let me return from the past to the present and offer some practical examples in which the visual is indeed serving these functions in our contemporary worship.

The Visual as Prop

The first time my wife and I visited Willow Creek Community Church outside of Chicago, they were having a baptismal service. The pastor, Bill Hybels, spoke on the meaning of baptism. Then, during the twenty to thirty minutes of the service of baptism, close to two hundred new Christians came forward to four baptismal stations placed across the front of the church. They answered simple questions about their belief in Christ and about their desire for Christian baptism, received the water of baptism on their forehead in what looked like the sign of the cross, and then moved to risers across the back of the stage, where they stood as a body. Most of those baptized were in their twenties and thirties, but the last to be baptized (by the pastor himself) was a small, older lady. When she approached the pastor, the microphone came on in time for all of us to hear her ask whether the pastor thought there was room in the kingdom of God for an "old lady" like herself. And after she was assured that there was, had confessed her faith and had been baptized, we celebrated the new birth of what would be for most congregations a new "mini-size" church.

Impressive, to say the least. Here was a congregation so alive to Christ and his Spirit that almost two hundred new believers wanted to celebrate their new faith through this act of faith. But what was more impressive than the numbers or the risers (a visual aid in its own right) was the visual "prop" that had been put in the center of the stage of the otherwise unadorned interior of the large auditorium that is Willow Creek's sanctuary. It was a large cross. To symbolically enact what their baptism meant to them, each initiate in turn took out a piece of paper on which they had written what they were confessing and tacked the paper to the cross. Here was the "old" person they were leaving behind at the cross as Jesus washed away their sins with his blood. The somber repetition of close to two hundred individuals showing the contemporary meaning of the atonement in visual terms did what no sermon of words alone could.

This visual theology also "taught" Willow Creek's understanding of the sacrament of baptism, something done in community by the initiate, in obedience to Christ's command and as a public witness to what they in faith believed Christ had accomplished on their behalf on the cross.

Stewart Hoover, in his essay on "The Cross at Willow Creek" points out that this church itself labels the use of the cross a "prop."[38] Some might think this trivializes the central symbol of the Christian faith. But that is not their intent, nor was it my experience as a worshiper. Rather, by using the cross as a visual aid to help the worshipers construct meaning, to quite literally "hammer" out a theology of the atonement, Willow Creek was breathing new life into a symbol that otherwise, and too easily, might simply adorn the wall of their church. Rather than risk having the visual representation of the cross be off-putting to those who have negative reactions to the institutional church and its symbols, Willow Creek used the cross for an enacted ritual, a "visual event" that had power and meaning. Here was experiential learning that involved more than intellect alone, learning that would not easily be forgotten. Luther would have been happy. But for me, the experience was even more than pedagogical. For in this event Christ was again present to me. That is, the visual aid proved sacramental. True, the event was the sacrament of baptism, but it was not through the baptism per se or even the symbolism of the water that Christ was present. Rather, Christ was made present to me through those pieces of paper tacked to a life-size cross.

The Visual as Conversation Partner

A second and very different visual experience in worship relates to the use of video as a dialogue partner to the sermon. In preaching one Sunday on "Sloth," the sin of laziness toward God, I used Psalm 19 as my text (or anti-text). The psalmist is someone who "hungers and thirsts after righteousness," someone who can't say enough about God's overpowering blessing as he reveals himself through both nature and Scripture. (It is interesting to note that the ancient practice of the church was to contrast the seven deadly sins not with the seven cardinal virtues, but with the Beatitudes.)

To help the congregation feel the contrast between the psalmist's desire to be in the presence of God and our own tendency toward sloth, I showed a five-minute clip from the Jay Leno show as part of my sermon. The clip is titled, "How Do I Know? The Bible Tells Me So." Leno shows his viewers an edited tape of interviews at the Beverly Center in Los Angeles, where he questioned people about their Bible knowledge. One man thought it was Pinnochio who had been swallowed by the whale. Another could identify the four Beatles but couldn't name one of the four Gospel writers. A woman was asked to name any of the Ten Commandments, and after saying that her daughter should be answering this because she had been sent to a Christian school, the mother finally blurted out, "You can't do anything you want to do." As the clip ends, Jay addresses the audience with these words: "Ladies and Gentlemen, we all are going to burn in hell."

Here is pedagogy by humorous reverse example. What is shown is as good a contrast to the portrayal in Psalm 19:10—"More to be desired are [the words of the Lord] than gold, even much fine gold; sweeter also than honey, and drippings of the honeycomb"—as our contemporary culture provides. The video also gives us the helpful statement of an informal "theologian," Jay Leno, whose final, ad lib response gets through our defenses in a way that most preachers' rhetoric would not. Such sloth over a lifetime will, indeed, prove deadly to one's spirit. Such laziness of spirit will, indeed, result in our "burning in hell."

As the congregation laughed at inanity after inanity, they also saw a caricature of themselves. Our own slothfulness toward the wonder of God's ongoing revelation to us in the Word and the world would also be laughable if it were not so potentially deadly. The interviews on the screen became a conversation partner for the Word. As a result, the congregation was enabled to hear the good news of the psalmist with fresh ears. The sound of laughter, the images on the screen, and the words of the late-night talk-show host all combined with the words of Scripture to open up our affection.

The Visual as Sacramental

In both of the previous examples, the line between the sacramental and the pedagogical proves to be a fuzzy one. This is because the sacramental is always a gift, an encounter with God that comes to us from beyond us. Alexander Solzhenitsyn is quoted as saying, "Through Art we are sometimes sent—indistinctly, briefly—revelations not to be achieved by rational thought."[39] Here is the point of a visual Christianity. Through the visual we learn something new about the God who has revealed himself in Word and words. We are also provided with an occasion for encountering our Lord afresh, as God transforms the stuff of life into a sacramental that reveals briefly, yet indelibly, something of his glory and grace.[40]

My wife, Catherine Barsotti, has preached from 2 Corinthians 4, where Paul describes the "light of the gospel of the glory of Christ" (v. 4) as a "treasure in clay jars, so that it may be made clear that this extraordinary power belongs to God and does not come from us" (v. 7). To help worshipers understand and experience the wonder of Christ being in them, she covers the front of the sanctuary with all types of pottery ("clay jars")—some tall and some pudgy, some glazed and some unfired, some beautiful and some broken into many pieces. In each pot she has placed a treasure, whether flowers, chocolate, or some small gift. After the sermon, Cathy invites those present to come forward and prayerfully choose the pot they most identify with. They are then to take some of the treasure found in "their" pot and in this way experience afresh the wonder of Christ being in us.

For some, the flowers and chocolate have served as a prop, a pedagogical device to help reinforce the scriptural message. For others, however, they have meant more. Coming to a broken pot in tears, a worshiper has received a piece of chocolate sacramentally. In it, they have encountered Christ's Spirit saying to them that the glory of God dwells within them, despite their unworthiness. The visual reinforcement allows for a liturgy of enactment that is transformative. The pedagogical has become the sacramental through the gracious presence of the Spirit of Christ, who fills it with his divine presence.

12

Penetrating the World with the Gospel

Three Approaches

Donald G. Bloesch

Since the period of the early church, Christians have been concerned with the momentous question of how to reach the world with the gospel. They see their mandate as being heralds and ambassadors of our Lord Jesus Christ, but they differ radically on the question of how to fulfill this mandate. When making a case for the credibility of Christian faith, the temptation to appeal to criteria acceptable to the intelligentsia is almost irresistible. Evangelical theologian Carl Henry gave voice to this concern when he urged, "Strike a blow in defense of the gospel!" For Henry, this means building a rationally persuasive case for the cardinal claims of the faith.

The parallel question that I shall deal with in this chapter is how one becomes a Christian. Reinhold Niebuhr gave one possible answer: "I am a Christian because Christianity makes more sense of more facts than any other way of thinking I know of."[1] Those belonging to the tradition of evangelical Pietism would express it another way: We are Christians because we have been convicted of sin by the Holy Spirit and have been led to trust in Christ for our deliverance and salvation.[2]

Apologetic Theology

One major strand of Christian thought that has its roots in the endeavor to uphold the missionary imperative of the faith is apologetic theology. Here the overriding concern is the defense of the faith in the public forum. We present a case for the claims of faith on the basis of a criterion that is held in common with the adversaries of faith. Our goal is to persuade the outsider of the credibility of the Christian message. We try to make the faith palatable to its "cultured despisers"[3] without compromising its integrity. Apologetic theology is a mediating theology—one that strives to build bridges of understanding to the non-Christian culture. Our rationale is not to water down the faith but to gain a hearing for the faith by speaking to the yearnings and questionings of the unbeliever. Apologetic theology seeks to relate to the age-old quest for meaning and purpose in life, which encompasses all cultures and religions. This kind of theology purports to show that the claims of the Christian faith are not unreasonable, that they merit serious consideration.

The apologetic tradition includes many notable figures in theology, including Clement of Alexandria, Origen, Justin Martyr, Augustine,[4] Thomas Aquinas, Joseph Butler, Friedrich Schleiermacher, Reinhold Niebuhr, Wolfhart Pannenberg, Emil Brunner, C. S. Lewis, Francis Schaeffer, Hans Küng, Carl Henry, and Paul Tillich. It should be evident from this list that apologetics can be utilized by various systems of theology—some liberal and some conservative. The common approach does not presuppose a common conclusion.

In this section I shall give special attention to Paul Tillich, whom Niebuhr astutely described as the Origen of our time. Like Origen, Tillich sought to relate positively to the cultural quest for meaning and to show how Christian faith is relevant to this quest. Also like Origen, Tillich was greatly indebted to Platonic philosophy and strove for a synthesis of Christ and culture. Tillich was more of a philosophical theologian than a biblical one. In his view, philosophy leads to theology just as theology presupposes a philosophical concern. Like many other apologists, Tillich saw philosophy as the precursor and handmaiden of theology and also as the goal of theology—a comprehensive understanding of faith and reality.

Tillich had an illustrious career as both teacher and author in Germany and subsequently in the United States.[5] After teaching in Frankfurt, Germany, he came to America in 1933, where he served as a professor of theology first at Union Theological Seminary in New York City, then at Harvard University Divinity School, and finally at the University of Chicago Divinity School. He was compelled to give up his teaching position in Germany because of his open opposition to National Socialism. He did not, however, align himself with the Confessing Church because of what appeared to him to be its authoritarianism and exclusivism.

While retaining a veneer of his Lutheran heritage, Tillich sought to address the concerns of modern culture. He saw value in the Bible as a record of profound religious experiences, but he did not view Scripture as an unerring rule for faith and practice. He believed the mythology of the Bible must be translated into an ontology if it is to make an imprint on the mind of the culture.

Tillich described his theology as apologetic rather than kerygmatic.[6] His theology is centered not in the apostolic proclamation (kerygma) but in the cultural and philosophical quest for meaning and beatitude. For Tillich, an apologetic theology is an answering theology. It begins with the creative questions of the culture and then proceeds to show how the Christian faith sheds new light on these questions. Its method is one of correlation: the goal is to correlate the cultural questions with the Christian answer—the "New Being" in Jesus Christ. All apologetics presuppose common ground with the outsider. In Tillich's view this common ground is the mystical a priori—the sense of unity with the all-encompassing divine presence. This mystical awareness functions as a point of contact between Christ and culture, revelation and reason. Other points of contact are the anxiety of guilt and the anxiety of meaninglessness, which trouble people in every culture. Our apologetic endeavors can also appeal to a sense of estrangement that mars human existence, as we present Christ as the healer of broken relationships.

It is interesting to compare Tillich with some other theological luminaries who have engaged in the apologetic task. For Carl Henry, the common ground with unbelief is logical thinking.[7] In his view, all thinking stands under the law of noncontradiction. We can argue the claims of Christian faith by showing that this faith is more logically consistent than any of its rivals. For Henry, logical consistency is a negative test for truth, while coherence is a subordinate test. In seeming opposition to Pietism, Henry holds that the two kinds of thinking are not regenerate and unregenerate, but valid and invalid. Natural reason by itself can recognize and articulate the claims of faith, though faith is necessary if these claims are to become normative in our lives. Tillich stands with Henry in holding that reason can prepare the way for faith, but Tillich also sees reason as standing under the threat of existential disruption and right reasoning as a matter of spiritual healing.

A theologian to the right of Tillich is Emil Brunner, who embraced apologetics as the way to penetrate the bastions of unbelief in the secular world.[8] Brunner called his apologetics "eristics," the method of attack. Similarly to Carl Henry and Cornelius Van Til, Brunner believed that our task is to undercut the presuppositions of the unbeliever to bring that person to the point of despair; then he or she will be ready and able to make a decision of faith.

An eristical element is also especially evident in the early work of Tillich, who held that despair is the precondition for faith. As he put it, "The message of the Protestant church . . . must insist upon the radical experience of the boundary-situation; it must destroy the secret reservations harbored by the modern man which prevent him from accepting resolutely the limits of his human existence."[9] As his theology evolved, Tillich made more room for correlation as opposed to confrontation and tried to see human culture in a more positive light. Both Brunner and Tillich presupposed that the human person has a moral capacity to respond to the gospel proclamation, for otherwise the apologetic endeavor itself would be called into question. In contrast to Henry, both of these existentialist theologians acknowledged the role of paradox in faith and the limitations of reason in its apprehension of the truth of faith.

By incorporating philosophical and cultural insights into theology, Tillich was compelled to reinterpret the claims of faith in order to reach a world increasingly removed from a Christian ethos. Tillich was highly critical of Karl Barth's theology, which espoused the direct proclamation of the Christian message on the basis that this is the primary medium of the Spirit's operation. According to Tillich, "The Protestant message cannot be a direct proclamation of religious truths as they are given in the Bible and in tradition, for the situation of the modern man of today is precisely one of doubt about all this and about the Protestant church itself."[10]

By taking his point of departure in the cultural quest for wisdom, Tillich was betrayed into compromising or revising the original claims of Christian faith. In his attempt to articulate the faith in a new way, Tillich relied on some old sources—Platonism and Neoplatonism. He also drew heavily on the rationalism of Hegel and the existentialism of Nietzsche. In Tillich's theology, God is no longer a living person but is now a God beyond the personal—the infinite ground of all being. With Plotinus, Tillich espoused a "God above God," a reality that eludes all precise conceptualization. Jesus Christ is no longer the preexistent Logos in human flesh but is now the paradigm of divine-human unity. Salvation becomes a process of healing rather than the act of reconciliation and redemption. Further, salvation is reconceived as reunion with the eternal rather than justification through a substitutionary atonement. Sin becomes separation from the ground of being instead of rebellion against a holy God. The fall of humanity is reinterpreted as an ontological fall as opposed to a historical fall. The fundamental problem of human existence is therefore finitude rather than sin, though Tillich would be uncomfortable with this way of formulating his position. The Bible becomes an aid in self-understanding rather than the written Word of God. The church becomes a community of shared experiences rather than a fellowship of faith in pilgrimage.

Tillich's departure from traditional faith is especially evident in his spirituality, an area in which he was immensely interested. In his reconception of love he tried to make a place for agape, the other-serving love of biblical faith, but it was definitely subordinated to eros, the self-aspiring love promulgated by Plato, Plotinus, and the Christian mystics. For Tillich, the motivation in Christian life is self-realization. Love is redefined as the drive for the unity of the separated. Its crowning symbol is a flock of birds soaring upward into the sky. The highest point in Christian faith is the fulfillment, not the sacrifice, of the self. Tillich tried to correlate the understanding of love in humanistic traditions with the biblical teaching, but he ended in espousing a humanistic ethic rather than the biblical one.

In Tillich's theology prayer becomes adoration and meditation as opposed to petition. Again he followed the mystical tradition by upholding wordless, silent prayer over pleading and remonstrating with God. Yet he tried to stay clear of the Neoplatonic ideal of "the flight of the alone to the alone." He was keenly aware of the need for community for a whole human existence and manifested a marked openness to communal experiments, though he fully realized the pitfalls of utopianism.[11]

With the rise of a postmodern theology of religions that celebrates the pluralism of the modern world, Tillich is regaining influence in theological circles. He looked forward to a "Religion of the Concrete Spirit" that would supersede the parochialism of traditional, empirical Christianity.[12] Tillich's ideal was a religion that would be open to new revelations, though he upheld Jesus Christ as the *final,* albeit not the *only,* revelation. Tillich acknowledged his spiritual father to be Schleiermacher, who, in his *On Religion: Speeches to Its Cultured Despisers,* foresaw the eclipse of historical Christianity and the emergence of a more inclusive religion that would take into account the religious aspirations of other cultures and religions.[13]

According to Tillich, the way to penetrate the outside world is through dialogue rather than evangelism. Because all people are in contact with the divine presence, there are no lost souls, only souls in the stage of latency. There are no absolute conversions, only relative ones. Our task as members of the believing community is to broaden understandings and build bridges between competing faith systems. We should never try to force people to change faiths but should instead encourage a fuller understanding, and possibly a deeper appreciation, of all faiths.

By contrast, conservative defenders of the Christian faith who have employed apologetics, such as J. Edward Carnell, Carl Henry, R. C. Sproul, the early Clark Pinnock, Norman Geisler, Cornelius Van Til, Francis Schaeffer, and many others, have kept close to traditional faith.[14] Yet it can be shown that they too have diverged markedly from the biblical pattern in their theological method by appealing to the wisdom of the world rather than the foolishness of preaching (see 1 Cor. 1:18–25).

Kerygmatic Theology

Standing in stark contrast to apologetic theology is kerygmatic theology, whose adherents place their trust in the apostolic proclamation, or kerygma, rather than in apologetic strategies. Tillich was one of the first to make the distinction between these two types of theology.[15] According to Tillich, in the kerygmatic approach we throw the gospel at our hearers as if it were a stone.[16] In apologetic theology we enter the existential situation of our hearers and try to make contact with their values and worldviews. We try to build on what we have in common with our hearers in order to lead them to an understanding and acceptance of the gospel.

Among those in the history of the church who have adopted a kerygmatic methodology are Irenaeus, Martin Luther, John Calvin, John Wesley, P. T. Forsyth, Dietrich Bonhoeffer, and Karl Barth. A theologian like Augustine combined the two approaches, but basically Augustine began with a philosophical perspective and then proceeded to a theological standpoint.[17] His motto was "I believe in order to understand," but this comprised only part of the dialectic that also included "I understand in order to believe."

The model I shall use for kerygmatic theology in this chapter is Karl Barth, the famed Reformed pastor and teacher and the author of the Barmen Declaration (1934).[18] Whereas Tillich's concern was the renewal of the culture, Barth's was the reform of the church. Like the Reformers, Barth emphasized the audible over the visual. He readily agreed with Luther: "We must learn to put our eyes into our ears." Faith comes from hearing, and hearing comes from the preaching of the Word of God (Rom. 10:17).

Barth was adamant that in and of ourselves we are incapable of communicating the Word of God; first, because the finite cannot appropriate the infinite (*finitum non capax infiniti*), and second, because sinful humanity cannot fathom the mystery of holiness. It is useless to try to join the message of faith to the religious quest because fallen humanity is not in quest of God but in flight from God. We seek not the righteousness of the kingdom but only our own glory. Our need is not to be enlightened but to be delivered, and this occurs when we hear and believe the gospel.

Like the Reformers, Barth regarded the preaching of the gospel as a sacramental sign—a channel of redemption. He believed the power of the gospel lies not in its formal articulation, but in the Holy Spirit, who acts and speaks as we act and speak. The point of contact with the natural or unredeemed person is not the sense of alienation or estrangement (as in Tillich) but the Holy Spirit, who gives us not only faith but also the very condition with which to receive faith.

According to Barth, faith is not a human possibility but a gift of God's grace. We cannot procure faith or create faith, but we can manifest faith in lives that give glory to God. We can make the gospel intelligible, but we cannot make it knowable. Only the Holy Spirit can do that as he works through the proclamation of Jesus Christ crucified.

For Barth, evangelism is not dialoguing with the unbelieving representatives of other positions but informing people of what God has done for us in Jesus Christ. There is a place for dialogue, but not as a substitute for preaching for conversion. We must strive to understand our faith as it interacts with the world, but we cannot hand out faith as if it were our possession. We can point others to faith, but only the Holy Spirit can bring faith to them. Whereas the symbol of the bridge is appropriate for Tillich's theology, the symbol of the fortress characterizes Barth's position. For Barth, our mandate is not to leave the fortress to battle our opponents on their own turf but to invite others into the fortress—not as adversaries but as potential converts. Whereas Tillich sought for a correlation between faith and unbelief, Barth's approach leads to a confrontation, yet one that has its roots not in an eristical attack but in the gospel itself, which is a stumbling block to Jews and foolishness to Greeks (1 Cor. 1:21–23).

Not surprisingly, Barth and Tillich have quite different views of revelation. Tillich sees revelation as an ecstatic experience that lifts us above ourselves in mystical union with God. Barth views revelation as an event or series of events in the sacred history mirrored in the Bible. For Tillich, revelation is being grasped by Being-itself; for Barth, revelation is being addressed by the living Lord.

Disagreements in theological method also account for differences in how one conceives God. Tillich championed a God of the depths—the infinite ground of all being. Tillich propounded an "ecstatic naturalism" and saw God as the immanent life force that inspires the universal religious quest. Barth, on the other hand, envisioned a God of the heights, one who descends into our midst from the beyond. Being a supernaturalist, Barth saw God as the Wholly Other.

In the area of spirituality, Tillich reduces prayer to meditation. For Barth, prayer is basically and primarily petition, even though it takes other forms, such as adoration and thanksgiving. The petitionary element, however, is present in these other forms as well, for we always approach God as people in need. In Tillich's theology we resign ourselves to God's will; in Barth's we seek to change God's will. The paradox is that in trying to alter God's will, we find that God's will is actually being done.

Barth was forever suspicious of a theology centered in a religious quest. The message of faith is not that we seek God but that God seeks us. It is not our ascent to God that characterizes the truly spiritual life but God's descent to a fallen humanity. Barth would heartily agree with James Denney: "I would rather be found in Christ than lost in God." Barth upheld an agape theology, one that takes us out of ourselves into the service of others, as opposed to an eros theology, in which we seek to secure our salvation through spiritual exercises that lead to union with God. Yet unlike Anders Nygren, Barth was not willing simply to posit an antithesis between agape and eros.[19] Eros is not annulled by agape, but transformed. Eros can be made to serve agape, just as works can be made to serve the outpouring of grace.

Further evidence of Barth's break with the mystical tradition of the faith is his prioritizing the gospel over the law. In mysticism, which also left its imprint on the Reformation, the law prepares us for the gospel by convicting us of sin and leading us into despair, thereby making us ripe for faith. According to Barth, such a view manifests a profound misreading of the New Testament. It is not the law by itself that leads us to faith, but the law in its unity with the gospel. Indeed, we cannot really know either our sin or the law until our inward eyes are opened to the reality of God's grace poured out for us in Jesus Christ. Just as reason does not lead to revelation, so the law does not lead to the gospel. But just as reason can be made to serve revelation, so the law can be brought into the service of the gospel and can therefore function as a veritable means of grace.

Charges that Barth is a fideist or even an irrationalist reflect a profound misunderstanding of his position. It is true that in his earlier writings he emphasized the disjunction between faith and reason, but a rereading of Anselm in the late 1920s led him to embrace the Anselmian method: faith seeking understanding. Reason cannot lead to faith, but it can be informed by faith. Faith moreover can give reason a sure anchor in transcendent reality and thereby enable reason to make an intelligible witness to faith. Although Barth looked with disdain upon apologetics as a propadeutic to dogmatics, he always recognized an apologetic dimension in faith. He believed that while we must always be prepared to give a reason for the hope that is in us (1 Peter 3:15) this reason is not evidence that the world can understand but a confession that can only be truly appreciated inside the circle of faith. For Barth, the most efficacious apologetic is a good dogmatic. We must be ready to answer attacks on the faith, yet always recognizing that while the cogency of our arguments may reinforce people in their faith commitment, it will not of itself move people toward such a commitment.

In my opinion, Barth can be justly criticized for his proclivity to objectivism, viewing salvation as having occurred completely in the past—in the life, death, and resurrection of Jesus Christ. In Barth's perspective salvation is something accomplished rather than something yet to be realized. Nevertheless, he also makes a place for the regenerating work of the Holy Spirit, who brings the fruits of Christ's sacrifice into our lives. This is especially evident in the last volume of his *Church Dogmatics*.[20] In his reaction against the experientialism of Schleiermacher, Barth tended to depreciate the role of religious experience in the life of faith. Yet we need to acknowledge that faith itself is an experience, one that paradoxically takes us out of our experience into the promises of Christ, which never deceive (Luther). In the commitment of faith we come to realize joy and peace in the Holy Spirit. We not only know the truth of salvation, but we come to feel the power of salvation. Barth was resistant to Pietism because he was poignantly aware that it so often leads into subjectivism and introversion. Yet he did not hesitate to draw on his Pietist heritage in espousing a theology of both Word and Spirit.[21]

Barth has had a measure of influence on some of the newer theological movements, including liberation theology and narrative theology. He would, however, be profoundly critical of these movements. Against liberation theology he would insist that the kingdom of God cannot be built by human hands.

It is instead an apocalyptic inbreaking of a new social order in history. We can nevertheless set up signs and parables of the coming kingdom. The kingdom must never be confounded with a just society, but human justice can be a sign or witness to the righteousness of the kingdom. Barth would object to narrative theology on the grounds that revelation cannot be reduced to the biblical narrative, for it always remains the transcendent Word of God, which can nevertheless make itself known through narrative as well as through other forms.

Charismatic Theology

One should bear in mind that there are other options besides apologetic and kerygmatic theologies.[22] Charismatic theology strives to impact the world through the power of spiritual gifts. These are the gifts that equip the saints for ministry; some of these gifts are enumerated in 1 Corinthians 12–14; Romans 12:4–8; and Ephesians 4:11–12. They include wisdom, knowledge, prophecy, suffering, love, preaching, teaching, lowly service, evangelism, hospitality, persevering prayer, healing, and leadership. Through these gifts we can penetrate non-Christian culture with the gospel. The exercise of these gifts does not necessarily exclude an apologetic or a kerygmatic stance, but they may be practiced apart from argumentation and kerygmatic preaching.

Just as apologetic and kerygmatic theologies have their roots in the mainstream of Christian tradition, the pentecostal gifts of the Spirit have been celebrated in traditions associated with dissent and nonconformity, including Montanism, mysticism, Anabaptism, Puritanism, Pietism, and in our day, Pentecostalism. In Catholic and Eastern Orthodox traditions the gifts of the Spirit are conspicuous in those esteemed as great saints or holy persons. In Protestantism, spiritual gifts are frequently present in missionaries and evangelists such as Johann Christoph Blumhardt (d. 1880), a German pastor whose ministry featured healings and exorcisms; Sundar Singh (d. 1929), who lived the life of a sadhu, or holy man, as a witness to Christ;[23] and Arthur Blessitt, who has been instrumental in winning souls for Christ by carrying a cross through many nations.

For the purposes of this chapter, I would like to give special attention to Frank Buchman (1878–1961), a charismatic Lutheran clergyman who had a remarkable ministry of personal evangelism.[24] His ministry, it seems, was geared to the up-and-outs, just as the Salvation Army tried to reach the down-and-outs. Buchman graduated from Mount Airy Lutheran seminary in Philadelphia (1902) and built the first Lutheran settlement house in this country. He was already regarded as a gifted person in this early stage of his ministry, but because of tensions with the board of directors of the settlement house, he gave up this ministry and embarked on a trip to Europe in order to find his true vocation. By the providence of God, Buchman was guided to a Keswick convention in northern England and there heard a sermon by a laywoman preacher on the miracle of the cross. His rancor against the board of directors at the settlement house dissipated, and he sensed a new power at work in his life. He immediately told others of his conversion experience and wrote a letter to each member of the board asking for their forgiveness. None of them replied, but this did not deter Buchman from embarking on a new and unconventional ministry. He prayed for a heightened sensitivity to the needs of others and received what is called in Catholic spirituality the "reading of hearts" and in Pentecostalism "the word of knowledge." He was endowed with a remarkable capacity to empathize with others and to see through the subterfuges that prevent people from acknowledging the demons within them. Like Francis of Assisi, with whom he has been compared, he began a ministry as an itinerant evangelist without any dependable source of income. Also like Francis and many of the mystics, Buchman embraced the single life, partly because of the demands of his ministry, though he always held marriage in high esteem. His new venture in ministry took him to various universities including Oxford, England, from which the movement derived its name—the Oxford Group.

What was the key to Buchman's remarkable success? He had the uncanny ability to discern the spiritual condition of people in need, and his answer in most cases was open confession of sin and obedience to God's commandment. His extraordinary power to communicate the Word of God became evident while on a world evangelistic tour with Sherwood Eddy. On one occasion, as an evangelistic meeting was coming to an end, a self-proclaimed atheist challenged the mission team to prove that there is a God. The team tried to answer his objections, but to no avail. Then Buchman, who had not yet spoken, stood up and fixed his diagnostic gaze on the questioner: "It's not unbelief that keeps you from God. You're an adulterer! Let's clean that up first, and then we'll get around to the God business."[25] The heckler sat down, palpably offended, but at the end of the meeting this man was surprisingly numbered among the converts. How was he converted? He had heard the gospel from the platform speakers, but he was not convicted of sin until he heard the words of the law addressed to him personally by Buchman. In this case, it seems law and gospel together constituted the means of grace, but the catalyst was the extraordinary way in which Buchman brought the interrogator to repentance.

On another occasion, Buchman was challenged by a young lecturer at Oxford University who conducted meetings on Sunday afternoons for the express purpose of exposing the claims of Christian faith.[26] Upon hearing of Buchman's impending visit to the university, he invited this ambassador of Christ to his apartment for a conversation on religious matters. Buchman graciously accepted. For an hour the young man presented the case for atheism, but Buchman did not reply to any of the arguments brought by his host. Finally the young lecturer said, "I wish you would tell me what you think of me." After some hesitation Buchman replied, "First, you are unhappy." The other agreed

that this was correct. Then Buchman asserted, "You have a very unhappy home."
He replied, "Yes, I have. I hate my father. I always have since I was a boy."
Buchman then said. "You are in the grip of an impure habit which you cannot bring yourself to talk about with anyone." The atheist blurted out, "That
is a lie." Then, following a period of silence, Buchman said, "I must go." The
young man persuaded Buchman to stay, however, with the admission that he
was indeed in the grip of an addiction. The two men talked honestly with one
another, and the evening ended with both on their knees and the atheist giving his life to God. What we have in this incident is neither apologetic nor
kerygmatic theology but a word of knowledge that proved to be the vehicle of
the Holy Spirit in bringing an outsider to faith in Christ and his gospel.

In the later 1930s, Buchman expanded his ministry to include leaders of
nations, and the Oxford Group became Moral Re-Armament. The distinctly
Christian character of the movement began to erode as Buchman sought to
bring leaders of all religions into a ministry that revolved around moral reno-
vation through surrender to the Spirit who resides in all people. Buchman was
committed to the truth that the key to social reformation and world peace was
personal transformation. But in this new venture, it was not so clear that inner
transformation depended on an explicit faith in Jesus Christ. Toward the end
of his life, however, Buchman tried to bring Moral Re-Armament into closer
accord with the ideas of the Oxford Group movement. In 1951 he asserted
that the Moral Re-Armament strategy to change the world "needs this stronger
dose . . . 'The blood of Jesus Christ His Son cleanseth us from all sin.' That is
the discovery everyone is looking for. That is the answer."[27]

Both the Oxford Group and Moral Re-Armament have been justly accused
of perfectionism, as though anyone could live fully according to the four
absolutes propounded by Buchman—purity, unselfishness, honesty, and love.
Yet Buchman himself saw that even the sanctified constantly fall short of the
moral ideal and that only Christ can save. The words he wrote in a letter to an
admirer are revealing:

> Just and holy is Thy Name,
> I am all unrighteousness;
> False and full of sin I am,
> Thou art full of truth and grace.[28]

Unlike Tillich and Barth, Buchman was not a professional theologian. His
life was a demonstration of practical Christianity. This dimension of the faith,
however, was not denied by either Barth or Tillich. Indeed, both of these scholars made a place for spiritual gifts, though they sought to bring these gifts into
the service of the wider Christian mission.

In contrast to most apologetic and kerygmatic theologies, charismatic theology is focused on a direct experience of the Spirit, which is both a means to
faith and a condition for faith. Buchman was not an irrationalist, but in con-

trast to Barth, his emphasis was on the cross of experience rather than the cross of history. He wished that every person would have "an experience of the Cross of Christ so that he could present it intelligently to anyone."[29] The question is whether in our evangelistic ministry we present simply our experience of Christ or the Christ of the Bible—who not only saved us personally but saved the whole world—at least in principle (*de jure*).

What distinguishes charismatic theology from traditional Reformed theology is the inclusion of signs and wonders as means of grace. Paul's words in Romans 15:17–21 give support to the charismatic position. The apostle confesses that he sought to win obedience from the Gentiles not only "by word and deed" but also "by the power of signs and wonders" (cf. Mark 16:20; Heb. 2:4). Yet the fuller biblical picture is that signs and wonders follow the preaching of the Word of God (as the Romans text also suggests). They ordinarily do not impart faith, but they reveal that the power of faith is at work in people's lives. Paul declares that the gospel is a stumbling block to Jews who seek signs and foolishness to Greeks who seek wisdom (1 Cor. 1:22–23). A feverish search for miracles may indicate an abdication of faith (cf. Matt. 12:39). The denial of miracles, on the other hand, casts doubt on the power of faith to change lives. The Bible does allow for the role of miracles in strengthening faith. Like arguments in defense of the faith, miracles can help people understand the mysteries of faith, but they do not in and of themselves make people believe. Only the Spirit can do that, as he acts through the preaching of the Word, but he may also act through signs and miracles when they are seen in the light of the one great miracle—the mystery of the incarnation of Christ, his atoning sacrifice, and his glorious resurrection. Yet this mystery does not give rise to faith unless we experience its grandeur and power in an act of decision and faith. If we are to benefit practically and salvifically, the message of the cross must become part of our lives through an evangelical experience. This is the truth of the Oxford Group movement and of Pietism in general.

The Road Ahead

We are living in a climate of relativism, postmodernism, and pluralism. Instead of embracing a strategy of defense (apologetics), it is incumbent on us to herald the coming of a new world order, the kingdom of God, which will be spearheaded by the preaching of the gospel. Every Christian is called to be a sign and witness of this heavenly kingdom. Every believer is under the mandate to put into operation the spiritual gifts that have been imparted to him or her by the Spirit of God. We do not all have the privilege of walking the way of Frank Buchman or Sundar Singh in a ministry of personal evangelism. Nor are we all called to be teachers or theologians like Paul Tillich or Karl Barth.

But as believers, all of us have some gift that Christ can use to advance his king-dom in this world of sin and death.

The pressing need in the years ahead is for a theology of world evangeliza-tion that would in some way be combined with a theology of social righ-teousness. Such a theological stance would necessarily be opposed to a global theology that tries to assimilate the values of all religions. It would also take pains to distinguish theology from every ideology, including a religious ideol-ogy like Moral Re-Armament. Theology must never be based on a set of ideas or principles designed to remold society. But it must never give up the hope that personal change will bring about a new social vision that speaks to the human yearning for peace and justice.

Because it heralds the dawning of a new social order, Christian faith will necessarily be countercultural. Its aim is not a synthesis with secular culture but the penetration of the culture by the gospel. The church will be a critic of the culture, not a pillar of the culture (as in neo-Protestantism). An authenti-cally biblical theology will not regard the Christian faith as a bridge to the cul-ture (as did Tillich), nor as a fortress that stands over against the culture (as did Barth). Instead, the metaphor that most nearly resonates with the biblical view is a foray. We carry out attacks on the idolatries of the culture but always remain close to our base (the Word of God). While the idea of a fortress is not dis-carded, the fortress mentality is transcended, since our goal is to get out of the fortress and into the world. This is indeed consonant with Barth's later work.

A theology of world evangelization will seek to bring the world into sub-mission to Jesus Christ, not through secular power, but through the evangeli-cal proclamation as set forth in Holy Scripture. It will also seek to win the world for the gospel by deeds of mercy, the fruits of the Holy Spirit. Signs and won-ders likewise play a role in the advancement of the kingdom in this world, but they will always point beyond themselves to the transcendent Word of God. They follow the preaching of the gospel rather than constitute the content of our proclamation. We must never place our faith in signs and wonders, but we minister with the expectation that the Spirit of God will be acting in marvelous ways wherever the Word of God is preached and obeyed.

In constructing a theology that serves the Christian mission, we must be alert to various pitfalls that substitute human strategy for the obedience of faith. One of these is moralism or legalism—making salvation contingent on pre-scribed rules or spiritual exercises. Another misstep is perfectionism—the illu-sion that we are no longer sinners in need of redemption because we have already realized the righteousness of faith. Closely related is utopianism, which claims that we have entered a stage in history in which the ambiguities of life are conquered.[30] Still another danger is sectarianism, in which we identify our own church fellowship with the holy catholic church or the kingdom of God. We must similarly be on guard against biblicism, in which the Bible becomes a law book that regulates the practice of faith rather than a missionary tract used by the Spirit to proclaim the message of faith. Finally, we must steer clear of restorationism, which simply means returning to the precepts and practices of biblical and apostolic tradition rather than listening to the voice of the Spirit guiding us to apply the treasures of the past to the present existential situation in which we live.

A theology of world evangelization will be not only evangelical (centered in the gospel) but also ecumenical (embracing the worldwide church). Only when Christians are united in thought and practice will their witness to Jesus Christ be credible to the world. Yet we should seek unity solely on the basis of truth. This does not imply a one world church, but it does presuppose altar and pulpit fellowship between the churches. We must refrain as much as possible from viewing other Christians as apostate, even if their theological systems are imperfect. To be sure, heresy must be combated, but in fulfilling this task we must be alert to our own vulnerability to heresy. We must strive to uproot the heresy within ourselves before we go after others.

A Protestantism that comes alive by the Spirit will be under the written Word of God and respectful of church tradition. It will be evangelical in its message and catholic in its concern to embrace all of God's people. It will not hesitate to acknowledge its indebtedness to the Protestant Reformation but will also be open to learning from the church fathers and the doctors and mystics of the medieval church. It will seek to draw not only on the tradition of Protestant orthodoxy but also on the spiritual movements of purification that came after the Reformation—Pietism, Puritanism, and Evangelicalism. It will be reserved toward religious enthusiasm but will realize that the forms and rituals of the church must be animated by the Spirit if they are to be effective in transmitting the treasure of the gospel.

A Spirit-filled church will strive for the union of structure and ecstasy.[31] It will not be monarchical or hierarchical in the sense of being under the rule of bishops or other clerics who are answerable only to themselves. Yet this does not imply that the office of bishop is excluded from the coming great church. In a church based on the Word of God, bishops and elders become servants of the Word and also servants of the people of God.

The church that I envision for the future will be respectful of the past but willing to chart a new course under the illumination of the Spirit. It will be open to innovations, but only if they are informed by the truth of Holy Scripture and sacred tradition. It will make a place for the rational defense of the faith, but a defense that is designed primarily to strengthen believers in the faith rather than to prove the truth of the faith to the outsider. It will be firmly kerygmatic in its emphasis on the preaching of the word, but it will also preach the law of God, which enables Christians to live out their faith in the world. It will be open to spiritual gifts without harboring the illusion that church growth is dependent on miraculous displays of power supposedly wrought by the Holy Spirit. It will see the value of hard theological thinking, what Calvin called the discipline of study. Faith needs not only to be proclaimed but also to be understood if we are to communicate this faith effectively to a pagan and secular culture.

I have discussed three figures in the life of the church who represent different theological responses to the challenges of secularism: Paul Tillich, Karl Barth, and Frank Buchman. The last is a pastoral, rather than academic, theologian. I might have included Jürgen Moltmann, whose theology duly recognizes the critical role of spiritual gifts in the Christian world mission.[32] Yet Buchman, more than Moltmann, epitomizes the legacy of Pietism by putting a greater emphasis on the practice of faith than on the interpretation of faith—though Buchman was also an interpreter. It should be noted that Barth, Tillich, and Buchman all stand in the tradition of Pietism or have been influenced by this tradition. Even Karl Barth, an avowed critic of Pietism, acknowledged the affinity of his concerns with such luminaries of Pietism as Johann Christoph Blumhardt, Christoph Blumhardt, Nicholas von Zinzendorf, J. A. Bengel, and Søren Kierkegaard. The current interest in spiritual formation in our centers of learning attests to the dawning of a new Pietism or a new venture in Pietism.[33] Yet we must keep in mind that Pietism can only be a source of renewal when it joins hands with orthodoxy. The truth of faith and the practice of faith go together. Only when faith is reconceived as freedom for obedience can the church be a transforming agent within society, spearheading the advance of the kingdom of God.

13

Robert Webber

Dennis Okholm

I was seventeen, a displaced Californian, slumming in a rented basement with two Wheaton College students for the summer, after which I would matriculate at the "citadel of evangelicalism." One of my roommates looked about as much like a hippie as a Wheaton student could in 1970—shoulder-length hair and wire rims. When we were first introduced, he was holding a book by some existentialist, one of many contemporary philosophers and theologians he was devouring that summer. Within minutes he made it clear that his reading list had been inspired by a fairly new Wheaton professor named Bob Webber. With convincing enthusiasm he gave me the first piece of advice I would receive regarding my Wheaton education: "You've got to take Webber!"

I did. With insider information, which I discovered about eighty other freshmen must have had, I enrolled in Bob Webber's section of the obligatory first-year course titled "Christ and Culture." We did not meet in the typical classroom; we met in the downstairs lounge of the freshman dorm, half of the time sitting cross-legged on a carpeted floor. We did not read Augustine's *City of God,* as all the other sections did. (As Bob's colleague for over a decade now, I have since discovered his mild disdain for the harbinger of medieval Christendom.) We read Schaeffer and Dooyeweerd and Niebuhr and existentialism, and we were obligated to attend Ingmar Bergman films. Our professor did not wear a tie and short-cropped hair like the others. He dressed in "mod" clothes, topped off with an ascot and curly neck-length locks. But the lectures were captivating, and the weekly challenge to rethink our fundamentalist-bred Christian convictions were both exhilarating and threatening. The Wheaton legends of Webber were in their infancy, but they were already well in place.[1]

Why were students like me and my "John Lennon wannabe" summer roommate so engaged by what Webber was saying? In part, it was because he was a fellow pilgrim—an honest Christian inquirer, reared in fundamentalism like most of his students, trying to figure out how to be an honest evangelical in the culture that had grown out of the 1960s, a world our parents never knew.

The Silence of God

This characterization of Webber as an honest Christian inquirer was quickly established the year before I enrolled at the college. On November 5, 1969, during his second year of teaching at Wheaton, Webber delivered his infamous "Silence of God" chapel address. If God was silent, the campus certainly was not after Webber's sermon. Classes were canceled in the afternoon. President Armerding followed with a special chapel redress the next morning. The college newspaper reverberated with articles and letters for the next three weeks. One of the more typical letters, by Frank Bellinger, associate professor of political science, echoes the enthusiasm of my summer roommate:

> Dr. Robert Webber's chapel message was the most courageous, honest and profound affirmation of a mature Christian faith that I have found in over 30 years of association with Wheaton College as a student and faculty member. . . . a modern day prophet Amos, telling it like it is, articulating the unspoken fears and hopes of many who have been increasingly uneasy about the stance of evangelicalism in today's secularized world.[2]

Still, the response was not unanimous adulation. Armerding and Webber reportedly discussed his resignation, though in the end, he was neither fired nor did he resign. Instead, Webber encouraged many of us to join him and others in uncharted waters of evangelicalism to appreciate both the church's common historical faith and the diverse cultural shapes it must take in each time and place. This new approach to evangelicalism would require "a chastening and a renewing": a chastening because the modernist culture had moved evangelicals away from historic and even biblical Christianity, and a renewal because the recovery of historic Christianity would make evangelicalism a better and more faithful Christian witness to the contemporary culture.

A decade after his chapel talk, Webber wrote:

> Twentieth-century evangelicalism is, as a matter of fact, a reflection of modern culture, shaped by the Renaissance, the Enlightenment, the romantic era, the industrial age, and modern technology. . . . If evangelicalism as a movement is going to be more representative of the historic faith it must become more conscious not only of the cultural shape of its own faith, but also by way of contrast, to the aspects of the historic Christian faith which it has forgotten. . . . The agenda for evangelicals must go in two directions simultaneously. On the one hand, we need to face the negative task of overcoming our modernity, while on the other hand we need to grow into a more mature and historic expression of the faith. Both will occur without the loss of "evangelical distinctives" if we

are successful in bringing together the "evangelical spirit" with the "historic substance" of Christianity.[3]

This became Webber's agenda. It was this passion to rescue evangelicalism from the slough of modernity by returning it to its Christian roots that found nascent articulation in the guttural cry of his chapel message. With practice that has come from answering those who misunderstand him, he later explained:

> My desire is not to modernize, not to secularize, not to water down or in any way dilute evangelical Christianity, but to challenge it to develop into biblically and historically informed adulthood. If we can overcome our modernity, retain our evangelical spirit, and recapture the historic substance of Christianity, we will have found a way to replenish and revitalize our tradition and, as a consequence, offer significant leadership to the church and to the world.[4]

Though he was unaware of it in 1969, Webber's burgeoning desire to return evangelicalism to its early church roots and to find strategies that effectively engage the contemporary culture would eventually mature into the passion that has engaged him for the past two decades—the reinvigoration of the church's worship. In fact, listening to Webber reflect on his "Silence of God" sermon a quarter century later helps us not only to understand better his self-examination of his life and scholarship but also to understand how he has arrived where he is today. Since the chapel address set the course for Webber's life from that point on, his reflection is worth quoting at length.

> November 1969 was a turning point in my life, a time that I will always remember and which I am still seeking to interpret and understand. . . .
> Fresh out of doctoral studies, I was prepared—or so I thought—to persuade the students of that era of the intellectual validity of the Christian faith. . . .
> I knew my intellectual answers lacked integrity because I myself could not connect my experience with my belief. That fact convinced me that I should not and could not offer the rational answers of my academic education to a student body hungering for the reality of God in their lives.
> As I prepared my sermon, a sense of God's absence kept running through my mind and was validated by my own experience. God was absent to me, to my inner person and the affective, emotional side of me. Sure, I could reason God's existence and discuss theological matters with a degree of intelligence, but I felt nothing.
> During this time, the Spirit gifted me with a willingness to experience the silence of God—and it was a deafening silence, a real absence of such intensity that I cried out with the fullness of my being for God to become present in my life. "God," I said, "I don't want more information about you. I want you!"
> Little did I know what God was doing at that time. Through the sermon I preached on the silence of God, he was moving me to a new—or perhaps should I say "old"—way of experiencing his presence. God was moving me from a purely

intellectual understanding based on propositions and analysis to a realized experience of him in worship. . . .

It was years before I grasped the significance of what had happened to me. Even more years before I realized how my experience—and that of others who sense the absence of God in their lives—is closely related to a vast cultural and spiritual shift taking place in the world today. . . .

In brief, the single most important thing the church can do is worship. A vibrant worship life will break through the sense that God is absent and reach the people in the world who are searching for meaning.[5]

Classical Christianity—The Common Core

Though expressed in a preliminary way in the chapel address, Webber's move from a parochial fundamentalism to what he would later call "classical Christianity"[6] (the common Christian core of the first six centuries of the church) was precipitated by an event that seems to be as paradigmatic and as formative as the 1969 sermon. To put it in perspective, we have to go back to what Webber calls the "familial faith" of his childhood.[7]

Until he was seven, Bob lived with his missionary parents and two siblings (younger brother Ken and older sister Eleanor) in what was then the Belgian Congo (now Zaire).

It wasn't really much of a village, but it was a home for my missionary parents. In addition to our mud house, there was a church, a barn where we kept pigs and sheep, and row after row of little mud huts which were home for about one thousand natives. And all of this was backed by a rather small, craggy mountain which was dotted with bushes and colorful wild flowers.[8]

After the Webbers left the Congo, they moved to Montgomeryville, Pennsylvania (about twenty-four miles west of Philadelphia), where Bob's father pastored a fundamentalist Baptist church that transferred its association with the American Baptists to the Conservative Baptist Association.

Bob later reflected that he left the mystery of the Congo to come to the West, where all mystery has a rational explanation, the Bible is a list to be memorized, and theology is the propositional revelation of God that reveals God's mind. Yet, as he put it, "the more certain I became about my ability to defend God's existence and explain his character, the less real he seemed to me."[9]

This sentiment is what he expressed in his chapel address out of his frustration with "answers" that no longer worked for the youth of the Vietnam generation, mired in despair and meaninglessness, that he came to teach in 1968. But if he could not find God in the intellectual systems he inherited, where was he to encounter God?

He would find God "on the Canterbury trail" a decade later. But Bob had been introduced to the head of that trail years before he expressed his discontent in chapel. The introduction took place during his doctoral studies and was capped by another paradigmatic experience.

Bob's wanderings from the straight and narrow path of his fundamentalist Baptist upbringing came after he left Bob Jones University. As he put it much later, "Instead of nurturing those seeds of prejudice, I chose to journey beyond the confines of my fundamentalist education into an Episcopal seminary, then a Presbyterian seminary, and finally a Lutheran school."[10]

It was the last of these, Concordia Theological Seminary, which he attended from 1965 to 1968, that would finally release him from his insular conception of the faith. It began with a course on the apostolic fathers. Though he had begun his doctoral work in New Testament studies, his belief that the New Testament was sufficient was being challenged. If God is the God of history, then God also speaks and acts in the life of the church. The question of continuity also arose: perhaps the brand of evangelicalism he knew was reductionistic and not clearly apostolic.[11]

The challenge to his preconceptions was heightened by Webber's doctoral thesis on William Perkins, the founder of Puritanism. Here was a progenitor of the evangelical faith who believed the Reformation was not an innovation but a return to the early church. Webber concluded that subsequent cultural changes moved the Protestant church increasingly farther from the spirit and substance of the Reformation and, consequently, from the early church.[12]

What seared the point of all this study in Webber's mind was an event that involved a praise and prayer group he had joined at Concordia. This ecumenical group of Catholics, Lutherans, Presbyterians, and evangelicals met monthly to discuss Scripture, pray, talk, and have fun.

> When the time came for many of us to graduate and move on to new places, we decided to bring our two-year fellowship to an end with a weekend retreat at a local Catholic conference center. It was there that we faced an issue we had never even discussed. Could we take Communion together? . . .
>
> Those memories [of my life in the church] said, "Go ahead. After all, there is only one Lord, one church, one faith, one baptism, one Holy Communion."
>
> In that moment, God broke through the walls I had allowed to separate me from my brothers and sisters of different denominations. . . . When God broke down my walls, he brought me into a richer fellowship with the body of Christ throughout the world. I'm convinced that the prejudices we hold and the walls we build between ourselves and other communities of Christians actually block our experience of God's presence in our lives.
>
> When I stepped into the small, inviting chapel, I also stepped into my first experience with the liturgical.[13]

Just as one peels the leaves of an artichoke to get at the heart, so Bob had come to "own" a faith that was not only common to the entire Christian church, but one that embraced mystery (which was unavailable to the rationalistic brand of Christianity in which he had been reared), worship (that went beyond the dichotomy of emotionalism and intellectualism), the sacraments (as visible and tangible symbols through which God works), and a holistic spirituality (that does not separate inner and outer, the spiritual and the physical). He himself would find an ecclesiastical home and historic identity for these features in the Episcopal church (though his ordination took place in the Reformed Presbyterian denomination).[14]

Breaking through the ecclesiastical prejudices eventually led Bob to inaugurate a very significant event among evangelicals—the "Chicago Call." Precipitated by a phone conversation he had had with Peter Gillquist (who would eventually move into the Antiochian Orthodox Church), Webber initiated a process that brought together forty-five evangelicals in May 1977 to call evangelicals back to historic Christianity. The group included Donald Bloesch, Donald Dayton, Tom Howard (who would subsequently enter the Roman Catholic Church), Virgil Cruz, Richard Lovelace, Roger Nicole, Luci Shaw, and Donald Tinder. They were to look "beyond the borders" of evangelical limits "toward a more inclusive and ultimately more historic Christianity" to a truly catholic faith.[15] The working assumption was that the true spirit of the Reformation is catholic, and departure from true catholicity is more a result of the Enlightenment than anything else. By recovering the fullness of the Christian church's heritage over against the reduction of historic faith and practice, evangelicals could counteract their "two basic failures." The first involved an insufficient recognition of the implications of the incarnation—a kind of gnostic rejection of creation. Instead, evangelicals needed to affirm the visible as good and as the means through which God communicates himself in saving grace to humans. In other words, the assembly was issuing a call to return to an incarnational view of theology. The second failure was evangelicalism's "amnesia"—the deficient recognition of the continuity of the church in history. This deficiency was evident in the evangelical disinterest in church history and in the traditions of the church preceding the Reformation.

The corrective was set out in a document—"The Chicago Call: An Appeal to Evangelicals." The prescription involved eight areas: a recovery of the church's historic roots and continuity (the major issue facing evangelical Christianity),[16] biblical fidelity, creedal identity, holistic salvation, sacramental integrity, spirituality, church authority, and church unity.

The Chicago Call represented what would become a common theme in Webber's lifework—discouraging wall building, looking for the common Christian basis, and seeking unity amidst diversity.

As mentioned, Webber found this unity and common basis in what he calls "classical Christianity." According to Webber, the good news is that this premodern (indeed, premedieval) Christianity has more in common with our postmodern culture than it does with the modernism out of which evangelicalism (and liberalism) grew. In fact, Webber is convinced that the postmodern world is a "rich cultural context" for the recovery of the classical view of the church and its message.[17] In answer to the question, Where does one go to find a Christianity that speaks meaningfully to the postmodern world? Webber answers:

> The classical tradition appears to be the most productive. It was shaped by mystery, holism, interpreted facts, community, and a combination of verbal and symbolic forms of communication. Therefore our challenge is not to reinvent Christianity, but to restore and then adapt classical Christianity to the postmodern cultural situation.[18]

In a sense, it was modernism that did reinvent Christianity. The modernist paradigm embraces individualism, rationalism, and factualism. (By the latter, Webber refers to the confidence that individuals can arrive at objective truth through reason.) These are built on the "convictions" of foundationalism, structuralism, and the notion of the metanarrative.[19] And modernism has reconfigured our conceptions of Christ, the church, worship, spirituality, mission, and authority.

To illustrate the modernist innovation, Webber cites the rationalistic approach to the Bible. The Bible has been lifted out of the context of the work of the Holy Spirit in the church, making it the object of rational criticism. The Bible's rightful authority can only be restored by returning it to its place in the development of the entire spectrum of Christian thought in the church's first six centuries and learning to read it canonically again.[20]

In a similar manner, the Enlightenment approach has led to a problematic conception of the church, emphasizing pragmatism in its atheological understanding of church and individualism in its ahistorical—we might say "chronocentric"—understanding of the church. This can only be corrected by a return to a biblically based theology of the church (emphasizing four New Testament images) and the four apostolic marks (as enumerated in the Apostles' Creed).[21]

Modernism has also failed the church in the area of spirituality. Its atemporal approach prompts us to ignore the resources the Holy Spirit has given to us through the history of the church. We act as though Christ's work does not relate to history and culture, due to a secular/sacred split engendered by secularization. With an overly confident dependence on human reason, we operate as though Christ did not save the mind. We confuse the Faith with conformity to subcultural standards (such as identifying Christianity with Western culture). We focus on rules and moralism that fail to help us grow into holistic and healthy relationships with all of life. And we stress overfamiliarity with God.[22]

Webber believes classical, premodern Christianity is just what the postmodern culture ordered to address what ails it. Classical Christianity emphasizes the unifying centrality of the Christ event, mystery rather than Enlightenment rationalism, community rather than modernist individualism, symbolic communication in addition to discursive communication, and holism rather than the fragmentation of life. But even more than all of that, what Webber has always found to be the most compelling feature of the early church's faith is its emphasis on the victorious Christ. More than anything else, this emphasis addresses postmodernism's difficulty with the problem of evil and the meaning of life.

> His victory over evil is the key not only to the early Christian tradition but to the renewal of our personal faith and to the renewal of the life of the church. I want to show how every aspect of the Christian life relates to Christ's victory over the power of evil and to the ultimate renewal of all things.[23]

The Incarnate Word and the Victorious Christ

The most consistently pressing theme in Webber's recovery of the early church for contemporary evangelicalism is his emphasis on *Christus victor*. When this is coupled with a proper understanding of the implications of the incarnation—an ignorance of which Webber argues lies at the root of much of the church's failure and its dependence on modernism[24]—an indispensable pattern is established for our conception of the church and its relation to the world. As God is in Christ and as the church is the body of Christ, so the church is to be in the world: "The church in her worship, her theology, her mission, and her spirituality, is to incarnate Jesus Christ in visible form."[25] The crucial question becomes, What kind of Christ have we incarnated? Though the cultural context to which this question is applied has changed, this same concern has haunted Webber throughout the twenty-five-year stretch from the publication of *Common Roots* to the release of *Ancient-Future Faith*.

The fusion of incarnation and *Christus victor* is clear in *The Church in the World*, where the overriding theme of the book is

> . . . a christological vision of the church and the world. Christ, the victor over the powers of evil, will restore the created order in the consummation with the final defeat of evil powers. The church, now commissioned to proclaim this message, heralds the defeat of evil with its power to distort the spheres of creation, and thus provides hope for humanity and the world in the eschatological vision which it declares and by which it seeks to live.[26]

An adequate conception of the church, then, must consider its christological source, its soteriological function, and its eschatological anticipation. The church is an extension of the incarnation—a continued presence of Christ in the world under the lordship of the one who has conquered the powers of evil that work through the structures of existence to distort God's creative and redeeming work.[27]

The church is to witness to Christ's defeat of the powers of evil through its worship, evangelism, and social action. The church is a new community in which loyalty to Christ determines how individuals relate to each other, to the world, and to the powers.

In fact, Webber celebrates the church's role as an agent of God's power in the world. As Satan wars against the church, the church exposes evil and acts as an agent of reconciliation. It unmasks Satan's power and uncovers his lies through its preaching, prayers, sacraments, and lifestyle. The church witnesses to Christ's dethronement of the powers that, as God's creation, have turned against God.[28]

In his emphasis on *Christus victor* and the church's role as the ongoing incarnation of Christ's presence in the world, Webber gives us a much fuller and richer sense of what it means to be a "witness." It is a role that engages us in every dimension of life (because Christ's work has cosmic significance) and in every activity (as opposed to just verbally sharing a tract).

Engaging the Culture

In keeping with the nature of the church's witness, Webber constantly refers to the church as a "counter" or "alternative" culture.[29] On the surface, one is tempted to see a preference for the Anabaptist or antithetical approach to culture. But such a conclusion would be premature. Webber consistently employs the incarnate Christ as a paradigm for the church's relation to the world: the church is to be *separate* from the ideologies that rule the world, *identified* with the world to whom it is communicating the gospel, and seeking to *transform* the world.[30]

In his usual fashion, Webber incorporates or balances the three historic and dominant responses the church has taken toward the world, emphasizing one or the other as the culture changes and as the church in human history attempts to fulfill its responsibility to be the kingdom of God. In *The Secular Saint,* he identifies the three options as "Separational," "Identificational," and "Transformational." In these three ways, the church serves the kingdom, the coming of which was foreseen in the Old Testament, was inaugurated by Christ, and will be consummated when the battle in which the church engages, in both personal and social dimensions, is over.[31]

Incorporating all three models does not imply that Webber is naïve about their shortcomings. The ultimate separation of sacred and secular and the denial of the incarnational nature of the church's presence in the world is precisely where the otherwise helpful Anabaptist response is deficient—a fault that Webber applauds John Howard Yoder for correcting. Webber appreciates Luther's view of the church in the world as incarnational, but criticizes it for suggesting that Christ's lordship over the world is not exercised by the church but through the government and the structures of existence; with its truncated eschatology this unhappily leads to a cultural conservatism. With Calvin, the incarnational presence of Christ works through the church and Christ's lordship over the structures of existence is affirmed. This is good, but the Reformed position tends in the opposite direction of Luther with equally bad effects, namely, leading the church to attempt the Christianization of the powers and ecclesial dominion over the structures of existence.[32]

What Webber is doing here is what he does in much of his work: he gives us a historical perspective so that we can avoid chronocentrism and learn from the entire church. This is his tactic, whether he is dealing with worship, the proper understanding of the atonement, or in this case, the evangelical church's response to the culture. And as we have demonstrated, his historical treatments usually employ instructive models or paradigms.

In fact, Webber wrote *The Secular Saint* in 1979 because, despite the awakening social consciousness of evangelicals in the 1970s (such as the Chicago Declaration[33]), he believed that

> many Evangelicals are still confused about how they are to be responsible Christians in the world . . . due, at least in part, to our failure to have a historical perspective on the question. For the most part we are calling for social concern without understanding the various ways in which Christians have functioned in the world in the past. . . . The Evangelical who has a good grasp of social theology and the historic models of Christian social action should be in a better position to understand his own responsibility in culture.[34]

Ultimately, *the* model for Webber is the incarnation of the one who is victorious over the powers through his death, resurrection, and second appearance. Cosmic redemption through the atoning work of Christ understood primarily as *Christus victor* and recapitulation[35] guides the church in her relation to the world and its powers. But precisely because the church's role is an incarnational one, the church's relation to the world is dynamic and responsive. So Webber brings together the disparate views of Yoder, Berkhof, and the "Epistle of Diognetus," for example, reminding us that there are no easy answers, formulae, exclusive strategies, or once-and-for-all models. The actual engagement of the world by the church is very complex and tension filled.[36]

Still, Webber has his preferences and criticisms of some strategies. He is less inclined to endorse the Constantinian church, for instance. He offers this poignant assessment: "Unfortunately, it was not civilization that was Christianized as much as Christianity that was civilized. . . . Thus, the church shifted from an incarnational approach to the world to one that assumed the lordship of Christ over the structures of existence."[37]

This is one of the reasons that Webber offered a critical assessment of Jerry Falwell and the Moral Majority in 1981.[38] Webber appreciated their biblical vision of reality, but their vision had been so acculturated as a response to secular humanism (about which Webber wrote another volume, *Secular Humanism, Threat and Challenge*) that traditional biblical categories had become greatly modified. For example, in the Moral Majority's vision creation has become creationism. The reality of sin is denied when it comes to "mighty men" in business and politics. The covenantal community is too closely aligned with the United States. God's holiness is stressed, but not God's mercy in saving the cosmos. Salvation rightly has political dimensions, but this soteriology is national rather than cosmic. The church has become politicized, and eschatology has become a timetable.

In the end, a Constantinian view of the relation of church and state wrongly identifies the United States as a Christian nation, weds Christianity to conservative politics, supports militarization, and ignores the reality of pluralism. Such civil religion (for which Webber had similar criticisms of John Richard Neuhaus) does not maintain the requisite tension between church and state, so the gospel and the church lose their prophetic edge and become tools of earthly powers.

Webber would not fault the Religious Right's attempt to wrestle the "new demons" of contemporary society, its opposition to secularism, and its sincerity and zeal, but it simply fails to maintain a clear biblical, christological, and cosmic concept of the church and the world. He favored a more "centrist" approach that parted company not only with the Religious Right but also with the ideologues of the left (such as the World Council of Churches), who are equally guilty of distorting the biblical perspective, politicizing the gospel, associating the faith with a particular political movement, and "spiritual legalism."[39]

Over against the extremes of the right and the left, Webber proposes a centrist and prophetic position that is maintained through a "radical understanding" of evil, Christ, and the church. On *this* basis, the church *should* be concerned about issues such as personal morality, abortion, the family, justice, the poor, racism, materialism, militarism, sexism, and stewardship of energy.[40] Further, in Webber's treatment of "secular humanism," he provided more specifics about the church's transforming role. The church should not enter into compromising political and economic alliances, nor try to accomplish its task in society through political power or legislative force. But it should take a more aggressive role in teaching Christian values without being moralistic or legalistic. The church can and should act as a social critic through prayer, the sacraments, preaching, and example. The church should engage in personal evangelism, intellectual competition, vocational servanthood, and organizational witness and impact on culture (but not through manipulation, coercion, or censorship).[41]

These are not themes that Webber has relegated to the 1980s. In his most recent work he defines the threefold mission of the church as evangelism, education, and making an impact on the world. This threefold mission has further implications for the church of the postmodern era.

> In evangelism there will be an increasing shift away from mass rallies to evangelism by the local church. Believers will bring friends and neighbors to the church, where people will be brought into the church through conversion and baptism. The process of evangelism will be connected with worship, and the emphasis on education will be on gaining wisdom.
> Finally, the church in the postmodern world will play a prophetic and priestly ministry in society. Believing that the gospel applies to every area of personal, social, moral, and national life, it will seek to exert an influence on society by being an alternative culture within society. Many congregations will recognize that the Christian vision of reality, informed by the politics of the kingdom, will keep the church free of particular political agendas so that it may speak to and serve the whole society as an alternative community.[42]

At one point in his ruminations about the church's role in the world, Webber takes a slightly different tack. The basis is the same: the church must be oriented by its theology, particularly in its understanding of the powers and Christ's victory, the "already and not yet" character of the kingdom, and the church's existence as an eschatological community. But under the influence of narrative theology and theologians such as Stanley Hauerwas, Webber wrestles with Rodney Clapp in *The People of the Truth* to understand how the church can focus on itself in worship and mission without withdrawing from the wider society and dwindling into an ineffective and sectarian body. Their answer is clear: "By recognizing and reaffirming its own distinctive identity and vision [from the biblical story learned in worship], the church can in fact be a more potent social and political presence than it now is."[43] Most importantly, this calls for "depth politics," effected primarily through worship, which is ultimately itself a kind of politics. "Depth politics is happening whenever anyone makes a deliberate and structured attempt to influence how people live in society."[44] The church effectively engages the culture not by commandeering political, economic, and social structures, as the far right and far left have attempted, but primarily by inculturating Christians who will then interpret their lives through the lens of God's story of the creation, redemption, and victorious recreation of the world through Jesus Christ.

Worship, then, becomes the "remembrance and reenactment of the story," or more specifically, it is "the rehearsal of the Christ event through which one's experience with God is established, maintained, and repaired."[45] In this recapitulation of the Christ event, we enact the Gospel.[46] Rather than being a retreat from the real world, worship enables Christians to see the world the way it

really is and it equips them to live in it."[47] In other words, worship is formative; it "grooms people to think theologically and act doxologically."[48]

Worship, then, is a political act, because people are shaped by God's action
on us, which is centered in Christ, and which necessitates a human response.
This involves more than discursive communication—an emphasis of the
Enlightenment that has influenced the way many evangelical churches think
about worship. Without neglecting discursive communication, worship is oriented more by "communal or cultural communication." *Lex orandi, lex credendi* ("The rule of prayer is the rule of belief").

> That is, the primary purpose of worship is not to provide discursive teaching
> about God, Christ, sin, salvation, the church, ethical behavior, and social con-
> cern. Instead, the primary purpose of worship is to experience faith in the com-
> munity of worship in such a way that the Christian faith is not merely known
> intellectually, but experienced as a reality.[49]

In a conversation over breakfast one morning Bob called this a "liturgical
epistemology."

Recovering the Church's Worship

Bringing worship into the realm of the church's political engagement with the
culture comes as no surprise to anyone who has followed Webber's career for the
last two decades. Worship has taken the central position in his life and in his writing. In fact, Bob has become one of the foremost evangelical voices on worship.
In the fall of 2000 he was installed as the Meyers Professor of Ministry, a chair
that he currently occupies at Northern Baptist Seminary. Previously, in 1994, he
founded the Institute for Worship Studies, which he still oversees.

Webber's prominence as an authority on worship in academic and ecclesial
circles is perhaps rooted in his past. But in another sense, worship has always
been influential in Bob's life—even under the modernist and fundamentalist
sway of his Baptist upbringing. The journey to a sacramental approach to life
really began with his baptism at age thirteen and continued with meaningful
communion services while growing up. Of his baptism Webber wrote,

> Little did I know at that tender age how much my baptism would mean to me
> at a later date. I have often reflected not only on the meaning of baptism, but
> also on its significance for me. That was no trivial event, no mere ritual of puberty.
> It was a life-changing event which I am still seeking to interpret and apply to
> my life.[50]

Indeed, his interpretation of the sacraments falls under the central motif we
have seen throughout this survey of his theology—that which he learned from

the early church, namely, the incarnational nature of Christianity. The sacraments "inflesh" the gospel, for the material world is the vehicle of our salvation. Webber also came to a deeper understanding of the word *sacrament* as he investigated the Latin Bible's translation of the Greek word *mysterion*. As he discovered, the word literally means "to make holy." The sacraments signify Christ to us and provide a sign of his transforming encounter with us. As he explained in *Evangelicals on the Canterbury Trail,*

> I no longer regard the sacraments as magical or pagan. Rather, I have come to believe they are visible means through which the saving and healing action of God through Jesus Christ is communicated to his people. The sacraments do not save us. They are vehicles through which the salvation of the world accomplished by Christ is extended to us. They bring Christ to us and touch us with his healing power.[51]

The modernist impulse has a difficult time with this conception. The evangelicalism that was nurtured by this impulse prefers to view the sacraments exclusively as human acts. Webber bemoans this impoverishment. Rather than just focusing on human actions, we need to recover an understanding of the sacraments as mysterious acts of *God* on us.

This sacramental activity is not confined to baptism and the Eucharist. As Webber understood the meaning of the word *sacrament* more fully, he also came to the realization that Jesus Christ *is* the sacrament—the only one who can make us holy.[52] Furthermore, *everything* in life points to the center—Jesus Christ, the Creator and Redeemer. Bob had already believed this as an evangelical. But now it had a name. And now it also helped him to appreciate the sacramental possibilities in all of life—from nature to the arts (which themselves are grounded in an incarnational theology).[53]

The same modernist impulse that has diminished the evangelical treatment of the sacraments has also forced us to develop a more biblical and historically informed theology of worship. Instead of organizing worship around stylistic preferences that perpetuate squabbles about the "right kind" of music, or instead of organizing worship around the concept of a performance dominated by the pastor, with the congregation serving as little more than an audience, Webber rightly insists that the key to the content and meaning of worship must be the Christian metanarrative (the story of God's saving work in history, culminating in the work of Christ to overthrow the powers of evil and eventually establish the kingdom of God). Even the *order* of worship is to be dictated by the Christian story. This would lead churches to move beyond the false options of heartfelt spontaneity versus dead ritual. Instead, the order of worship must be centered around Word and Table as vehicles through which the story of Christ's work is proclaimed and enacted.

And over against the modernist's preoccupation with words and cognitive understanding, symbolic communication must be reintroduced into the church's worship, which means giving more attention to the way we use space, how we select music and its place in the order of service, how we employ the arts to serve the theme of worship, how biblically and historically informed our celebrations of baptism and communion are, and how we participate in the gospel by ordering our lives around the church year ("*Christus victor* time, a time that lives in the expectation of the recapitulation").[54]

And so we come back to where we started—namely, Webber's recognition of postmodernism's receptive bent toward classical Christianity's understanding of worship, his unwillingness to allow reason to dominate over mystery, or verbal communication over the symbolic. True, the metanarrative of Christianity must be unapologetically rehearsed and proclaimed in Christian worship as the only true story of the cosmos—an affirmation that does not set well with most postmoderns. But the communication of this story in the active *event* of Christian worship[55] will be welcomed by postmoderns, if we draw on the entire history of worship that contributes direction for its order in the ancient church's ritual (preparation, hearing the Word, responding at the Table, dismissal), as well as the Reformation emphasis on the Word, the Free Church's Christocentric focus, and the contemporary church's sense of the Spirit's presence and greater intimacy. This is the "blended worship" that Webber endorses, one that is energized by a "convergence" of the charismatic movement and liturgical renewal.[56] It is a blending and convergence that is perhaps appropriate for a postmodern culture in which life is seen more as a collage than as a linear progression of reasoned arguments and carefully aligned evidences. Through such worship, Webber insists, we will find a source of empowerment, evangelism, education, spirituality, and social action.[57] If Webber is not right, then we *must* find another alternative, for Webber has always been correct about one thing—"the church is the primary focus of God's activity in the world."[58]

A Postscript

It took little prodding to convice me to write a chapter for this book. It was an honor to be asked, for Bob has not only been a very influential teacher in my life, but also, for the past thirteen years, a highly respected and cherished colleague. My late colleague Tim Phillips (who was my contemporary at Wheaton as a student and was equally affected by Bob) was right when he assessed that Bob was the best lecturer in our department. He was (and is) the master of using charts and diagrams to get his point across.

Bob's celebration of "blended worship" and his charitable critical assessment of the Moral Majority *and* the World Council of Churches exemplify what I know firsthand: Bob is not only evenhanded but gracious toward all. When he writes, "Christianity is like a diamond. To see it in all of its fullness and beauty, we must see it from all of its sides,"[59] he is not simply waxing theoretical. His treatment of others belies that this is a deep-seated conviction. He does indeed look for the common core while celebrating the diversity of God's kingdom.

Of course, Bob's magnanimity shows up in his eagerness to collaborate with and learn from others. This is evident in his books and his inclusion of others in leading seminars and workshops that he has coordinated.

The one incident I will never forget from the time when Bob and I shared small offices next to each other at Wheaton is the bleak, slushy, cold Chicago winter morning when I trudged into the office and sarcastically said, "Well, Bob, this is the day the Lord has made." Without missing a beat, Bob replied, "Yeah, but he's done better."

In leaving Wheaton, Bob offered a retirement speech to the department that included a lighthearted list of "Ten Things They Said About Bob Webber," betraying that Bob is even humble enough to describe himself as he would the weather. God may have done better. But for the church's sake, I'm glad that God saw fit to make Bob Webber, and that so many have had the opportunity to celebrate this gift of God. Let us rejoice and give thanks for him.

Notes

Chapter 1

1. Carolyn Gratton, noted for her work in psychology and spiritual direction, describes this threefold movement as a process for spiritual formation. She uses the terms "integration, collapse, and new integration." See Carolyn Gratton, *The Art of Spiritual Guidance* (New York: Crossroad, 1993). James Fowler, in his studies of human and faith development, discusses Piaget's model of moving from equilibrium to trust (resolution), with a period of dislocation leading to trust. See James W. Fowler, *Stages of Faith: The Psychology of Human Development and the Quest for Meaning* (San Francisco: Harper and Row, 1981). For an analysis of certain psalms by applying the sequence of "orientation, disorientation, and reorientation," see Walter Brueggemann, *The Message of the Psalms* (Minneapolis: Augsburg, 1984).

2. Gratton, *Art of Spiritual Guidance,* 40–41.

3. Though some theorists argue that tradition provides continuity during times of disorientation (religious tradition, for example), in the case of worship, it is tradition itself that is being tested and therefore serves as the actual source of the disorientation. I suggest this is one reason worship trends of the past two decades have been so disruptive to congregations; the very thing that typically provides continuity is being threatened.

4. Mary Ann Zollman, "Introduction to Spiritual Direction," (class lecture, Dusquesne University, 16 June 1993).

5. John Fenwick and Bryan Spinks, *Worship in Transition: The Liturgical Movement in the Twentieth Century* (New York: Continuum, 1995), 7–8.

6. Gordon S. Wakefield, *An Outline of Christian Worship* (Edinburgh: T and T Clark, 1998), 153–54.

7. John Fenwick and Bryan Spinks, *Worship in Transition: The Liturgical Movement in the Twentieth Century* (New York: Continuum, 1995), 5–10.

8. Robert Webber, "Preparing for Ministry in a Postmodern World: The Worship-Driven Church," *Creator* (May/June 2000): 5.

9. Ibid.

10. Barry Liesch, *The New Worship* (Grand Rapids: Baker, 1996), 75–76.

11. David Tracy, "Theology and the Many Faces of Postmodernity," in *Readings in Modern Theology,* ed. Robin Gill (Nashville: Abingdon, 1995), 225.

12. C. S. Lewis, *The Screwtape Letters* (New York: Simon and Schuster, 1961), 91–92. Emphasis mine.

13. Richard M. Riss, "The Charismatic Renewal," in *The Complete Library of Christian Worship,* vol. 2 (Nashville: Star Song; Peabody, Mass.: Hendrickson, 1994), 121.

14. See James F. White, *Protestant Worship: Traditions in Transition* (Louisville: Westminster/John Knox, 1989), chapter 11.

15. Julie Bogart, "What You Can Learn about Leading Worship from a Rock Star" *Worship Leader* 10, no. 5 (July/August 2001): 24.

16. Robert Webber, "The Praise and Worship Renewal," in *The Complete Library of Christian Worship,* vol. 2 (Nashville: Star Song; Peabody, Mass.: Hendrickson, 1994), 131.

17. German Martinez, "The Impact of the Constitution on the Sacred Liturgy," in *The Complete Library of Christian Worship,* vol. 2 (Nashville: Star Song; Peabody, Mass.: Hendrickson, 1994), 108.

18. "The Constitution on the Sacred Liturgy," in *The Complete Library of Christian Worship,* vol. 2 (Nashville: Star Song; Peabody, Mass.: Hendrickson, 1994), 317–22.

19. For a solid review of the reception of the reforms of Vatican II, see Lawrence Madden, ed., *The Awakening Church: Twenty-five Years of Liturgical Renewal* (Collegeville, Minn.: Liturgical, 1992). For a more recent analysis, see Regis Duffy, *An American Emmaus* (New York: Crossroad, 1995).

20. George Barna, "Worship in the Third Millennium," in *Experience God in Worship* (Loveland, Colo.: Group, 2000) 18–19.

21. For a detailed analysis of the various types of postmodernism and their implications, see Pauline Marie Rosenau, *Post-Modernism and the Social Sciences: Insights, Inroads, and Intrusions* (Princeton: Princeton University Press, 1992), especially pages 3–20.

22. Stanley J. Grenz, *A Primer on Postmodernism* (Grand Rapids: Eerdmans, 1996), 14.

23. Robert Webber, *Ancient-Future Faith: Rethinking Evangelicalism for a Postmodern World* (Grand Rapids: Baker, 1999), 81–82.

24. J. Richard Middleton and Brian J. Walsh, *Truth Is Stranger than It Used to Be: Biblical Faith in a Postmodern Age* (Downers Grove, Ill.: InterVarsity Press, 1995), 11.

25. Sally Morganthaler, *Worship Evangelism: Inviting Unbelievers into the Presence of God* (Grand Rapids: Zondervan, 1995), 18.

26. The length of each cultural era has, to date, encompassed multiple generations. For instance, the Enlightenment, beginning approximately 1648, at the end of the Thirty Years War, extended to around 1800, marked by the publication of Immanuel Kant's *Critique of Reason*. Likewise, the modern era lasted from about 1750 to 1900 (overlapping the Enlightenment period). In the early 1970s, postmodernism was recognized as the beginning of an era, marked by some as the failure of the Pruitt-Igoe housing project in St. Louis, Missouri, a project that attempted to create the utopian society thought possible by the modern mindset. For more on the beginnings of postmodernism, see Grenz, *A Primer on Postmodernism* and Terry Eagleton, *The Illusions of Postmodernism* (Cambridge, Mass.: Blackwell, 1996). Because each era overlaps in time, and because we are near the beginning of the postmodern era, it may be concluded that our culture is presently in a transition from one era to another.

27. See Richard Cimino and Don Latin, *Shopping for Faith: American Religion in the New Millennium* (San Francisco: Jossey-Bass, 1998).

28. Pierre Babin, *The New Era in Religious Communication* (Minneapolis: Fortress, 1991).

29. For example, see chapter 11 of this book, Robert K. Johnston, "Visual Christianity: The Peril of Pleasure and the Value of the Experience"

30. Babin, *The New Era*, 21.

31. Regarding the influence of the printing press on Christianity, see Edward Muir, *Ritual in Early Modern Europe* (New York: Cambridge University Press, 1997).

32. Babin, *The New Era*, 29.

Chapter 2

1. As found in recent Youth Specialties training material. Cited by permission of Dan Kimball, Santa Cruz Bible Church, Santa Cruz, California, in an e-mail to the author, 14 March 2001. These terms refer to the logical sequencing of actions within worship. An organic approach to worship provides opportunity for the multilayering of actions.

2. From the online forum accessed through <http://www.easumbandy.com/forums.htm> (July and August 2000).

3. Kathy Black, *Worship across Cultures: A Handbook* (Nashville: Abingdon, 1998). In this book, Black

analyzes worship in Southern California among twenty-one different ethnic groups.

4. For "multimedia worship," see Paul Franklyn, "Tech-Knowledge for Ministry: Multimedia Worship," *Net Results* 18, no. 7 (July 1997): 4; for "authentic worship," see Sally Morganthaler, "Out of the Box: Authentic Worship in a Postmodern Culture," *Worship Leader* (May/June 1998): 24–32; for "liturgical worship," "praise and worship," and "seeker services," see Andy Langford, *Transitions in Worship: Moving from Traditional to Contemporary* (Nashville: Abingdon, 1999), 18.

5. Timothy Wright, *A Community of Joy: How to Create Contemporary Worship* (Nashville: Abingdon, 1994), 57.

6. George Barna, et al., *Experience God in Worship* (Loveland, Colo.: Group, 2000). The categories used included "convergence," "liturgical," "contemporary," "evangelical," "African-American," "Charismatic," and "Gen-X."

7. Compare the characterization of contemporary worship in Daniel T. Benedict and Craig Kennet Miller, *Contemporary Worship for the Twenty-first Century: Worship or Evangelism?* (Nashville: Discipleship Resources, 1994), 10–16 and 120.

8. See, for example, Eva Stimson, "Praise God with Guitars and Organ?" *Presbyterians Today* (September 1998): 12.

9. See Robert Webber, *Signs of Wonder: The Phenomenon of Convergence in Modern Liturgical and Charismatic Churches* (Nashville: Abbott Martyn, 1992); republished as *The Worship Phenomenon: A Dynamic New Awakening in Worship Is Reviving the Body of Christ* (Nashville: Star Song, 1994); republished as *Blended Worship: Achieving Substance and Relevance in Worship* (Peabody, Mass.: Hendrickson, 1996). See also Robert Webber, *Renew Your Worship: A Study in the Blending of Traditional and Contemporary Worship* (Peabody, Mass.: Hendrickson, 1997); Rober Webber, *Planning Blended Worship: The Creative Mixture of Old and New* (Nashville: Abingdon, 1998); and Robert Webber et al., *Renew! Songs and Hymns for Blended Worship* (Carol Stream, Ill.: Hope, 1995).

10. Langford, *Transitions in Worship*, 18. See also Benedict and Miller, *Contemporary Worship for the Twenty-first Century*.

11. Leonard Sweet, *Soul Tsunami: Sink or Swim in New Millennium Culture* (Grand Rapids: Zondervan, 1999), 390–91.

12. L. Edward Phillips and Sara Webb Phillips, *In Spirit and Truth: United Methodist Worship for the Emerging Church* (Nashville: Discipleship Resources, 2000), 30. See also Thomas G. Long, *Beyond the Worship Wars: Building Vital and Faithful Worship* (Alban Institute, 2001), 3; and Marianne Sawicki, "How Can Christian Worship Be Contemporary?" in *What Is*

"Contemporary" Worship? ed. Gordon Lathrop (Minneapolis: Augsburg Fortress, 1995), 27.

13. Long, *Beyond the Worship Wars,* 12.

14. Constance Cherry, "Blended Worship: What It Is, What It Isn't," *Reformed Worship* 55 (March 2000): 6–8.

15. "About Us. Easum, Bandy, and Associates Organizational Assumptions," <http://www.easumbandy.com/about.htm#Mission> (12 July 2001).

16. William M. Easum, "Worship in a Changing Culture," in *Contemporary Worship: A Sourcebook for Spirited-Traditional, Praise and Seeker Services,* ed. Tim Wright and Jan Wright (Nashville: Abingdon, 1997), 17–18.

17. William M. Easum and Thomas G. Bandy, *Growing Spiritual Redwoods* (Nashville: Abingdon, 1997), 73. A comparative chart is provided on pages 73–74.

18. Ibid., 74–75.

19. Ibid., 72.

20. Ibid., 76–77. These categories are not defined very clearly. They appear to deal with individual types of interactions with the gospel message.

21. Ibid., 80–83.

22. Ibid., 94–95.

23. Thomas G. Bandy, "How Do We Multi-Track Our Worship?" *Net Results* 21, no. 7 (July 2000): 17.

24. William M. Easum, "What I Now See in Worship," *Net Results* 21, no. 6 (June 2000): 20–22.

25. Ibid., 22.

26. Bandy, "How Do We Multi-Track Our Worship?" 15.

27. Only a few statements in the writings of Easum and Bandy indicate a concern with the theological content of worship. See Easum and Bandy, *Growing Spiritual Redwoods,* 51–52.

28. For a similar critique of Easum, see Frank Burch Brown, *Good Taste, Bad Taste, and Christian Taste: Aesthetics in Religious Life* (New York: Oxford University Press, 2000), 238–42.

29. Easum and Bandy, *Growing Spiritual Redwoods,* 74; and Easum, "Worship in a Changing Culture," 17.

30. Easum and Bandy, *Growing Spiritual Redwoods,* 75.

31. See Brown, *Good Taste, Bad Taste, and Christian Taste,* 243.

32. Paul Basden, *The Worship Maze: Finding a Style to Fit Your Church* (Downers Grove, Ill.: InterVarsity Press, 1999).

33. Ibid., 101–3.

34. Ibid., 36.

35. Ibid.

36. Ibid., 54.

37. Ibid., 55.

38. Ibid., 66.

39. Ibid., 77.

40. Ibid., 89.

41. Ibid., 67.

42. Ibid., 42.

43. Ibid., 60, 85–86.

44. James White's earliest attempt came in the mid-1970s: "Traditions of Protestant Worship," *Worship* 49, no. 5 (May 1975): 272–81. This article was substantially reproduced in *Christian Worship in Transition* (Nashville: Abingdon, 1976), 61–75. Refinement continued in the 1980s: *Introduction to Christian Worship,* 1st ed. (Nashville: Abingdon, 1980), 41–43; "Creativity: The Free Church Tradition," in *Liturgy: A Creative Tradition,* vol. 162 of *Concilium,* ed. Mary Collins and David Power (New York: Seabury, 1983), 47–52; "The Classification of Protestant Traditions of Worship," *Studia Liturgica* 17 (1987): 264–72. In 1989 a mature form of the taxonomy became the basis for a whole book: *Protestant Worship: Traditions in Transition* (Louisville: Westminster/John Knox, 1989), 21–24.

45. White, *Protestant Worship,* 22. For his earlier version, see White, "Traditions of Protestant Worship," 272.

46. White, *Protestant Worship,* 22.

47. One of the major changes in White's later forms of the taxonomy is the elimination of the "Free Church" terminology to define certain Protestant traditions. Earlier forms of the taxonomy speak of three different historic manifestations of a Free Church approach to worship. Later forms of the taxonomy use different terms instead: Anabaptist, Puritan/separatist, and frontier. For further consideration of the term "frontier," see Lester Ruth, "Reconsidering the Emergence of the Second Great Awakening and Camp Meetings among Early Methodists," *Worship* 75 , no.4 (July 2001): 354–55.

48. White, *Protestant Worship,* 23.

49. James White, *Documents of Christian Worship: Descriptive and Interpretive Sources* (Louisville: Westminster/John Knox, 1992), 7, 9.

50. See the similar critique in Keith Watkins, "Protestant Worship: Many Traditions or One?" *Worship* 64, no. 4 (July 1990): 309. Another critique of White's taxonomy is given by Frank C. Senn in "Protestant Worship: Does It Exist?" *Worship* 64, no. 4 (July 1990): 322–30. Both scholars argue, not persuasively I believe, that Protestantism properly defined constitutes a single worship tradition.

51. White, *Protestant Worship,* 22. White, "The Classification of Protestant Traditions," 266. White also notes an awkwardness in his taxonomy in that certain groups (Moravians, Shakers, Brethren) do not easily fit within his tradition labels. See White, *Protestant Worship,* 23.

52. White, "The Classification of Protestant Traditions," 267.

53. Ibid., 272; White, "Traditions of Protestant Worship," 282. White has in mind primarily the shar-

ing within the liturgical movement, but the same point could be made about more popular influences, such as megachurches like Willow Creek and Saddleback Community churches.

54. White, "Traditions of Protestant Worship," 282.

55. To a lesser degree, Basden's analysis of the inner character of different liturgical approaches is also helpful.

56. Robert Webber, *Planning Blended Worship,* 20. See also Robert Webber, *Worship Old and New,* rev. ed. (Grand Rapids: Zondervan, 1994), 149–51; and Webber, *Renew Your Worship,* 32.

57. See, for example, Webber, *Worship Old and New,* 149–50.

58. *The United Methodist Book of Worship* (Nashville: United Methodist Publishing House, 1992), 87.

59. Kim Miller et al., *Handbook for Multi-Sensory Worship* (Nashville: Abingdon, 1999), 9.

60. For an example, see Webber, *Signs of Wonder,* 37.

61. John D. Witvliet, "At Play in the House of the Lord: Why Worship Matters," *Books and Culture* 4, no. 6 (November/December 1998): 23. For a popular description of the sacramentality of music, against which Robert Webber reacted negatively, see Robert Webber, "Reducing God to Music? We Experience God in More than Songs and Segues," *Leadership* 20 (spring 1999): 35.

62. Could the internal fights many congregations have over worship style actually be disputes about different approaches to liturgical sacramentality, not about the styles themselves?

63. John D. Witvliet, "The Blessing and Bane of the North American Mega-Church," *Jahrbuch für Liturgik und Hymnologie* (1998): 201–2. Witvliet provides an extensive bibliography in note 15 of the same article.

64. Ruth Ann Ashton, *God's Presence through Music* (South Bend, Ind.: Lesea, 1993).

65. Carl S. Dudley and David A. Roozen, *Faith Communities Today: A Report on Religion in the United States Today* (Hartford, Conn.: Hartford Institute for Religion Research at Hartford Seminary, March 2001), <http://fact.hartsem.edu/Final percent20FAC-Trpt.pdf>, (12 July 2001), 40.

66. To be truly accurate, two other possibilities for different kinds of sacramentality must be included in this scheme: fellowship-organized and aesthetics-organized. In the former, emphasis is placed on the community itself as the locus of God's presence. Classic Quaker worship might place in this category. In aesthetics-organized sacramentality, the worshipers sense God's presence through the worship environment itself. The aesthetics-organized approach could apply to everything from the Precious Moments Chapel in Carthage, Missouri, to the National Cathe-

dral in Washington, D.C., and is determined as much by taste as by theology.

67. White, *Traditions in Transition,* 22.

Chapter 3

1. Michael Hamilton, "Willow Creek's Place in History," *Christianity Today* 44, no.13 (13 November 2000): 62–68.

2. Gordon Lathrop, "New Pentecost or Joseph's Britches? Reflections on the History and Meaning of the Worship Ordo in the Megachurches," *Worship* 72 no.6 (Nov. 1998): 527. Tracy Hartman follows Lathrop and another Lutheran liturgist, Frank Senn, in her assessment of Willow Creek's liturgical pedigree, though her reading of the history is more favorable than either Senn's or Lathrop's. See Tracy Hartman, "Problems and Possibilities: Willow Creek Community Church and Implications for Preaching in the Twenty-first Century," *The Academy of Homiletics* 35 (2000): 87–96; see also Frank Senn, "Worship Alive: An Analysis and Critique of 'Alternative Worship Services'," *Worship* 69, no.3 (May 1995): 194–224.

3. See Leigh E. Schmidt, *Holy Fairs: Scottish Communions and American Revivals in the Early Modern Period* (Princeton: Princeton University Press, 1989).

4. White, *Protestant Worship,* 171–91.

5. The adage often used to embody this concept is *lex orandi, lex credendi,* which means that the law of prayer shapes the law of belief. This suggests that theology is picked up primarily inductively, by praying it. See Aidan Kavanaugh, *On Liturgical Theology* (New York: Pueblo, 1984). See also Avery Dulles, "Theology and Worship: The Reciprocity of Belief and Prayer" *Ex Auditu* 8 (1993): 85–94.

6. For a thorough examination of this, see William Harmless, *Augustine and the Catechumenate* (Collegeville, Minn.: Liturgical Press, 1995).

7. For example, see Robert Webber, *Liturgical Evangelism* (Harrisburg, Pa.: Morehouse, 1992); Sonja Stewart and Jerome Berryman, *Young Children and Worship.* (Louisville: Westminster, 1989); and Tina Lillig, *The Catechesis of the Good Shepherd in a Parish Setting* (Chicago: Catechesis of the Good Shepherd, 1998).

8. Robert Wuthnow, *The Reconstructing of American Religion* (Princeton: Princeton University Press, 1988), 37–63.

9. Ibid., 30–31.

10. Ibid., 64.

11. Dean Hoge, Benton Johnson, and Donald Luidens, *Vanishing Boundaries: The Religion of Mainline Protestant Baby Boomers* (Louisville: Westminster/John Knox, 1994), 1.

12. Ibid., 7–9. Studies have identified that the factors attributing to this phenomenon were an increased educational level among the laity, a rise in pluralism, as well as growing privatism and individualism and the

correlating decline of community. Within the church there is a perceived lack of relevance of both the message and the programs; see ibid., 13–17.

13. Wuthnow, *Reconstructing of American Religion,* 71.

14. See Peter Berger, *The Sacred Canopy* (New York: Doubleday, 1967), especially chapter 6, "Secularization and the Problem of Plausibility." This phenomenon of interiorization is supported by Robert Bellah's concept of "Shelia-ism" in *Habits of the Heart* (New York: Perennial Library, 1985), 219–20.

15. David Bakan, "Adolescence in America: From Idea to Social Fact," *Studies in Adolescence,* ed. Robert Grinder (New York: Macmillan, 1975), 3–14.

16. David Barnhart and Allan Metcalf, *America in So Many Words* (New York: Houghton Mifflin, 1999).

17. Mark Senter, *The Coming Revolution in Youth Ministry* (Wheaton: Victor, 1992), 69.

18. Ibid., 53.

19. Ibid., 42.

20. Ibid., 56.

21. For a formidable study of this trial and its lasting cultural and religious impact on American society, see Edward Larson, *Summer for the Gods: The Scopes Trial and America's Continuing Debate over Science and Religion* (New York: Basic, 1997).

22. Senter, *Coming Revolution,* 127.

23. Mark Senter, "The Youth for Christ Movement as an Educational Agency and Its Impact upon Protestant Churches, 1931–1979." (Ph.D. diss., Loyola University Chicago, 1989), 269.

24. Ibid., 273.

25. Ibid., 274.

26. Ibid., 329–32. One of the primary sources disseminating resources for implementing this youth ministry model was Youth Specialties in El Cajon, California.

27. James Twitchell, *AdcultUSA: The Triumph of Advertising in American Culture* (New York: Columbia University Press, 1996), 31–33.

28. Ibid., 36–37.

29. James Mellando, *Willow Creek Community Church* (Harvard Business School Brief #9-691-102, 1991), 5.

30. Senter, *Coming Revolution,* 23–24.

31. Michael Maudlin and Edward Gilbreath, "Selling Out the House of God?" *Christianity Today* 33, no.8 (18 July 1994): 20–25.

32. Verla Gillmor, "Community Is Their Middle Name," *Christianity Today* 44, no. 13 (13 November 2000): 50.

33. James White, "The Americanization of Christian Worship or New Lebanon to Nashville," (unpublished paper, 1995), 6.

34. Donald McGavran, *Understanding Church Growth,* 3d ed. (Grand Rapids: Eerdmans, 1990), 8. This observation was challenged by Lester Ruth who

suggests that church growth does have much to say about worship. See "Lex Agendi, Lex Orandi: Toward an Understanding of Seeker Services as a New Kind of Liturgy," *Worship* 70 (1996): 386–405.

35. Mallado, *Willow Creek Community Church,* 7–13.

36. This pattern has gone through some interesting adaptations, as numerous people now come to Willow Creek's seeker service without a personal invitation, which means there is no way to follow up on their visit and still retain the intentionally anonymous atmosphere of the seeker service. There are also scores of people who find their way to Willow Creek through small groups. This has forced Willow Creek to adjust its seven-step pattern to accommodate these new entry points into the life of the church (Gillmor, "Community Is Their Middle Name," 50–51).

37. Lester Ruth, "The Use of Seeker Services: Models and Questions," *Reformed Liturgy and Music* 30, no. 2 (1996): 48–53.

38. One of the four guiding principals of Willow Creek is "The needs of the seeker differ from those of the believer" (Mellado, *Willow Creek Community Church,* 7).

39. Gustav Niebuhr, "Where Religion Gets a Big Dose of Shopping Mall Culture" *New York Times,* Sunday Late Edition, 16 April 1995, Section 1, 1, 14.

40. Gregory Pritchard, "The Strategy of Willow Creek Community Church: A Study in the Sociology of Religion" (Ph.D. diss., Northwestern University, 1994), 755.

41. Trip Gabriel, "MTV-Inspired Images, but the Message for Children is a Moral One" *New York Times,* Sunday Late Edition, 16 April 1995, Section 1, 14.

42. Hartman, "Problems and Possibilities," 94.

43. For more detailed analysis see Ruth, "Lex Agendi, Lex Orandi."

44. Neibuhr, "Shopping Mall Culture," 14.

45. Hoge et al., *Vanishing Boundaries,* 23.

46. The figure of 75 percent is one that has been used consistently over the last two decades regarding the percentage of Protestants of all denominations who had a primary faith experience through youth ministry. In light of recent studies, this figure may be conservative. Cf "Christian Camps, Conference and Retreat Centers: 1990 Survey Report." (Wheaton, Ill.: Christian Camping International, USA, 1990).

47. E. Byron Anderson, "Liturgical Catechesis," *Religious Education* 92, no. 3 (Summer 1997): 350.

48. Ibid., 352.

49. Keith Roberts, "Ritual and the Transmission of a Cultural Tradition: An Ethnographic Perspective," in *Beyond Establishment: Protestant Identity in a Post-Christian Age,* ed. Jackson Carroll and Wade Clark Roof (Louisville: Westminster/John Knox, 1993), 74–98.

50. Thomas Troeger, "How Culture Shapes the Religious Imagination," *The Academy of Homiletics* 35 (2000): 107–16.

51. See Paul Goldberger, "The Gospel of Church Architecture, Revised" *New York Times*, 20 April 1995, Section C, 1–6; and Gustav Niebuhr, "Protestantism Shifts toward a New Model of How 'Church' is Done" *New York Times*, 29 April 1995, Section 1, 12.

52. Emphasis mine. Stewart Hoover, "The Cross at Willow Creek: Seeker Religion and the Contemporary Marketplace," in *Religion and Popular Culture in America*, ed. Bruce Forbes and Jeffery Mahan (Berkeley: University of California Press, 2000), 145. See also chapter 11 of this book.

53. A focal religious symbol is a symbol that is central to the identity of a religion. Although the symbol may be found in other religions, as in the case of the cross, it has a unique importance to the mythology of the religion for which it is focal. The cross is an archetypal focal symbol for Christians as it symbolizes the death and resurrection of Christ. See Robert Ellwood, *Introducing Religion: From Inside Out*, 3d ed. (Englewood Cliffs, N.J.: Prentice Hall, 1993), 70–72.

54. Hoover, "The Cross at Willow Creek," 154–58. I find Hoover's unique interpretation of John Calvin's theology of symbols *vis-à-vis* contemporary culture especially fascinating.

55. Ellwood, *Introducing Religion*, 70–72.

56. For two Lutheran examples, see Ralph Quere, "Catechetical and Evangelistic Theology," *Currents in Theology and Mission* 22 (August 1995): 280–83; and Ralph Smith, "Youth and Worship," *Currents in Theology and Mission* 22 (August 1995): 275–79.

57. Pete Ward, *Growing Up Evangelical: Youthwork and the Making of a Subculture* (London: SPCK, 1996).

58. Mark Yaconelli, "Youth Ministry: A Contemplative Approach," *Christian Century* 116 (21–28 April 1999): 450–54.

59. For example, see Webber, *Ancient-Future Faith*. Often the use of signs and symbols in liturgical worship connects with postmodern youth, who eschew spiritual truth as propositional.

60. Pritchard, "The Strategy of Willow Creek," 806.

61. Ibid., 809.

62. Ibid., 810.

Chapter 4

1. The use of the term "blended worship" is frequently associated with the contribution of Robert Webber. Importantly, Webber's use of the term goes far beyond musical style to include all aspects of worship. Webber calls for worship leaders to look in a wide range of resources for texts, songs, gestures, and practices that will help a congregation celebrate Christ through the historic pattern of worship. Unfortunately,

many people seem more excited about the "wide range of resources" than the "historic pattern of Christian worship," resulting in services that are eclectic but not well grounded.

2. For a recent account of these changes, see Michael S. Hamilton, "A Generation Changes North American Hymnody," *The Hymn: A Journal of Congregational Song* 52, no. 3 (July 2001): 11–20; and Karen B. Westerfield Tucker, "Liturgical Perspectives on Changes in North American Hymnody in the Past Twenty-five Years," *The Hymn: A Journal of Congregational Song* 52, no. 3 (July 2001): 22–27.

3. Since the mid-1970s, nearly every denomination has published a new hymnal. In the late 1990s and early 2000s, many have published hymnal supplements. More than ever before, these hymnals and supplements have been produced with cooperation among hymnal editors of various worship traditions. This ferment has led to a small industry of related efforts: the publication of dozens of single-author hymn collections, regular hymn-writing competitions, and conferences on hymn writing and hymn accompaniment. There has probably never been as many single-author hymn collections in print as there are today. In the journal *The Hymn*, the Hymn Society's book service is printed in a smaller and smaller type size with each issue in an attempt to cram all the new publications into those four pages.

4. See Paul Westermeyer, *The Church Musician*, rev. ed. (Minneapolis: Augsburg Fortress), 130–35. Here Westermeyer, in conversation with other leading voices regarding church music, dispels the myth that Martin Luther actually said the words "Why should the devil have all the good tunes?" It is very difficult (perhaps impossible) to make an honest comparison between Luther and Wesley (who themselves lived in remarkably different contexts) and our own day. Such a comparison needs to do justice to all the implications of vernacularization, without confusing it with unrestrained popularization.

5. Augustine, *Against the Manichaens*, Book 15, para. 25.

6. See chapter 2 of this book.

7. Augustine, *Confessions*, trans. R. S. Pine-Coffin (Harmondsworth: Penguin Classics, 1961), 239.

8. From John Wesley, *Select Hymns, 1761*, quoted in preface of the *United Methodist Hymnal*, (Nashville: United Methodist Publishing House, 1989), vii.

9. Thomas G. Long, *Beyond the Worship Wars* (Alban Institute, 2001), 32. Long is reflecting on a passage by theologian Hendrikus Berkhof.

10. Webber, *Worship Old and New*, 195. Emphasis mine.

11. Nicholas Wolterstorf, *Art in Action* (Grand Rapids: Eerdmans, 1981), 184.

12. Ibid., 185. This is one application of Wolterstorff's comprehensive theory of art: "I want to argue . . . that works of art are objects and instruments of

action. They are all inextricably embedded in the fabric of human intention. They are objects and instruments of action whereby we carry out our intentions with respect to the world, our fellows, ourselves, and our gods. Understanding art requires understanding art in [hu]man life" (3). Wolterstorff sees this understanding of art as broader and more inclusive than other explanatory theories: "Over and over one comes across the claims to the effect that such-and-such is 'the essential function of art.' 'Art is mimesis.' 'Art is self-expression.' 'Art is significant form.' All such formulae fall prey to the same dilemma. Either what is said to be characteristic of art is true of more than art, or, if true only of art, it is not true of all art. The universality of art corresponds only to a diversity and flux of purposes, not to some pervasive and unique purpose. . . . Seldom do we have before our mind's eye the whole broad sweep of the purposes of art." (18, 20)

13. Robert Webber, *Worship Old and New*, 195; and *Signs of Wonder*, 83.

14. Webber, *Signs of Wonder*, 97.

15. Gordon Lathrop, *Holy Things: A Liturgical Theology* (Minneapolis: Fortress, 1993), 223.

16. "Constitutions of the Holy Apostles," in *Ante-Nicene Fathers*, vol. 7, ed. Alexander Roberts and James Donaldson (Grand Rapids: Eerdmans, 1951), 421.

17. Alice Parker, *Melodious Accord* (Chicago: GIA, 1991), 6.

18. Dietrich Bonhöffer, *Life Together* (London: SCM Press, 1949), 51.

19. Frank Burch Brown, *Religious Aesthetics: A Theological Study of Making and Meaning* (Princeton: Princeton University Press, 1989), 152–54.

20. John Calvin, *Institutes of the Christian Religion*, ed. John T. McNeill (Philadelphia: Westminster, 1960), 4.10.30.

21. For example, see Anscar J. Chupungco, *Liturgies of the Future: The Process and Methods of Inculturation* (New York: Paulist, 1989); and *So We Believe, So We Pray: Toward Koinonia in Worship*, ed. Thomas F. Best and Dagmar Heller (Geneva: WCC, 1995).

22. Kenneth Smits, "Liturgical Reform in a Cultural Perspective," *Worship* 50, no.2 (March 1976): 98.

23. A summary of this statement is printed in Gordon Lathrop, *Holy People: A Liturgical Ecclesiology* (Minneapolis: Fortress, 1999), 233–36.

Chapter 5

1. *The Book of Alternative Services* of the Anglican Church of Canada (Toronto: Anglican Book Centre, 1985), 150–64, 321–32; *Lutheran Book of Worship* (Minneapolis: Augsburg, 1978), 121–25; *Lutheran Book of Worship: Ministers Desk Edition* (Minneapolis: Augsburg, 1978), 143–53; *Book of Common Worship*, prepared for the Presbyterian Church USA and the Cumberland Presbyterian Church (Louisville: Westminster/John Knox, 1993), 294–314, 403–29; *Book of Worship* (New York: United Church of Christ Office for Church Life and Leadership, 1986); *The United Methodist Book of Worship* (Nashville: United Methodist Publishing House, 1992), 86–114, 368–76; Hoyt L. Hickman, Don E. Saliers, Laurence Hull Stookey, and James F. White, *The New Handbook of the Christian Year* (Nashville: Abingdon, 1992), 191–201.

2. Laurence Hull Stookey, *Baptism: Christ's Act in the Church* (Nashville: Abingdon, 1982), 129–30.

3. Daniel B. Stevick, *Baptismal Moments, Baptismal Meanings* (New York: Church Hymnal Corporation, 1987), xv.

4. *The Book of Common Prayer* (New York: Church Hymnal Corporation, 1979), 298; hereafter referred to as *BCP 1979*.

5. Or "ready and desirous to be confirmed," a clause added to address situations in which the ministry of a bishop, who in Anglicanism is the only allowable minister of confirmation, is not readily available.

6. *The Book of Occasional Services 1994* (New York: Church Hymnal Corporation, 1995), 161.

7. *BCP 1979*, 312. Occasions when a bishop is present are also recommended for baptism.

8. *BCP 1979*, 307.

9. Paul V. Marshall, *Prayer Book Parallels*, vol. 1, *Anglican Liturgy in America* (New York: Church Hymnal Corporation, 1989), 254–55

10. *Ephphatha* literally means "opening" the ears and mouth or nostrils by placing saliva on them, a practice derived from the biblical account of Jesus' healing of a man who was deaf and mute (see Mark 7:32–35).

11. Paul Turner, *The Hallelujah Highway: A History of the Catechumenate* (Chicago: Liturgy Training Publications, 2000), 120.

12. Ibid., 140–48.

13. Ibid., 151–55.

14. Maxwell Johnson, *The Rites of Christian Initiation: Their Evolution and Interpretation* (Collegeville, Minn.: Liturgical, 1999), 301–2; see also Turner, *Hallelujah Highway*, 151.

15. See, for example, Edward Yarnold, S.J., *The Awe-Inspiring Rites of Initiation: The Origins of the RCIA* (Edinburgh: T and T Clark; Collegeville, Minn.: Liturgical, 1994), which includes excerpts from several fourth-century baptismal homilies as well as a description of the catechumenate developed from those homilies and other ancient documents.

16. Turner, *Hallelujah Highway*, 157–69.

17. *Rite of Christian Initiation of Adults*, study edition (Collegeville, Minn.: Liturgical, 1988), para. 36; hereafter referred to as *RCIA*.

18. *RCIA*, para. 52.

19. *RCIA*, para. 60.

20. "National [U.S.] Statutes for the Catechumenate," para. 6. These statutes are included as Appendix III to *RCIA.*

21. *RCIA,* para. 78.

22. Johnson, *Rites of Christian Initiation,* 309.

23. *RCIA,* para. 141.

24. When confirmation does not immediately follow baptism, the explanatory rites also include anointing with chrism.

25. The texts of the prayer and the formula for anointing are similar to the postbaptismal action in the *BCP 1979,* 308. What the Episcopal Church calls "confirmation" is a rite of reaffirmation of faith, notably different from the Roman Catholic form of confirmation.

26. *RCIA,* para. 244.

27. These monthly assemblies are not specified in *RCIA* but are part of the "National Statutes for the Catechumenate," para. 22–24.

28. *RCIA,* para. 250.

29. *The Book of Occasional Services 1994,* 114–30; *Living Witness: The Adult Catechumenate* (Winnepeg: Evangelical Lutheran Church in Canada, 1992); *Welcome to Christ: Lutheran Rites for the Catechumenate, A Lutheran Catechetical Guide,* and *A Lutheran Introduction to the Catechumenate* (Minneapolis: Augsburg Fortress, 1997); Daniel T. Benedict Jr., *Come to the Waters* (Nashville: Discipleship Resources, 1996).

30. Information can be obtained from the NAAC website: <www.catechumenate.org>.

31. "National Statutes for the Catechumenate," para. 33.

32. "Additional (Combined) Rites," Appendix 1 in *RCIA,* para. 505–94.

33. *Book of Occasional Services 1994,* 136–45.

34. Benedict, *Come to the Waters,* 138–50.

35. *Welcome to Christ,* 14–15, 26, 30, 34.

36. "The Preparation of Parents and Godparents for the Baptism of Infants and Young Children," in *The Book of Occasional Services 1994,* 159–62; "A Thanksgiving for the Birth or Adoption of a Child," in *BCP 1979,* 439–45.

37. Benedict, *Come to the Waters,* 123–37.

38. *This Is the Night* (Chicago: Liturgy Training Publications, 1992), videocassette.

Chapter 6

1. E. Brooks Holifield, *A History of Pastoral Care in America: From Salvation to Self-Realization* (Nashville: Abingdon, 1983).

2. Donald S. Browning makes this point very persuasively in his *The Moral Context of Pastoral Care* (Philadelphia: Westminster, 1976).

3. Robert Webber, ed., *The Renewal of Sunday Worship* (Peabody, Mass.: Hendrickson, 1993); Robert Webber, *Evangelicals on the Canterbury Trail: Why*

Evangelicals Are Attracted to the Liturgical Church (Waco: Word, 1985).

4. William H. Willimon, *Worship as Pastoral Care* (Nashville: Abingdon, 1979).

5. Among the most interesting subsequent treatments of the subject are Elaine Ramshaw, *Ritual and Pastoral Care* (Philadelphia: Fortress 1987); Elaine Ramshaw, "Ritual and Pastoral Care: The Vital Connection," in Eleanor Bernstein, C.S.J., ed., *Disciples at the Crossroads: Perspectives on Worship and Church Leadership* (Collegeville, Minn.: Liturgical, 1993), 92–105; Howard W. Roberts, *Pastoral Care through Worship* (Macon, Ga.: Smyth and Helwys, 1995); H. P. V. Renner, "The Use of Ritual in Pastoral Care," *The Journal of Pastoral Care* 33, no. 3 (September 1979): 164–74; Kenneth R. Mitchell, "Ritual in Pastoral Care," *The Journal of Pastoral Care* 63, no. 1 (spring 1989): 68–77.

6. John H. Westerhoff III and William H. Willimon, *Liturgy and Learning through the Life Cycle* (Akron: OSL, 1980, 1994).

7. Vatican Council II, *The Conciliar and Post Conciliar Documents,* ed. Austin Flannery, O.P. (Collegeville, Minn.: Liturgical, 1975), 107.

8. For an overview of ritual theories and their application to worship, see *Studia Liturigica* 23, no. 1 (1993); and *Liturgy Digest* 1, no. 1 (spring 1993). For an introductory text on ritual studies and their pastoral application see Gerard Pottebaum, *The Rites of People,* rev. ed. (Washington, D.C.: Pastoral, 1992).

9. See Pam Couture, "Ritual and Pastoral Care," in Rodney J. Hunter, ed., *Dictionary of Pastoral Care and Counseling* (Nashville: Abingdon, 1990), 1089.

10. Erik Erickson, *Toys and Reasons: Stages in the Ritualization of Experience* (New York: Norton, 1977). For an appropriation of Erickson to pastoral ministry see Donald Capps, *Life Cycle Theory and Pastoral Care* (Philadelphia: Fortress, 1983).

11. Victor W. Turner, *The Ritual Process: Structure and Anti-Structure* (Chicago: Aldine, 1969).

12. Arnold Van Gennep, *The Rites of Passage* (Chicago: University of Chicago Press, 1960).

13. Gregory Dix, ed. *The Treatise on the Apostolic Tradition of St. Hippolytus of Rome* (London: SPCK, 1968).

14. For further reading see Westerhoff and Willimon, *Liturgy and Learning through the Life Cycle;* and Paul Bradshaw and Lawrence Hoffman, eds., *Life Cycles in Jewish and Christian Worship* (Notre Dame, Ind.: University of Notre Dame Press, 1996).

15. As discussed in Adam Phillips, "On Being Bored," in *On Kissing, Tickling, and Being Bored: Psychoanalytic Essays on the Unexamined Life* (Cambridge: Harvard University Press, 1993), 68–74.

16. See Janet Liebman Jacobs and Donald Capps, eds., *Religion, Society, and Psychoanalysis: Readings in Contemporary Theory* (Boulder: Westview, 1997). A number of chapters in this book discuss Winnicott's

contributions both to psychoanalysis and to our images of human development.

17. D. W. Winnicott, *Playing and Reality* (New York: Routledge, 1992).

Chapter 7

1. A la Marva J. Dawn, *A Royal 'Waste' of Time: The Splendor of Worshiping God and Being Church for the World* (Grand Rapids: Eerdmans, 1999).

2. Cyril, *Ad Quirininum* 3, para. 26, as cited in Alan Kreider, *Worship and Evangelism in Pre-Christendom* (Cambridge: Grove, 1995), 33.

3. Hugh of St. Victor is cited in Talal Asad, *Genealogies of Religion* (Baltimore: Johns Hopkins University Press, 1993), 78.

4. A helpful and concise account of the liturgical renewal movement is Paul McPartlan, *Sacrament of Salvation* (Edinburgh: T and T Clark, 1995). The Vatican II document *Sacrosanctum Concilium* is foremost among the numerous texts that explicitly point to the centrality of corporate worship in the formation of Christians. For example, "It is through the liturgy, especially, that the faithful are enabled to express in their lives and manifest to others the mystery of Christ and the real nature of the true Church. . . . The liturgy daily builds up those who are in the church, making of them a holy temple of the Lord, a dwelling-place for God in the Spirit" (para. 2). And, "The liturgy is the summit toward which the activity of the Church is directed; it is also the fount from which all her power flows" (para. 10). From Austin P. Flannery, ed., *Documents of Vatican II* (Grand Rapids: Eerdmans, 1984), 1, 6. The fruits of the liturgical renewal movement have, of course, spread beyond the Roman Catholic communion. Certainly the points of liturgy being an action of the entire gathered body and formative of Christian community and character are widely shared by Protestant and Eastern Orthodox Christians, as well as Roman Catholics.

5. MacIntyre's signal work in this regard is, of course, *After Virtue,* 2d ed. (Notre Dame, Ind.: University of Notre Dame Press, 1984). Hauerwas's central arguments and appropriation of virtue for theological ethics are put forth in *A Community of Character* (Notre Dame, Ind.: University of Notre Dame Press, 1981) and *The Peaceable Kingdom* (Notre Dame, Ind.: University of Notre Dame Press, 1983). For a sense of the influence of virtue ethics in several Christian traditions, from the Catholic to the Anabaptist, see Nancey Murphy, Brad J. Kallenberg, and Mark Thiessen Nation, eds., *Virtues and Practices in the Christian Tradition* (Harrisburg, Pa.: Trinity, 1997). Hauerwas has now trained a generation of theologians. For an outstanding autobiographical and theological account of worship and formation by one of his former students, see Michael G. Cartwright, "Sharing the House of God: Learning to Read (Scripture) with

Anabaptists," *The Mennonite Quarterly Review* 74, no. 4 (October 2000): 593–621.

6. Catherine Bell, *Ritual: Perspectives and Dimensions* (New York and Oxford: Oxford University Press, 1997), 221.

7. Cited in Ibid., 230.

8. Ibid.

9. Ibid., 225.

10. Ibid., 228. It is noteworthy how the construction of sociopolitical rituals necessitated the reconstruction/destruction of religio-political rituals as Communism sought to supplant the Orthodox Church.

11. History is to a large degree written in the terms of the confrontation between cultures and their ritualistic systems. Think of conquering powers determined that a subjugated power worship the conqueror's gods and, often, throw over the previously existing, cultural-formative rituals. The Christian missionary endeavor was essential to a consciousness of cultural and ritualistic differences throughout the world, with missionaries (and the later secular missionizers, such as generals and anthropologists) recognizing that if the newly "discovered" people would be made like them, many preexisting rituals would have to be abolished or reformed. For a splendid account of such early encounters and confrontation of rituals, see Tom Hiney, *On the Missionary Trail: A Journey through Polynesia, Asia, and Africa with the London Missionary Society* (New York: Atlantic Monthly, 2000).

I take the passionate resistance—often unto death—to change or to abolition of rituals as an indication of how important rituals are to the formation of cultural and individual identity. To destroy my ritual can destroy me, since to eliminate what is essential to forming and sustaining my identity eliminates me. I will either literally die in resistance or be adopted into the new culture and ritual system, and so die figuratively and be born again as a new self—which, of course, is exactly what baptism and other initiation rites suppose.

12. For the influence of speech act theory in ritual studies, see Bell, *Ritual*, 68–69. For an important assessment of speech act theory for theology, see James Wm. McClendon Jr. and James M. Smith, *Convictions*, rev. ed. (Valley Forge, Pa.: Trinity, 1994), 47–79.

13. Robin Gill, *Churchgoing and Christian Ethics* (Cambridge: Cambridge University Press, 1999), 41–42.

14. Ibid., 42.

15. Ibid., 193–94.

16. Ibid., 197.

17. Ibid.

18. Robert D. Putnam, *Bowling Alone: The Collapse of Revival of American Community* (New York: Simon and Schuster, 2000), 66–67.

19. David G. Myers, *The American Paradox: Spiritual Hunger in an Age of Plenty* (New Haven: Yale Uni-

versity Press, 2000), 269, 278, 273, and 285, respectively.

Lest I confine comments on churchgoing and behavior entirely to English-speaking countries, I note also Myers' citation of an international study of Jews in Israel, Catholics in Spain, Calvinists in the Netherlands, Orthodox in Greece, and Catholics in West Germany "consistently found that highly religious people tended to be less hedonistic and self-centered" (270).

20. See Robert Wuthnow, *God and Mammon in America* (New York: Free Press, 1994).

21. I am not discounting the reality that Christian rituals, like other rituals, can be misguided and evil in their effect. Rituals can be dangerous exactly because they are effective, and not all ritual is good—think of Hitler's diabolically effective use of ritual. Church rituals, to the church's shame, have played a role in inculcating bigotry as well as altruism. In South Africa, for instance, the segregation of eucharistic observances by race paved the way for apartheid. Such possibilities, in my estimate, only underscore the need for the church to appreciate—and properly discern—the power of its worship.

22. The classic account of this bereft political condition, and subsequently of the God-responsive church as the only true polity, is Augustine's *City of God,* book 19.

23. All quotations in this paragraph are from Robert Webber, *Worship Old and New,* 98–99.

24. I quote the translation and wording of my own communion, the Episcopal Church: "Holy Eucharist Rite II," *Book of Common Prayer,* 362.

25. Cited in David McCarthy Matzko, "The Performance of the Good: Ritual Action and the Moral Life," *Pro Ecclesia* 7, no. 2 (spring 1998): 200.

26. Dom Gregory Dix, *The Shape of the Liturgy* (New York: Seabury, 1983), 161. Dix is by no means idiosyncratic on this reading. The Anglican-Roman International Commission on Eucharistic Devotion, for instance, parses *anamnesis* as "the making effective in the present of an event in the past." Cited in Robert W. Jenson, *Systematic Theology,* vol. 2, *The Works of God* (New York and Oxford: Oxford University Press, 1999), 258.

27. Jenson, *Systematic Theology,* 258.

28. Liturgical theologian Todd E. Johnson reminds us that the opposite of anamnesis, "re-member," is not forget, but "dis-member." Anamnesis reconnects us with the living God—re-membering us as part of the body of Christ.

29. Hendrik Berkhof, *Christ and the Powers,* trans. John H. Yoder (Scottdale, Pa.: Herald, 1967), 43.

30. See the excellent treatment of this subject by Marva J. Dawn, *Powers, Weakness, and the Tabernacling of God* (Grand Rapids: Eerdmans, 2001), 24–29.

31. On this point, see Oliver O'Donovan's magisterial *The Desire of the Nations* (Cambridge: Cambridge University Press, 1996); and Pierre Manent, *An Intellectual History of Liberalism,* trans. Rebecca Balinski (Princeton: Princeton University Press, 1995), especially chapter 1, "Europe and the Theologico-Political Problem," 3–9.

32. For development of these and related points, see my *A Peculiar People: The Church as Culture in a Post-Christian Society* (Downers Grove, Ill.: InterVarsity Press, 1996), especially pages 76–93.

33. Bell, *Ritual,* 182.

34. See Asad, *Genealogies of Religion,* 55.

35. Bell, *Ritual,* 241.

36. Ibid., 244.

37. For argument and demonstration of this contention, see my "The Theology of Consumption and the Consumption of Theology: Toward a Christian Response to Consumerism," in Rodney Clapp, *Border Crossings: Christian Trespasses on Popular Culture and Public Affairs* (Grand Rapids: Brazos Press, 2000), 126–56. Also, the extraordinarily insightful theological reflections of Philip D. Kenneson suggest both profound and down-to-earth ways to foster faithfulness in an age of advanced capitalism. See his *Life on the Vine: Cultivating the Fruit of the Spirit in Christian Community* (Downers Grove, Ill.: InterVarsity Press, 1999).

Chapter 8

1. From "News" in *America* 185, no.10 (10 September 2001): 4.

2. My memory of a conversation that took place in a Luther faculty forum on September 29, 2001.

3. This is my paraphrase of Robert Kegan's quotation of Burbules and Rice's formulation of postmodernism, found in Robert Kegan, *In Over Our Heads: The Mental Demands of Modern Life* (Cambridge: Harvard University Press, 1994), 325.

4. Louis Charles Willard, ed., *Fact Book on Theological Education,* The Association of Theological Schools, for the academic year 2000-2001 (Pittsburgh: ATS, 2001). It is noteworthy that Roman Catholic lay ministry programs, such as Loyola University Chicago's Institute of Pastoral Studies, consistently have 70 percent female students.

5. Taken from the definition for "context" in *Merriam Webster's Dictionary.*

6. Thomas Boomershine noted in a presentation that he gave in Ottawa, Ontario, in May 1999 that in our contemporary cultural contexts, we reason "more by means of sympathetic identification than through philosophical argumentation."

7. See chapter 9 of this book.

8. Adán Medrano, "Media Trends and Contemporary Ministries: Changing Our Assumptions about Media," (presented to the Catholic Bishops' Conference of the Netherlands, Hilversum, The Netherlands,

May 6, 1998). Available online at: <http://www.jmcommunications.com/english/medrano.html>.

9. Elliott Eisner, *The Educational Imagination* (New York: MacMillan, 1985).

10. Maryellen Weiner, *Improving Your Teaching* (Sage, 1993), as cited by the "Tomorrow's Professor" listserv, available online at: <http://sll.stanford.edu/projects/tomprof/newtomprof/postings/73.html>.

11. Parker Palmer, *The Courage to Teach* (San Francisco: Jossey-Bass, 1998), 107–8.

12. Tom Beaudoin, *Virtual Faith: The Irreverent Spiritual Quest of Generation X* (San Francisco: Jossey-Bass, 1998).

13. Palmer, *Courage to Teach,* 107–8.

14. See, for example, Mary Hess, "Media Literacy as a Support for the Development of a Responsible Imagination in Religious Community," in *Religion and Popular Culture: Studies on the Interaction of Worldviews,* ed. Daniel Stout and Judith Buddenbaum (Ames: Iowa State University Press, 2001), 289–311; and Mary Hess, "The Bible and Popular Culture: Engaging Sacred Text in a World of Others," in *New Paradigms for Bible Study* (New York: ABS, forthcoming).

15. Richard Shweder, *Thinking through Others: Expeditions in Cultural Psychology* (Cambridge: Harvard University Press, 1991), 108.

16. Ibid., 109.

17. Ibid., 109–10.

18. Ibid., 110.

19. Hanan Alexander, *Reclaiming Goodness: Education and the Spiritual Quest* (Notre Dame, Ind.: University of Notre Dame Press, 2001), 173.

20. Ibid., 184. Emphasis in original.

21. By "practice" I am not in any way making a theological claim about the outcome of our call. Rather, I am pointing to a logistic issue—what flows from our redemption on a daily basis? What are the fruits of the Spirit in this context?

22. *America* (10 September 2001).

23. Alexander, *Reclaiming Goodness,* 186.

24. Ibid., 205.

25. Kenneth Bruffee, *Collaborative Learning: Higher Education, Interdependence, and the Authority of Knowledge* (Baltimore: Johns Hopkins University Press, 1993).

26. I do not think it is a coincidence that one of the most popular crossover hits from a Christian rock band in recent years is a tune from the group Jars of Clay.

Chapter 9

1. The Congregations Project (funded by Lily Endowment and housed at Rice University) that is researching multiethnic Christian congregations identifies a "mixed church," or a multiethnic church, as a congregation with "at least 20 percent of its members

providing racial or ethnic diversity." *The Christian Century* 118, no. 7 (28 February 2001): 6–8.

2. *The Dictionary of Cultural Literacy,* ed. E. D. Hirsch, Jr., Joseph F. Kett, and James Trefil. 2d ed. (Boston: Houghton Mifflin: 1993), 412.

3. See Kathy Black, *Culturally Conscious Worship* (St. Louis: Chalice, 2000).

4. See ibid.

5. Ibid., 83–115.

6. See Thomas Long, *The Witness of Preaching,* (Louisville: Westminster/John Knox, 1989).

7. Edward Hall, *Understanding Cultural Differences* (Yarmouth, Maine: Interculutural, 1990), 43–50.

8. For further exploration of these concepts see Duane Elmer, *Cross-Cultural Conflict* (Downers Grove, Ill.: InterVarsity Press, 1995); and Hall, *Understanding Cultural Differences.*

9. Ada Maria Isasi-Diaz coined the term "kindom" in "Solidarity: Love of Neighbor in the 1980s," in *Lift Every Voice and Sing,* ed. Susan Brooks (Thistlethwaite and San Francisco: Harper and Row, 1990).

Chapter 10

1. The multiple forms within the Lutheran family are a good example of this. See the chart inside the front cover of E. Clifford Nelson, *Lutheranism in North America, 1914–1970* (Minneapolis: Augsburg, 1972).

2. Gilson A. C. Waldkoenig, "Henry Melchior Muhlenberg: Friend of Revivalism," *Lutheran Theological Seminary Bulletin* 72, no. 4 (fall 1992).

3. Martin E. Marty, "Ethnicity: The Skeleton of Religion in America," *Church History* 41, no. 1 (March 1972); and Gerald Brauer, "Regionalism and Religion in America," *Church History* 54, no. 3 (September 1985).

4. Sidney Mead, *The Lively Experiment* (Harper and Row, 1963).

5. H. Richard Niebuhr, *The Social Sources of Denominationalism* (New York: Harper and Row, 1921).

6. Ernst Troeltsch, *The Social Teaching of the Christian Churches,* trans. Olive Wyon, (Chicago: University of Chicago Press, 1976 and 1981).

7. H. Richard Niebuhr, *The Kingdom of God in America* (New York: Harper and Row, 1937).

8. Jon Butler, *Awash in a Sea of Faith: Christianizing the American People* (Cambridge: Harvard University Press, 1990).

9. Roger Finke and Rodney Stark, *The Churching of America, 1776–1990* (New Brunswick, N.J.: Rutgers University Press, 1992).

10. Putnam, *Bowling Alone.*

11. Nancy Ammerman, "Bowling Together: Congregations and the American Civil Order," 1996, lecture posted at <http://www.asu.edu/clas/religious_studies/home/1996lec.html>.

12. Robert Bellah et al., *Habits of the Heart*, anniversary ed. (Berkeley: University of California Press, 1996); and Amitai Etzioni, *The Spirit of Community* (New York: Crown, 1993).

13. Randall Balmer and Jesse T. Todd Jr., "Calvary Chapel, Costa Mesa, California," in *American Congregations*, vol. 1, ed., James P. Wind and James W. Lewis (Chicago: University of Chicago Press, 1994).

14. Marty makes this argument in several works, including *The Noise of Conflict*, vol. 2 of *Modern American Religion* (Chicago: University of Chicago Press, 1997)

15. Wuthnow, *Restructuring of American Religion*.

16. For an account of this split, begin with Bryan Hillis, *Can Two Walk Together Unless They Be Agreed?* (Brooklyn, N.Y.: Carlson, 1991).

Chapter 11

1. Andrew Delbanco, *The Real American Dream: A Meditation on Hope* (Cambridge: Harvard University Press, 1999), 5, 24.

2. Edwin Muir, "The Incarnate One," in *Collected Poems* (London: Faber, 1960), 228.

3. Douglas Gomery, "As the Dial Turns," *Wilson Quarterly* (autumn 1993), quoted in Mitchell Stephens, *The Rise of the Image, the Fall of the Word* (New York: Oxford University Press, 1998), 6.

4. Ibid.

5. Beaudoin, *Virtual Faith*, 13.

6. Roger Ebert, preface to Albert J. Bergesen and Andrew M. Greeley, *God in the Movies* (New Brunswick: Transaction, 2000), viii.

7. Augustine, *The Confessions of St. Augustine*, F. J. Sheed, trans. (New York: Sheed and Ward, 1942), 198.

8. Jeffrey C. Pugh, *The Matrix of Faith: Reclaiming a Christian Vision* (New York: Crossroad, 2001), 40.

9. In his excellent article, "I Renounce the Devil and All His Ways," in Carl Braaten and Robert Jenson, eds., *Sin, Death, and the Devil* (Grand Rapids: Eerdmans, 2000), 76–93, Gilbert Meilaender comments that there is a place not only for the banana but also for the banana split, but that Augustine doesn't see it.

10. Augustine, *The Confessions of St. Augustine*, 198.

11. Martin Luther, *Luther's Works, American Edition, 40* (Philadelphia 1958), 99–100, quoted in Carl C. Christensen, "Luther's Theology and the Use of Religious Art," *Lutheran Quarterly* 22, no. 2 (May 1970): 148–49.

12. Martin Luther, *D. Martin Luthers Werke, Kritische Gesamtausgabe*, 10ii, 458, quoted in Christensen, "Luther's Theology," 158.

13. Ibid.

14. Martin Luther, quoted in Christensen, "Luther's Theology," 157.

15. Martin Luther, *Luther's Works*, 40i, 548, quoted in Christensen, "Luther's Theology," 156.

16. Andrew Greeley, *The Catholic Imagination* (Berkeley: University of California Press, 2000), 77–78.

17. Desiderius Erasmus, *The Enchiridion* (Bloomington: Indiana University Press, 1963), 112, 109, quoted in Harry Boonstra, "Of Images and Image Breakers," *Calvin Theological Journal* 32 (November 1997): 425.

18. Zwingli wrote in the margin of his edition of Erasmus's *Lucubrationes*, "But even since God himself is spirit: mind: not body, it is obvious that like rejoices in like: doubtless he is above all to be worshipped by purity of mind. . . . For the father seeks worshippers as will worship him in spirit, since he is spirit." Quoted in P. Auksi, "Simplicity and Silence: The Influence of Scripture on the Aesthetic Thought of the Major Reformers," *Journal of Religious History* 10 (December 1979): 345, note 8.

19. Ulrich Zwingli (III.853), quoted in Auksi, "Simplicity and Silence," 345.

20. Ulrich Zwingli, quoted in Charles Garside Jr., *Zwingli and the Arts* (New Haven: Yale University Press, 1966), 159–60. Cf. John Dillenberger, "The Seductive Power of the Visual Arts: Shall the Response Be Iconoclasm or Baptism?" *Andover Newton Quarterly* 17 (March 1977): 305.

21. Karl Plank, "Of Unity and Distinction," *Calvin Theological Journal* 13, no.1 (April 1978): 19.

22. John Calvin, *OS* 1.43, quoted in David C. Steinmetz, *Calvin in Context* (New York: Oxford University Press, 1995), 60.

23. To allow for this new commandment and still keep the number at ten (!), the Reformers combined what previously had been the ninth and tenth commandments having to do with coveting physical and personal property.

24. Charles Hodge, quoted in James I. Packer, *Knowing God* (Downers Grove, Ill.: InterVarsity Press, 1973), 39.

25. John of Damascus, quoted in Gennadios Limouris, "The Microcosm and Macrocosm of the Icon: Theology, Spirituality and Worship in Colour," in Gennadios Limouris, ed., *Icons: Windows on Eternity* (Geneva: WCC, 1990), 106.

26. "The Doctrine (Horos) of the Veneration of Icons as Formulated by the Seventh Ecumenical Council (787)," in Limouris, *Icons*, 1.

27. Cf. Dan-Ilie Ciobotea and William H. Lazareth, "The Triune God: The Supreme Source of Life. Thought Inspired by Rublev's Icon of the Trinity," in Limouris, *Icons*, 202–4.

28. Emilio Castro, "The Ecumenical Significance of Icons," in Limouris, *Icons*, 5.

29. Bishop Ambrosius of Joensuu, "'Jesus Christ—the Life of the World' in "Orthodox Iconography," in Limouris, *Icons,* 205.

30. Alain Blancy, "Protestantism and the Ecumenical Council: Toward a Reformed Theology of the Icon," in Limouris, *Icons,* 42–43.

31. Castro, "Ecumenical Significance," 4–9.

32. Andrew Greeley, *The Catholic Imagination* (Berkeley: University of California Press, 2000), 5. Cf. David Tracy, *The Analogical Imagination* (New York: Crossroad, 1982).

33. Richard P. McBrien, *Catholicism,* study ed. (Minneapolis: Winston), 1180.

34. Richard A. Blake, *Afterimage: The Indelible Catholic Imagination of Six American Filmmakers* (Chicago: Loyola, 2000), 17.

35. McBrien, *Catholicism,* 1183.

36. Greeley, *Catholic Imagination,* 184.

37. Ibid., 12. Greeley's observations, though insightful into the relationship between Christianity and culture may be on historically shaky ground. Historians have raised significant doubts as to whether any such goddess was ever venerated. Scholars instead are leaning toward thinking the origins of Easter were rooted in a derivation of the term "East," which was commonly understood as a symbol of resurrection. Other scholars suggest it may actually come from the German term "Urstand," which means resurrection. See Adolf Adam, *The Liturgical Year* (New York: Pueblo, 1981) 62–63.

38. Hoover, "The Cross at Willow Creek," 145–59.

39. Alexander Solzhenitsyn, *Our Word of Truth,* quoted in Alister McGrath, *The Unknown God* (Grand Rapids: Eerdmans, 1999), 10.

40. I would like to thank my research assistant Brian Ebersole for combing the church's tradition to locate the relevant material for this chapter.

Chapter 12

1. Quoted in Richard Neuhaus, "While We're At It," *First Things,* no. 108, (December 2000): 74.

2. Niebuhr also came out of the Pietist tradition, but he tried to transcend Pietism, with its otherworldly emphasis, by embracing an ethic of "Christian realism" that employs creative compromise in its effort to change the structures of society.

3. See Friedrich Schleiermacher, *On Religion: Speeches to Its Cultured Despisers,* trans. John Oman (New York: Harper and Row, 1958).

4. See note 17.

5. See Wilhelm and Marion Pauck, *Paul Tillich: His Life and Thought* (New York: Harper and Row, 1976).

6. Paul Tillich, *Systematic Theology* (Chicago: University of Chicago Press, 1951), 1:30–31, 59–68.

7. See Bob E. Patterson, *Carl F. H. Henry* (Waco: Word, 1983).

8. See Peter Vogelsanger, "Brunner as Apologist," in Charles W. Kegley, ed., *The Theology of Emil Brunner* (New York: Macmillan, 1962), 289–301; and Emil Brunner, *The Christian Doctrine of God,* trans. Olive Wyon (Philadelphia: Westminster, 1950), 98–103.

9. Paul Tillich, *The Protestant Era,* trans. James Luther Adams (Chicago: University of Chicago Press, 1948), 203.

10. Ibid., 202.

11. Tillich, *Systematic Theology* 3:354–55; 358–60.

12. Paul Tillich, *The Future of Religions* (New York: Harper and Row, 1966), 87.

13. See Friedrich Schleiermacher, *On Religion: Speeches to Its Cultured Despisers,* 251–53.

14. On the apologetic character of much conservative evangelical theology, see Stanley J. Grenz, *Renewing the Center: Evangelical Theology in a Post-Theological Era* (Grand Rapids: Baker, 2000), 85–150.

15. See Tillich, *Systematic Theology,* 1:6–8.

16. Ibid., 7. Tillich fails to recognize that when using a kerygmatic approach like Karl Barth's, we do seek for sociological and psychological points of contact with the outsider, though not for theological points of contact.

17. For the apologetic thrust of Augustine's theology, in which philosophy becomes a preparation for theology, see Augustine, *Confessions,* trans. J. G. Pilkington, in *Basic Writings of Saint Augustine,* ed. Whitney J. Oates (New York: Random House, 1948), 1:3–256.

18. See Eberhard Busch, *Karl Barth: His Life from Letters and Autobiographical Texts,* trans. John Bowden (Philadelphia: Fortress, 1976).

19. See Anders Nygren, *Agape and Eros,* trans. Philip S. Watson (1932 and 1938; rev. ed., Philadelphia: Westminster, 1953).

20. Karl Barth, *Church Dogmatics,* trans. G. W. Bromiley (Edinburgh: T and T Clark, 1969), 4:4.

21. See Eberhard Busch, *Karl Barth und die Pietisten* (Munich: Chr. Kaiser Verlag, 1978). Also see Karl Barth, *Protestant Theology in the Nineteenth Century* (Valley Forge, Pa.: Judson, 1973), 508–18, 643–53.

22. Besides charismatic theology, other theological options are confessional and ecclesiastical theologies that emphasize maintaining continuity with church tradition. Philip Schaff might be a suitable model for this kind of approach.

23. See Kim Comer, ed., *Wisdom of the Sadhu: Teachings of Sundar Singh* (Farmington, Pa.: Plough, 2000); and Cyril J. Davey, *The Story of Sadhu Sundar Singh* (1950; reprint, Chicago: Moody Press, 1963).

24. See Garth Lean, *Frank Buchman: A Life* (London: Constable, 1985). Note that when I refer to Buchman as charismatic, I am not thereby linking him

with any specific religious movement, such as Pentecostalism. He is charismatic only in the sense that he was ready to manifest the spiritual gifts that were implanted in him by the Holy Spirit.

25. Cited in Marcus Bach, *They Have Found a Faith* (Indianapolis: Bobbs-Merrill, 1946), 135.

26. See Peter Howard, *Frank Buchman's Secret* (London: Heinemann, 1961), 9–10.

27. Lean, *Frank Buchman: A Life,* 388.

28. Ibid., 318.

29. Ibid., 449.

30. On Tillich's critique of utopianism see note 11.

31. See Tillich, *Systematic Theology,* 3:114–20.

32. See Jürgen Moltmann, *The Spirit of Life,* trans. Margaret Kohl (Minneapolis: Fortress, 1992). Moltmann's theology has, on the whole, a marked apologetic bent, though he opposes natural theology in the traditional sense of a propaedeutic to faith. He claims that Christian theology can prove its truth by speaking to the questions that proceed out of the struggles of human existence. See Moltmann, *Theology of Hope,* trans. James W. Leitch (New York: Harper and Row, 1967).

33. A pietist theology, or a theology of the spiritual life, is viable only when united with a theology of the Word of God. It must be grounded in the truth of divine revelation rather than in religious experience per se (as in radical Pietism).

Chapter 13

1. A student's 1988 history project in the Wheaton College archives states: "As I was flipping through *The Record* [the student newspaper], I began to see a trend, that whenever there was a controversial issue, Dr. Webber was usually there." Actually, the student's perception is accurate, at least until a year or two after this student's paper was written, when Webber was given a presidential order to make no more public statements on controversial issues that would involve the college.

2. From the *Wheaton Record* in November 1969.

3. Robert Webber, *Common Roots: A Call to Evangelical Maturity* (Grand Rapids: Zondervan, 1978), 16–17.

4. Webber, *Common Roots,* 23.

5. Robert Webber, *Signs of Wonder: The Phenomenon of Convergence in Modern Liturgical and Charismatic Churches* (Nashville: Abbot Martyn, 1992), 14–16.

6. See Webber, *Ancient-Future Faith* (Grand Rapids: Baker, 1999).

7. Much of what follows can be found in Robert Webber and Donald Bloesch, *The Orthodox Evangelicals: Who They Are and What They Are Saying* (Nashville: Nelson, 1978); and in Webber, *Evangelicals on the Canterbury Trail* (Waco: Word, 1985).

8. Robert Webber, *Worship Is a Verb* (Waco: Word, 1985), 27.

9. Webber, *Evangelicals on the Canterbury Trail,* 25.

10. Webber, *Signs of Wonder,* 7. The schools he was referring to are Reformed Episcopal Seminary in Philadelphia, Covenant Theological Seminary, and Concordia Theological Seminary both in St. Louis.

11. See Webber, *Orthodox Evangelicals,* 21.

12. See Webber, *Ancient-Future Faith,* 25.

13. Webber, *Signs of Wonder,* 3–4.

14. Webber, *Evangelicals on the Canterbury Trail,* 15–16.

15. Webber, *Orthodox Evangelicals,* 19. The story of the Chicago Call is detailed in this book.

16. See Webber, *Common Roots,* 15.

17. Webber, *Ancient-Future Faith,* 91. The juxtaposition of classical Christianity and postmodernism is the burden of this entire book. Webber finds the plurality of the pre-Constantinian church a helpful reference point for the church in our pluralistic, postmodern world. This is an explicit proposal in this book that has been implicit throughout most of Webber's career.

18. Ibid., 24.

19. Ibid., 18–19.

20. Ibid., 31; cf. 45–46.

21. The four New Testament images are: the people of God, new creation, fellowship in faith, and the body of Christ. See ibid., chs. 8–10, especially pp. 78–82.

22. Ibid., 123–35.

23. Ibid., 66.

24. Ibid., 125.

25. Webber, *Common Roots,* 245.

26. Robert Webber, *The Church in the World: Opposition, Tensions, or Transformation?* (Grand Rapids: Academie, 1986), 8.

27. See ibid., 31, 45. On pages 264–69, Webber clearly enumerates the five theological ideas that are necessary for a "new" model of the relation of the church to the world: (1) the orders of creation and structures of existence are under God; (2) evil powers work through the structures of existence; (3) Christ is victorious over these evil powers; (4) the church is Christ's witness to the powers of evil; (5) the church lives in eschatological hope of Christ's return.

28. See ibid., chapters 2–3.

29. For example, see Robert Webber, *The Secular Saint: The Role of the Christian in the Secular World* (Grand Rapids: Zondervan, 1981), chapter 5; and Webber, *Ancient-Future Faith,* 165–70.

30. These three dimensions of the church's relation to the world are found in many of Webber's writings: for example, *The Moral Majority: Right or Wrong?* (Westchester, Ill.: Crossway, 1981), 131-40; Webber, *Ancient-Future Faith,* 168–69.

31. See Webber, *Secular Saint,* chapter 4.

32. See Webber, *Church in the World,* 94–96, 100, 118, 140.

33. In 1973, over fifty evangelicals gathered in Chicago to draft the Chicago Declaration, which challenged evangelicals to a have a greater concern for the ills of society. It was coordinated by Ron Sider and involved leaders such as Jim Wallis, John Alexander, and Webber. See Webber, *Secular Saint,* 23–24, 175–76.

34. Ibid., 13–14.

35. Recapitulation is a theory of Christ's work most often associated with Irenaeus in the second century (hence, one of Webber's favored soteriological paradigms). Irenaeus taught that Christ, the second Adam, undoes the work of the fallen first Adam.

36. See Webber, *Secular Saint,* 188–201.

37. Webber, *Church in the World,* 67.

38. For what follows, see Webber, *Moral Majority.* Also, see Webber, *Church in the World,* chapter 15.

39. See more on Webber's assessment of the World Council of Churches in Webber, *Moral Majority,* 84–86. He chastised the WCC for lack of involvement in moral issues that touch personal and family life, for not adequately rooting liberation in the biblical Christ and liberation from sin in Christ's death and resurrection and for having an inadequate view of the church as a distinct supernatural society to which the redeemed give ultimate allegiance (*vis-à-vis* the primacy of God's work in a specific political order).

40. See ibid., 108–15.

41. Robert Webber, *Secular Humanism, Threat and Challenge* (Grand Rapids: Zondervan, 1982), 109–25.

42. Webber, *Ancient-Future Faith,* 171–72.

43. Robert Webber and Rodney Clapp, *People of the Truth: A Christian Challenge to Contemporary Culture* (Harrisburg, Pa: Morehouse. 1993), 6.

44. Ibid., 12.

45. Webber, *Ancient-Future Faith,* 93, 106. Cf. Webber, *Worship Is a Verb,* 38–46.

46. Webber, *Ancient-Future Faith,* 106; Webber, *Worship Is a Verb,* 67–68. See also page 12: "It (worship) is not something done to us or for us, but by us."

47. Ibid., 90.

48. Ibid., 102.

49. Webber, *Signs of Wonder,* 75.

50. Ibid., 117.

51. Webber, *Evangelicals on the Canterbury Trail,* 55–56.

52. Ibid., 118.

53. Extending the concept of "sacrament" beyond baptism and the Eucharist was one of the points to which David Wells objected in his response to the "Chicago Call"; see Webber, *Orthodox Evangelicals,* 218–19.

54. See Webber, *Ancient-Future Faith,* chapters 11–13.

55. Webber emphasizes that worship is an *event,* which corresponds to Webber's preference for understanding the essence of Christianity as an event rather than a doctrinal statement. See Webber, *Worship, Old and New* (Grand Rapids: Ministry Resources Library, 1982), chapter 2.

56. See Webber, *Ancient-Future Faith,* 99; Webber, *Worship, Old and New;* and Webber, *Blended Worship* (Peabody, Mass.: Hendrickson, 1996).

57. Webber, *Signs of Wonder,* chapter 10.

58. Webber, *Moral Majority,* 129.

59. Webber, *Evangelicals on the Canterbury Trail,* 12.

Bibliography

Books by Robert Webber
(Arranged by date of publication)

Reshaping Evangelical Higher Education. With Larry Richards and Marvin Keene Mayers. Grand Rapids: Zondervan, 1972.

How to Choose a Christian College. Carol Stream, Ill.: Creation House, 1974.

Common Roots: A Call to Evangelical Maturity. Grand Rapids: Zondervan, 1978.

God Still Speaks: A Biblical View of Christian Communication. Nashville: Nelson, 1978.

The Orthodox Evangelicals: Who They Are and What They Are Saying. With Donald Bloesch. Nashville: Nelson, 1978.

The Moral Majority: Right or Wrong? Westchester, Ill.: Crossway, 1981.

The Secular Saint: The Role of the Christian in the Secular World. Grand Rapids: Zondervan, 1981.

Secular Humanism, Threat and Challenge. Grand Rapids: Zondervan, 1982.

Worship, Old and New. With Maureen LeLacheur and Gerard Terpstra. Grand Rapids: Ministry Resources Library, 1982.

In Heart and Home: A Woman's Workshop on Worship, With Helps for Leaders. Grand Rapids: Lamplighter, 1985.

Evangelicals on the Canterbury Trail: Why Evangelicals Are Attracted to the Liturgical Church. Waco: Word, 1985.

Worship Is a Verb. Waco: Word, 1985.

Celebrating Our Faith: Evangelicalism through Worship. San Francisco: Harper and Row, 1986.

The Church in the World: Opposition, Tensions, or Transformation? Grand Rapids: Academie, 1986.

I Believe: A Woman's Workshop on Relational Doctrine. Grand Rapids: Zondervan, 1986.

The Majestic Tapestry. Nashville: Nelson, 1986.

People of the Truth: The Power of the Worshiping Community in the Modern World. With Rodney Clapp. San Francisco: Harper and Row, 1988. (Later published as *People of the Truth: A Christian Challenge to Contemporary Culture.* With Rodney Clapp. Harrisburg, Pa.: Morehouse, 1993.)

Signs of Wonder: The Phenomenon of Convergence in Modern Liturgical and Charismatic Churches. Nashville: Abbott Martyn, 1992.

Liturgical Evangelicalism. Harrisburg, Pa.: Morehouse, 1992.

The Biblical Foundations of Christian Worship (vol. 1 of *The Complete Library of Christian Worship* [CLCW]). Peabody, Mass.: Hendrickson; Nashville: Star Song, 1993.

The Renewal of Sunday Worship (CLCW vol. 3). Peabody, Mass.: Hendrickson, 1993.

The Daily Book of Prayer. Grand Rapids: Eerdmans, 1993.

In This Sanctuary: An Invitation to Worship the Savior. With Twila Paris. Nashville: Star Song, 1993.

The Services of the Christian Year (CLCW vol. 5). Nashville: Star Song ,1993; Peabody, Mass.: Hendrickson, 1996.

What Christians Believe: A Biblical and Historical Summary. With Alan F. Johnson.

Grand Rapids: Academie, 1989; Grand Rapids: Zondervan. 1993.

The Sacred Actions of Christian Worship (CLCW vol. 6). Nashville: Star Song, 1994; Peabody, Mass.: Hendrickson, 1994.

Music and the Arts in Christian Worship (CLCW vol. 4). Nashville: Star Song; Peabody, Mass.: Hendrickson, 1994.

Twenty Centuries of Christian Worship (CLCW vol. 2). Nashville: Star Song; Peabody, Mass.: Hendrickson, 1994.

The Ministries of Christian Worship (CLCW vol. 7). Nashville: Star Song, 1994; Peabody, Mass.: Hendrickson, 1996

Worship Old and New: A Biblical Historical, and Practical Introduction. Rev. ed. Grand Rapids: Zondervan, 1994.

The Worship Phenomenon. Nashville: Star Song, 1994.

Blended Worship: Achieving Substance and Relevance in Worship. Peabody, Mass.: Hendrickson, 1996.

The Book of Family Prayer. Peabody, Mass.: Hendrickson, 1996.

Learning to Worship with Your Heart: A Study in the Biblical Foundations of Christian Worship. Wheaton, Ill.: Institute for Worship Studies, 1994; Peabody, Mass.: Hendrickson, 1996.

Rediscovering the Missing Jewel: A Study of Worship through the Centuries. Peabody, Mass.: Hendrickson, 1996.

Church Music in the Twenty-first Century: A Symposium. With Harold M. Best, Louis Ball, and Mary Charlotte Ball. Jefferson City, Tenn.: Louis and Mary Charlotte Ball Institute of Church Music, The Center for Church Music, Carson-Newman College, 1997.

Enter His Courts with Praise: A Study of the Role of Music and the Arts in Worship. Peabody, Mass.: Hendrickson, 1997.

Renew Your Worship: A Study in the Blending of Traditional and Contemporary Worship. Peabody, Mass.: Hendrickson, 1997.

Empowered by the Holy Spirit: A Study in the Ministries of Worship. Peabody, Mass.: Hendrickson, 1998.

Encountering the Healing Power of God: A Study in the Sacred Actions of Worship. Peabody, Mass.: Hendrickson, 1998.

Planning Blended Worship: The Creative Mixture of Old and New. Nashville: Abingdon, 1998.

Rediscovering the Christian Feasts: A Study in the Services of the Christian Year. Peabody, Mass.: Hendrickson, 1998.

Worship: Journey into His Presence. Mansfield, Pa.: Kingdom, 1999.

Ancient-Future Faith: Rethinking Evangelicalism for a Postmodern World. Grand Rapids: Baker, 1999.

The Prymer: The Prayer Book of the Medieval Era Adapted for Contemporary Use. Brewster, Mass.: Paraclete, 2000.

The Younger Evangelicals: Facing the Challenges of the New World. Grand Rapids: Baker, 2002.

Notable Essays and Articles by Robert Webber
(Arranged by date of publication)

"Living in the World." *Post American* 3 (June/July 1974): 26–28.

"Church Buildings: Shapes of Worship." *Christianity Today* 25 (7 August 1981): 18–20.

"Worship: A Methodology for Evangelical Renewal." *Theological Students Fellowship Bulletin* 7, no. 1 (September/October 1983): 8–10.

"Let's Put Worship into the Worship Service: Let's End Gospel Pep Rallies and Sunday Morning Variety Shows." *Christianity Today* 28, no. 3 (17 February 1984): 52.

"Are Evangelicals Becoming Sacramental?" *Ecumenical Trends* 14, no. 3 (March 1985): 36–38.

"Easter: Reliving the Mystery." *Christianity Today* 30, no. 5 (21 March 1986): 16–18.

"Ethics and Evangelism: Learning from the Third-Century Church." *Christian Century* 103, no. 27 (24 September 1986): 806–8.

"Worship and Spirituality." *Reformed Liturgy and Music* 20, no. 2 (spring 1986): 67–71.

"The Impact of the Liturgical Movement on the Evangelical Church." *Reformed Worship* 21 (spring 1987): 111–14.

"As for Me and My House: Learning from a Jewish Model of Worship." *Reformed Liturgy and Music*, no. 12 (summer 1989): 33–35.

"Ecumenical Influences on Evangelical Worship." *Ecumenical Trends* 19 (May 1990): 73–76.

"Enter His Courts with Praise: A New Style of Worship Is Sweeping the Reformed Church." *Reformed Worship*, no. 20 (June 1991): 9–12.

"Preconditions for Renewal: New Attention to the Biblical and Historical Sources." *Evangelical Journal* 9 (spring 1991): 3–10.

"Bring Them In: Three Models for Evangelism through Worship." *Reformed Worship*, no. 23 (March 1992): 4–6.

"The Future Direction of Christian Worship." *Ex Auditu* 8 (1992): 113–28.

"Worship and Sound." *Cross Point* 9 (spring 1996): 27–35.

"Reducing God to Music? We Experience God in More than Songs and Segues." *Leadership* 20 (spring 1999): 35.

Contributors

Kathy Black is the Gerald Kennedy Chair of Homiletics and Liturgics at the Claremont School of Theology in Southern California. Dr. Black is the author of *Signs of Solidarity: Ministry with Persons who are Deaf, Deafened, and Hard of Hearing; Worship Across Cultures;* and *Culturally-Conscious Worship.*

Donald Bloesch is professor of theology emeritus at the University of Dubuque Theological Seminary, Dubuque, Iowa. Dr. Bloesch is presently working on a seven-volume systematic theology called *Christian Foundations.* The fifth volume, entitled *The Holy Spirit: Works and Gifts,* has recently been released.

Constance M. Cherry serves as executive director of worship and music at the First Presbyterian Church of Hollywood, California. Dr. Cherry is on the faculty of Robert Webber's Institute for Worship Studies, and along with teachesing worship as an adjunct professor at several seminaries and in cross-cultural settings. She is a recognized hymn writer, with her work featured in a one-author collection of hymns, *Proclaim New Hope.*

Rodney Clapp is editorial director of Brazos Press. His books include *Border Crossings* and *A Peculiar People.* A popular speaker on theology and culture, he contributes frequently to theological and ministerial journals and is senior editor of *Prism* magazine.

Mary Hess is assistant professor of educational leadership at Luther Seminary in St. Paul, Minnesota. Dr. Hess, a Roman Catholic layperson, is a member of the International Study Commission on Media, Religion, and Culture. Her work is regularly published in the journal *Religious Education,* and she maintains a web site at <www.luthersem.edu/mhess>.

Todd E. Johnson is director of the master of divinity program and assistant professor of pastoral studies at Loyola University Chicago's Institute of Pastoral Studies, where he teaches liturgical, sacramental, and systematic theology. Author of numerous articles on liturgical history and theology, Dr. Johnson is on the editorial board of *Questions Liturgique* and is completing a book on Evelyn Underhill's ecumenical theology of symbols and sacraments. He also teaches for Robert Webber in his Institute for Worship Studies.

Robert K. Johnston is professor of theology and culture at Fuller Theological Seminary in Pasadena, California. Dr. Johnston's recent books include *Reel Spirituality: Theology and Film in Dialogue* and *Life Is Not Work/ Work Is Not Life: Simple Reminders for Finding Balance in a 24/7 World.*

Ruth Meyers is associate professor of liturgics at Seabury-Western Theological Seminary (Episcopal Church), Evanston, Illinois. Dr. Meyers is a participant in the language consultation of the Renewing Worship Project in the Evangelical Lutheran Church in America. Dr. Meyers is coeditor of *Gleanings: Essays on Expansive Language with Prayers for Various Occasions,* and author of *Continuing the Reformation.*

Dennis Okholm is professor of theology at Wheaton College, an ordained minister in the Presbyterian Church (USA), and an oblate of a Benedictine order. He has authored and edited several books, and is coauthor of *A Family of Faith: An Introduction to Evangelical Theology.*

Lester Ruth is assistant professor of worship and liturgy at Asbury Theological Seminary in Wilmore, Kentucky. Dr. Ruth is the author of *A Little Heaven Below: Worship at Early Methodist Quarterly Meetings* and coauthor of *Creative Preaching on the Sacraments.* Dr. Ruth teaches for Robert Webber in his Institute for Worship Studies.

Gilson Waldkoenig is associate professor of church in society and director of the Town and Country Church Institute at the Lutheran Theological Seminary at Gettysburg, Pennsylvania. Dr. Waldkoenig also teaches rural ministry and ecclesiology and is the author of *Symbiotic Community* and coauthor of *Cooperating Congregations.*

William H. Willimon is dean of the chapel and professor of Christian ministry at Duke University in Durham, North Carolina. Dr. Willimon has published widely in pastoral fields, including *Worship as Pastoral Care* and *Pastor: The Theology and Practice of Ordained Leadership.*

John D. Witvliet is director of the Calvin Institute of Christian Worship at Calvin College and Calvin Theological Seminary in Grand Rapids, Michigan, where he has oversight of the Institute's practical and scholarly programs as well as being the project director of the Worship Renewal Grants Program, funded by Lilly Endowment Inc. Dr. Witvliet also teaches courses in worship, theology, and music. He has published widely in the areas of music and worship, and is the editor of *A Child Shall Lead: Children in Worship.* Dr. Witvliet teaches for Robert Webber in his Institute for Worship Studies.